Roots of Respect

Roots of Respect

A Historic-Philosophical Itinerary

Edited by
Giovanni Giorgini and Elena Irrera

DE GRUYTER

ISBN 978-3-11-044814-6
e-ISBN (PDF) 978-3-11-052628-8

This work is licensed under the Creative Commons Attribution-NonCommercial-NoDerivs 3.0 License.
For details go to http://creativecommons.org/licenses/by-nc-nd/3.0/.

Library of Congress Cataloging-in-Publication Data
A CIP catalog record for this book has been applied for at the Library of Congress.

Bibliografic information published by the Deutsche Nationalbibliothek
The Deutsche Nationalbibliothek lists this publication in the Deutschen Nationalbibliografie;
detailed bibliografic data are available on the Internet at http://dnb.dnb.de.

© 2018 Walter de Gruyter GmbH, Berlin/Boston
This volume is text- and page-identical with the hardback published in 2017.
Printing and binding: CPI books GmbH, Leck

♾ Printed on acid-free paper
Printed in Germany

www.degruyter.com

Preface

The last four decades have witnessed a remarkable upsurge of interest in the nature of respect. Despite the prominence gained by the principle of respect for persons in ethical, political and legal discourse, one of the most largely unexplored issues remains the problem of the historical-philosophical roots of this notion. In the hope of contributing to filling in this lacuna, the present collection of essays aims to outline and critically discuss some of the most prominent theoretical expressions of the notion of respect in ancient, modern and contemporary times.

The idea of writing this volume came from working with Emanuela Ceva (University of Pavia), director of the FIRB Research Project "Feeding Respect", funded by the Italian Ministry of Education, University and Research (RBFR107AN0_002). The editors of the volume, members of the research-group set up within the framework of the project, jointly organized a two-day conference entitled *Dignity, Respect, and Self-Respect. Ancient, Modern, and Contemporary Perspectives*, hosted by the University of Bologna in May 2014, with the support of the University of Pavia (Department of Social and Political Sciences). The conference, which examined the issue of respect under a variety of approaches (political theory, philosophy of right and the history of philosophy), attracted the attention of a large number of international scholars and post-graduate students.

With the help of the other members of the FIRB research-group, the organizers selected six papers on respect for persons from the many delivered at the conference by PhD students, research fellows and established academics (including the papers written by the editors themselves). The volume also includes three essays by scholars who did not take part in the conference (Rowe, Knoll and Laitinen), but were invited to contribute by virtue of their expertise on subjects not adequately treated from a historic-philosophical point of view at the conference itself.

It is our pleasure to acknowledge the debts we have contracted as we have been working on this collection of essays. Our first debt is to Emanuela Ceva, director of the "Feeding Respect"-FIRB Project, who has strongly encouraged us to put together this collection of essays and suggested to confine ourselves to a purely historic-philosophical approach to the issue of respect for persons. We are also grateful to Ian Carter, Corrado del Bo', Francesco Ferraro, Chiara Testino and Federico Zuolo for engaging and stimulating discussions on the topics addressed by this volume on the occasion of various meetings organized by the Universities of Pavia and Milan.

A special thanks goes to Giuseppe Sassatelli, director of the Department of History, Cultures and Civilizations in 2014, for his support in the organization of the conference from which the present work takes its origins.

Giovanni Giorgini and Elena Irrera
Bologna, 17/10/2016

Table of Contents

Preface —— V

Note on Citations and Abbreviations —— IX

Giovanni Giorgini and Elena Irrera
Introduction —— 1

Giovanni Giorgini and Elena Irrera
Recognition: A Philosophical Problem —— 17

Part I: Respect in Ancient Philosophy

Giovanni Giorgini
The Notion of Respect in Ancient Greek Poetry —— 41

Christopher J. Rowe
Plato on Respect, and What "Belongs to" Oneself —— 67

Simon Weber
Aristotle and Respect for Persons —— 83

Part II: Respect in Modern Philosophy

Elena Irrera
Human Interaction in the State of Nature: Hobbes on Respect for Persons and Self-Respect —— 109

Christine Bratu
The Source of Moral Motivation and Actions We Owe to Others: Kant's Theory of Respect —— 131

Marie Göbel
Respect as the Foundation of Human Rights: To What Extent Can This View Be Attributed to Kant? —— 149

Part III: From Modern to Contemporary Perspectives on Respect

Arto Laitinen
Hegel and Respect for Persons — 171

Antis Loizides
John Stuart Mill: Individuality, Dignity, and Respect for Persons — 187

Manuel Knoll
The Cardinal Role of Respect and Self-Respect for Rawls's and Walzer's Theories of Justice — 207

List of Contributors — 225

Index — 227

Note on Citations and Abbreviations

Note on Citations

References to Kant's works are to the Akademie-Ausgabe of *Kants gesammelte Schriften* (AK), edited by the Royal Prussian, subsequently German, then Berlin-Brandenburg Academy of Sciences (1900 ff., Reimer/De Gruyter), citing volume and page numbers, with the exception of the *Critique of Pure Reason*, which is cited in terms of the A (first edition)/B (second edition) page numbers.

References to Hobbes's works are by title, followed by volume and page number of *The Complete Works of Thomas Hobbes* (EW), edited by Sir William Molesworth (1839–1845, London: J. Bohn).

References to John Stuart Mill's works are by title, followed by volume and page number of the *Collected Works of John Stuart Mill* (CW), edited by J.M. Robson (1963–1991, Toronto: University of Toronto Press, London: Routledge and Kegan Paul).

Abbreviations

Aeschylus
Coephorae: *Coeph.*
Eumenides: *Eum.*

Aeschynes

Against Timarchus: *Contra Tim.*

Aristotle

Constitution of the Athenians: *AP*
Eudemian Ethics: *EE*
Magna Moralia: *MM*
Metaphysics: *Met.*
Nicomachean Ethics: *NE*
Poetics: *Poet.*
Politics: *Pol.*
Rhetoric: *Rhet.*

Cicero

De Finibus: *De Fin.*
De Officiis: *Off.*

Dêmosthenes (Dem.)

Against Philip 3 (IX): *Phil. 3*
Against Meidias (XXI): *c. Meid.*

Hegel

Philosophy of Right: PR

Herodotus (Hdt.)

Hobbes

The Elements of Law: Natural and Politic: EL
De Cive: DC
Leviathan: L

Homer

Iliad: *Il.*
Odyssey: *Od.*

Kant

Metaphysics of Morals: MM
Metaphysics of Morals Vigilantius: MMV
Groundwork of the Metaphysics of Morals: G
Critique of Practical Reason: CPrR

Plato

Charmides: *Charm.*
Hippias Major: *Hipp. Ma.*
Lysis: *Lys.*
Parmenides: *Parm.*
Protagoras: *Prot.*
Republic: *Rep.*
Sophist: *Soph.*
Symposium: *Symp.*
Theaetetus: *Theaet.*
Timaeus: *Tim.*

Sophocles

Electra: *El.*

Xenophon

Memorabilia: *Mem.*
Oeconomicus: *Oec.*
Constitution of Lacedaemonians: *Resp. Lac.*

Giovanni Giorgini and Elena Irrera
Introduction

If you can see me I can see you
David Bowie

In recent years, the notion of "respect" has come to occupy an increasingly important role in contemporary ethical and political theory. More specifically, the idea of equal respect for persons has often been invoked by scholars and policy-makers as a principle capable of informing a wide array of human interactions in pluralistic societies, especially those which, albeit featuring various forms of conflict, appear ultimately to be rooted in the fundamental values of equality, freedom and dignity. A conspicuous number of scholarly attempts in the philosophy of law,[1] social theory,[2] ethical theory[3] and political philosophy[4] have shown not only that respect represents an appropriate response to a rich array of practical issues, but also that no application of such an ideal can be neatly separated from a preliminary analysis of its theoretical grounds. While, in the area of contemporary political philosophy, a great deal of attention has been devoted to the normative import of the ideal of respect in liberally oriented political communities,[5] scant attention has been accorded to its historic-philosophical roots.

Such a noticeable lacuna in the field of philosophical studies appears even more lamentable when considered in the light of the possible benefits that a treatment of respect across the history of philosophy might produce. These benefits will be evident in connection with at least two aims. First and foremost, a conceptual clarification of the ways in which the notion of respect and its mani-

---

1 See for instance the pioneering work of Ronald Dworkin and his attempt to ground law and right on moral principles. In his theory of law, pride of place is held by the right of each individual to equal respect and concern (1977 and 1985). See also Joseph Raz, who addresses the issue of law as an object of respect (Raz 1979). For a recent reconstruction of how the ideal of respect (framed in terms of respect for the dignity of individual human beings) figures in national and international jurisprudence, see Brownsword 2014.
2 See Honneth 1996; Sennett 2002 and 2003; Honneth and Fraser 2003.
3 See Dillon 1992; Raz 2001; Bird 2004; Carter 2009 and 2011.
4 See for instance Michael Walzer's theory of recognition in Walzer 1983; Taylor 1992; Carter, Galeotti and Ottonelli 2008; Galeotti 2010.
5 See for instance Galeotti 2002, who provides a contribution to a theory of multicultural liberalism in which practices of toleration are premised on the ideal of equal respect for persons. Cf. Ceva and Zuolo 2013. See also Carter 2011, who proposes a model of respect able to supply a justification for equal treatment of persons.

fold connotations is articulated in ancient, modern and contemporary philosophy might act as a suitable historic and theoretical basis for a fruitful discussion of the supposed normative role of respect in the public domain. This suggests that a preliminary conceptualization of respect in terms of a value able to shape ethically acceptable patterns of political behavior might inspire the practice of institutional decision-makers, especially those committed to finding practical ways of implementing equal respect for persons in the political arena (for instance, within the framework of deliberative processes aimed at establishing the principles from which fair distributive measures ought to stem.[6] Alternatively, the ideal of equal respect for persons might shape some institutionally-based responses to a number of specific substantive claims and requests of recognition advanced by citizens and community-members[7]).

Secondly, addressing the theme of respect for persons from the point of view of the history of philosophy may fruitfully contribute to a deeper understanding of the nature and implications of issues such as ethical virtues, political justice and the human good. A work committed to a critical engagement with the key passages through which the evolution of the notion of respect for persons takes place over the centuries may offer a fresh new lens through which elements of analogy, continuity and rupture between philosophical theories belonging to different times and contexts might be put in better focus. Moreover, a methodological approach of this kind in relation to the issue of respect would benefit considerably from treatment of an idea which several scholars have considered the possibly underlying rationale of the notion of respect. This idea is expressed by the English word *recognition*. Indeed, a reconstruction of the varieties of expressions using the term "recognition", over the centuries of philosophical thought, could help readers towards a theoretical reconfiguration of various types of respect;[8] furthermore, it would enable them to identify the criteria on the basis of which these types of respect are accorded to persons. Viewed in such a light, a historic-philosophical investigation of the nature of respect and the related notion of recognition could be considered as an intellectual endeavor to be taken seriously in its own right.

---

[6] The kind of justice concerning the fairness of the procedures by which decisions are made is generally labeled as "procedural justice". A notable case of procedural justice is supplied by Rawls 1999.
[7] See for instance Galeotti 2010. See also Fraser 2003.
[8] Types that, according to some well-known accounts, include esteem for the moral excellence of individuals, the reverential recognition of their role in society and reciprocal acknowledgment of an equal status as moral agents. Cf. above all Darwall 1977 and 2006; Hudson 1980; Hill 1998; Buss 1999; Green 2010.

Although there exist studies in which respect is addressed in a historical-philosophical perspective,[9] the (short) genealogies they supply appear mainly designed to promote a clearer understanding of related concepts like "rights" and "dignity".[10] In fact, most of these studies do not generally provide a full-scale treatment of how the notion is developed across the history of philosophy, being mostly committed to singling out specific moments and characters (especially Kant's reflection on respect for persons and its relationship to respect for the moral law[11]).

The collection of essays presented here aims at providing a conceptualization of this notion by highlighting the key passages of its theoretical development from its very embryonic stages in classical times. In view of this task, the volume brings together the expertise of classicists and scholars specialized in modern and contemporary philosophy. The following set of basic questions will guide the authors: 1) How many kinds of respect can be traced in the history of philosophy? To what extent do they differ? Do they present aspects of convergence? 2) What are the most seminal attempts to conceptualize such kinds of respect? 3) Did such attempts affect the contemporary reflection on the problems of respect, justice and human rights, and how? 4) How do various kinds of respect for persons interlace with the value of "self-respect"? Do the two notions contribute to reciprocally shape their meaning and range of implications?

The working hypothesis underlying this volume is that the contemporary formulation of respect presents itself as the upshot of a process of theoretical reflection which finds its roots in classical antiquity and incorporates a collection of themes already at work in philosophers like Plato and Aristotle: the feeling of shame, rational agency, ethical virtue, justice, reciprocity, moral equality and abidance by the law. By analysis of pivotal texts of ancient, modern and contemporary philosophy, the volume will try to offer an articulated account of respect which, starting from its primeval connection with the search for esteem and the pursuit of human excellence, gradually evolves towards the recognition of the political status of each citizen and culminates into a true politics of human rights. As the essays contained in this anthology will show, equal respect, although being grounded on a full and aware recognition of individuals as human beings, appears to coexist and to entertain significant relations with non-egalitarian patterns of recognition.

---

9 See for instance Mordacci 2012.
10 See for instance Kateb 2011.
11 See for instance Hill 2000; Neumann 2000; Timmons and Johnson 2015.

Far from offering an exhaustive treatment of the subject, this anthology focuses on a small number of authors: Theognis, Plato, Aristotle, Hobbes, Kant, Hegel, Rawls and Walzer. The reader will notice that the volume addresses not only well-defined philosophical accounts of respect, but also some philosophical views in which the issue of respect is neither fully nor consciously brought into focus. With reference to such views, we believe that an examination of the role played by the notion of respect for persons (however undeveloped) could conceivably provide valuable material for a critical re-assessment of the philosophical contexts in which these views are situated.

In the first part of this introductory chapter we will provide a general introduction to the issue of respect for persons, trying to bring to light different perspectives from which the nature of this concept can be investigated. In the second part we will propose a short summary of the essays included in this volume.

1 Respect for Persons: Its Nature and Different Kinds

When considered from a purely formal point of view, respect consists in a complex relationship between three key aspects: (i) the presence of two subjects, i.e. the respecter and the respected object (either animate or inanimate); (ii) what might be called "the basis of respect", i.e. some feature or fact that, being possessed or experienced by an individual, makes her worthy of respectful treatment; (iii) an evaluative point of view, from which the property is assessed in positive terms. According to this pattern, scholars like Carl Cranor (1975) and Stephen Darwall (1977) have argued that

> This relationship [i.e. respect] consists, roughly, in the respecter's judging that the person's having the characteristic is a good thing (from the relevant point of view), his appreciating why it is a good thing, and his being disposed to do what is appropriate to the person's having that characteristic.[12]

The definition of the word "respect" provided by Cranor and Darwall reflects a widespread tendency to think of respect in terms of an "attitude", that is, as a consolidated disposition to respond to oneself or others which is prompted by a previous identification and evaluation of specific properties. Along this line, Robin Dillon (2007, pp. 202–203) has proposed that respect, as an attitude, rep-

---

[12] This is Darwall's reformulation of Cranor's view of respect in Darwall 1977, p. 37.

resents a complex phenomenon produced by an intersection of beliefs, perceptions, judgments, emotions, feelings and ways of experiencing things. Viewed under this light, the attitude of respect encompasses a range of cognitive, affective, motivational, and evaluative dimensions (Dillon 2007, pp. 202–203) that cannot find actualization without some form of regard and sensitivity[13] for both the addressee of respect and the property/ies that make/s her worthy of a respectful response. On Dillon's view, respect itself can be considered a form of regard, that is,

> a mode of attention to and perception and acknowledgement of an object as having a certain importance, worth, authority, status, or power. (Dillon 2007, p. 202)

An appeal to the etymology of the word "respect" may provide a deeper understanding of the notion of "regard" and its distinctive relevance in connection with respect. As the Latin root *respicere* is generally taken to suggest, respecting a person involves one's act of "looking back"[14] at her, presumably in response to that person's having first cast a gaze on one (that is, the one who is called to respect that person). The idea of a reciprocated vision between human subjects might work as a metaphor for the view that, in many circumstances, respect is a responsive attitude towards persons who entertain legitimate expectations of being treated with a certain form of regard. One of the most notable formulations of this thesis is found in Stephen Darwall's *The Second Person Standpoint: Morality, Respect, and Accountability* (2006). By focusing on equal respect for persons, i.e. a form of respect that abstracts from social and professional standing or individual talents, Darwall suggests that each person, *qua* moral agent, is endowed with an equal authority to be kept into account by her human fellows (Darwall 2006, p. 142). On Darwall's view, a relationship of mutual accountability can flourish only when each of the involved subjects takes up a perspective from which each can make and acknowledge claims on one another's conduct and will (Darwall 2006, p. 3). This perspective is called by Darwall "second-person standpoint", and it proves to be a source of normative reasons (among them those that prevent persons from doing damage to each other, as well as those that bind each of them to view the others as subjects worthy of regard).

---

[13] This is also suggested by Leslie Green (Green 2010), who has argued that one cannot treat people with authentic respect without being a "respecter", that is, a person able to show some form of sensitivity towards the addressee of respect.
[14] Cf. the entry "*respicere*" in the Oxford Latin Dictionary; cf. the entry "respect" in the Online Etymology Dictionary (http://www.etymonline.com).

Ideas similar to those endorsed by Darwall are shared even by scholars who deny that respect ought to be considered an attitude. Joseph Raz, for instance, believes that respect is simply a matter of actions, a practical way of treating persons (Raz 2001, p. 138), and also a duty to observe in societies (Raz 2001, p. 159). However, like Darwall, Raz maintains that the duty of respect consists in giving "due weight" to the interests of other persons, which implies that each person has a right-claim to assert her status as moral agent (not that each person has a right-claim for any specific benefit). As he explains in his *The Morality of Freedom* (Raz 1986, p. 190),

> [T]o say "I have a right to have my interest taken into account" is like saying "I too am a person".

Under this light, experiencing people as respect-worthy presupposes "viewing" them as possessors of an irreducible authority.[15]

The metaphor of vision can also explain a second sense (a relatively unexplored one, in our view) in which the Latin word *respicere* might convey: "to look again" (Dillon 2007, p. 202). This meaning adds a slightly different twist to the idea of respect for persons as a response to someone's claims. First and foremost, to "look again" might imply that respect is a matter of paying attention to a certain subject (which, in its turn, might prompt the respecter to give the addressee of respect adequate care; cf. Dillon 1992). In the second place, looking at a certain person again might be tantamount to seeing that person in a new light.[16] In this sense, the act of *re-spicere* appears to be premised on the capacity of the respecter to undertake a closer inspection of people, and thus to identify the relevant properties by which they can be recognized as worthy of respect.

Leaving aside the existence of generic accounts of the idea of respect in different branches of philosophy, it is an undeniable fact that showing respect for people varies depending on the nature of the properties that are assumed to rightly prompt it, as well as the particular contexts in which respect is invoked. The existence of different ways of respecting persons is matched by polysemy of the word "respect" and the multifarious uses of this word in our everyday language.

Two well-known characterizations of different types of respect have been proposed by Stephen Hudson and Darwall respectively. On Hudson's view, respect can be either (1) directive, (2) evaluative, (3) "obstacle-respect" or (4) institutional, depending on the circumstances that shape it (Hudson 1980). In the

---

15 This is how Buss (1999, p. 519) rephrases Raz's ideas.
16 This is one of the meanings of the intensive prefix "*re*" (cf. Oxford Latin Dictionary): "anew".

case of directive respect, the addressee of respect ought to be regarded as a guide to action for the respecting subject (for instance, a person issuing commands, rules or advices, or one that legitimately invokes right-claims).[17] Evaluative respect, on the other hand, is the one accorded to persons endowed with some kind of outstanding excellence (either natural or acquired through experience; cf. Hudson 1980, pp. 72–73). Hudson's view of evaluative respect shows some degree of correspondence with Darwall's view of "appraisal respect", although Darwall, unlike Hudson, qualifies it as one that ought to be accorded only to those persons that display an outstanding moral behavior towards others (not only those people who show equal respect for others without possessing other outstanding talents, but also those who, by possessing some excellence that is not "moral" in its own right, employ it in ways that either foster respect for others or do not prevent it; Darwall 1977, pp. 41–45).

The third form of respect identified by Hudson is one felt for things or persons that, by virtue of their characteristics or the limits they impose, are perceived by people as "barriers" to their agential paths. This kind of respect is called by Hudson "obstacle-respect", and it is generally referred to as a mode of conduct (not an attitude) towards rules (like speed-limits) or dangerous beings (like ferocious animals) that elicit careful behavior (Hudson 1980, pp. 74–75).

Finally, Hudson outlines a kind of respect that, being addressed to institutional authorities, is not accorded on the basis of the personal characteristics of the authority holders, but simply as recognition of status. The same kind of respect is described by Darwall in terms of "honor". Darwall takes issue with respect for institutional authorities within the framework of a discussion of the differences between two broad categories under which various kinds of respect fall: *appraisal respect* and *recognition respect*.

Unlike esteem for moral excellence, which does not by itself bind the respecting subjects to accommodate their conduct in relation to the existence, the qualities and/or the claims of the addressees of respect, recognition respect for someone as a person means

> to give appropriate weight to the fact that he or she is a person by being willing to constrain one's behavior in ways required by that fact. (Darwall 1977, p. 45)

According to the taxonomy of respect outlined by Darwall, respect as "honor" stands out as an "asymmetric" form of recognition. Accordingly, to recognize the authority and peculiar standing of someone binds the respecter to make her-

---

[17] Hudson includes among the addressees of directive respect even abstract entities like laws and rights (pp. 71–72).

self accountable towards the addressee of respect (that is to say, the respected subject possesses a legitimate "second-personal" authority). Respect as honor is not by itself reciprocated, nor is it premised on equality of entitlements, although this does not prevent those who honor and revere some institutional authority to be the addressees of respect by that authority simply in virtue of their being "human". This type of respect, being the one which human beings owe to each other *qua* human beings endowed with agential capacities, can be considered "equal respect", and it features acts of reciprocal, symmetric recognition.

On Darwall's view, equal respect binds each person to pursue her life plans in a way that is compatible with the recognition of the fact that other human beings, *qua* human, can legitimately vindicate the same authority to shape their lives. This kind of respect, which has been addressed by philosophers like John Rawls and Ronald Dworkin, underlies a conception of justice that rests on the assumption that human beings, independently of features like gender and race, are entitled to equal concern.[18]

Finally, a kind of recognition respect that, without being second-personal, is based on a supposed asymmetry between the respecter and the respected concerning a certain competence is the one that Darwall names "respect for epistemic authority".[19] This is the type of respect that brings the respecting subjects to trust and accept advice issued by expert people without binding them in a normative sense. As a form of recognition respect, however, respect for epistemic authority compels the respecting subjects to take indications by competent people into account, and so to impart a specific direction to their conduct on relevant matters.

2 Outline of the Present Volume

The present volume consists of ten chapters: an introductory chapter in which the co-editors discuss the notion of "recognition" (a notion which plays a fundamental role in any theory of respect for persons), and nine chapters in which the notion of "respect for persons" is examined in relation to specific philosophers. The volume is divided into three parts: (I) a study of respect for persons (and self-respect) in Ancient Philosophy; (II) an investigation of the notion of respect in

---

18 See for instance J. Rawls (1971), *A Theory of Justice*; R. Dworkin (1977), *Taking Rights Seriously*, especially p. 182.
19 See also Hudson (1980, p. 71), who includes this kind of respect in the category of "directive respect".

Modern Philosophy; (III) a reconstruction of the evolution that the notion of respect undergoes in the transition from Modern to Contemporary Philosophy.

In the first of the nine essays of this volume, *The Notion of Respect in Ancient Greek Poetry*, Giovanni Giorgini examines the appearance of the concept of "respect" in early Greek poetry, with special regard to the poets Homer, Solon and Theognis. After taking into consideration the most likely candidates for a Greek notion of respect – the words *aidôs* and *timê* – Giorgini goes on to argue that the idea of respect emerged in Greek culture inside the aristocracy. The nobles considered themselves the possessors of outstanding moral value and saw themselves as "peers" and as such worthy of respect: to respect their equals and be respected by them was the appropriate behavior of an aristocrat. Giorgini shows that the vicissitudes of aristocracy were mirrored in the evolution of the notion of respect. The poems of Solon and Theognis, both active in the 6th century BCE, are used as case studies. Particular emphasis is accorded to the notion of *aidôs*, which, from the Homeric poems up to Plato, conveys a fragile sense of self-respect that may be not only nurtured, but also threatened, by one's fellow-citizens. The emergence of democracy, first in Athens and then in other Greek cities, paved the way to a new ideology which saw the Athenian citizens as collectively noble and as such inherently worthy of respect. Democratic theory appropriated the notion of equality among peers and extended it to the entire Athenian citizenry: in this new perspective, a person was considered worthy of respect regardless of his status or his belonging to a noble family. Giorgini then investigates the institutionalization of this concept in the notions of *timê* ("honor", but also "office") and *atimia* (disenfranchisement) and examines their implications: lack of virtue or unjust behavior lead to forms of institutionalized lack of respect, as in those processes which bring those who have been convicted of certain crimes to the condition of *atimia*, that is, of deprivation of honor and good social status. Giorgini concludes with a section on the ritualistic aspect of respect, namely deliberate disrespectful behavior which causes dishonor to other people.

Plato either has no word for, or no word that coincides significantly with, "respect"; what he does have is a concept – of love, and/or of friendship – through and around which he discusses the questions that underlie the notions of respect and self-respect, i.e., all those questions concerned with our relationships to others and to ourselves. It has been proposed, notoriously, that Plato's universe has room only for a kind of self-love, insofar as he seems to insist that we not only do but should see everything and everyone through the prism of our own interests and our own good. In his essay *Plato on Respect, and What "Belongs to" Oneself*, Rowe argues that this is to misunderstand Plato completely: for one thing, it makes it hard, if not impossible, to see how Plato could at the same time insist that even as a person will do everything for the sake of his or her own good, he or she will never – if he or she is a good person – do anything to harm another. Leaving aside the considerable complexities surrounding the notion of "harm" in Plato, the general upshot still is that the Platonic agent will ideally behave in the same ways as we ourselves might expect people to behave "out of respect" (however this is to be understood) for others, or for themselves. One of the chief aims of Rowe's paper is to show how Plato, although being the kind of egoist he seems to be (a very refined kind of egoist, but an egoist nonetheless), manages to justify his emphasis on the requirement for us to be just, or fair, or considerate – or pious. The most important claim made by Rowe in his chapter is that Plato effects the necessary combination between egoism and other-regardingness by using the notion of what is "ours", or "belongs to" – is *oikeion* to – ourselves, so that it includes others and others' interests as well as our own. A second relevant claim, made already by one ancient voice but hardly recognized in modern times, is that the Platonic approach has much in common with the Stoic idea of *oikeiôsis*.

Many of the difficulties regarding a proper conceptualization of respect for persons in Plato can be found in Aristotle. In his *Aristotle and Respect for Persons*, Weber points out that Aristotle has neither a single technical term that corresponds to our notion of "respect" nor one that tallies with our concept of "person". The Greek word that may come closest to the concept of "respect" in Aristotle's writings is probably the verb *"timaô"* and the corresponding noun *"timê"*. *"Timaô"* and *"timê"* in Aristotle relate either to a form of "appraisal respect", the esteem for an agent's outstanding moral qualities, or a form of "respect as honor", which means the attitude and conduct which is owed to a (good) statesman and other officeholders. However, as Weber points out, *timaô/timê* are definitely not related to "recognition respect", i.e., the recognition of the equal, inherent and absolute moral value of human beings qua persons independently of their deserts (which is the morally significant kind of respect we refer to by talking of "respect for persons"). Moreover, Aristotle's distinctively eudaimonistic approach to the human good rules out a proper account of respect as a deontological notion, that is, as a morally binding conduct which commits every human being to recognize persons as ends in themselves and in all circumstances (as Kant instead would suggest).

Despite these possible grounds for objection, Weber contends that Aristotle develops a concept of morally required attitudes towards other persons that seems to present significant analogies with the modern idea of respect for persons. More to the point, by analysis of some relevant passages of the *Politics*, Weber proposes that this concept can be found within the framework of Aristotle's theory of rulership over free men, i.e. the kind of rule that aims at the subject's and not at the ruler's benefit. The respect that rulers owe to citizens in right constitutions finds its sense within an eudaimonistic-paternalistic framework, and is premised on recognition in every citizen of the human deliberative faculty, the same faculty which, if brought to its full-fledged actuality in a virtue-oriented political community, ensures individual happiness. The same capacity makes individuals free by nature, and existing "not for someone else's sake", as slaves by nature do, but for their own sake (*hautou esti*).

As the first three chapters of this volume suggest, respect stands out primarily as a principle of virtuous conduct. Nevertheless, when we conceive of respect as a philosophical notion, its uncontroversial practical import appears to coexist with a primarily "descriptive" function. In her *Human Interaction in the State of Nature: Hobbes on Respect for Persons and Self-Respect*, Irrera argues that self-respect and respect for persons can be viewed in Hobbes's thought not only as prescriptive ideals, but also and especially as notions that help to clarify crucial aspects of human nature and behavior. What is more, as the author contends, an attempt to identify various forms of respect in Hobbes's work (esteem, honor, equal respect and recognition of authority) may foster a clearer and deeper understanding of his discussion of the state of nature and the transition to the civil state. By leaving aside the civil state, Irrera focuses on the state of nature as described by Hobbes in *The Elements of Law: Natural and Politic*, and *Leviathan*. As Irrera argues, Hobbes's theory of "power" provides the fundamentals of two broad categories into which the notion of respect can fall: a well-grounded respect, based on sound personal experience of one's own powers and the powers possessed by others, and ill-grounded forms of respect, which do not rely on the same kind of experience.

Irrera maintains that mutually conflicting claims arise primarily when everyone, by developing a personal (and not always well-grounded) sense of his or her own worth, cultivates expectations about his or her own good that end up being thwarted, due to similar expectations held by other human beings. Moreover, a form of equal respect that might be identified in the state of nature, that is, the one based on recognition of the mutual power to inflict damage to others, must be replaced by the one prescribed by the laws of nature. Only this form of respect ensures an authentic regard for others, grounded in recognition of the legitimacy of their individual pursuits.

The principle that every person deserves respect and the idea that every person deserves it unconditionally represent the most relevant conditions of adequacy for any philosophical theory about equal respect. For many contemporary authors who work on the concept of "equal respect" and its conceptual underpinnings, the writings of Immanuel Kant constitute a crucial point of reference. On the other hand, what exactly Kant means when he talks about respect (*Ach-

tung) is debatable. In *The Source of Moral Motivation and Actions We Owe to Others: Kant's Theory of Respect*, Bratu discusses two different senses in which Kant understands respect: (1) the feeling that constitutes the source of moral motivation (*reverentia*), and (2) a specific set of actions we are obliged to perform in response to certain morally relevant features of persons (*observantia*). By analyzing some passages of CRP and MM, Bratu proposes that, although both respect as *reverentia* and respect as *observantia* are premised on the *acknowledgment of some morally relevant feature* of persons, in the case of *reverentia* this acknowledgment takes place at the level of feelings and motivations, and it is directed to the things that the moral law requires, while respect as *observantia* takes place at the level of actions, and it concerns primarily recognition of human dignity.

This second form of respect requires that each and every person ought to be treated as *human*, being effectively entitled to such a treatment. On the other hand, it is a matter of debate whether Kant has a proper conception of human rights, and, if so, what he regards as their "normative ground" or "foundation". Those who argue that he does have such a conception typically invoke, among other things, the "one innate right to freedom" as formulated in the *Doctrine of Right*, as the most promising candidate for a human right in Kant. Additionally, one often encounters the view that this right – and maybe other rights related to it – is ultimately grounded in dignity and "respect" for human or rational beings. Given both the prominence of the topic and the frequency with which this "foundational claim" is made, it is remarkably unclear what precisely it could actually amount to in Kantian terms. Most crucially, it is not clear how we should properly understand the claim that respect is the foundation of human rights in Kant. Göbel's essay *Respect as the Foundation of Human Rights: To What Extent Can This View Be Attributed to Kant?* aims to reduce these unclarities by considering to what extent the view that respect for persons is the foundation of human rights might be an adequate characterization of Kant's philosophical position on this subject. Goebel distinguishes the claim that Kant was a defender of human rights (which she rejects) from the possibility of a Kantian theory of human rights (which she affirms). Göbel then addresses the question of how Kant's concept of respect might fit into the latter as a foundation. The answer is developed via a systematic (re)construction of two concepts of respect in Kant, i.e. respect as a moral obligation to recognize human beings as ends in themselves, and respect as the only possible motive or "drive" (*Triebfeder*) to morally good action.

Kant's view of self-respect and respect for persons substantiates the thesis that, in order to be autonomous and self-governed, a fully rational agent must also be "moral". As Kant presents it, this view is nevertheless open to a number of objections, the most relevant of which is the one which presents the Kantian moral law as empty, in that not only does it not even attempt to indicate particular moral duties, but also appears detached from concrete practical action (Geiger 2007; Priest 1987).

The insufficiency of a universal moral law which is not well-connected to action has led several philosophers to attempts to reconcile abstract universality and concrete particularity in morality. The most well-known of them is Hegel-whose philosophy of personhood and morality can be seen as a reformulation and enrichment of some Kantian views (Wallace 1995). Laitinen's essay assesses Hegel's theory of respect and its relevance to contemporary accounts of respect. Following Fichte's initiative, Hegel considered recognition (and, more properly, relations of recognition) as a crucial component of human personhood. Far from being merely a social status, "personhood in Hegel's sense" concerns different aspects of human personhood or selfhood and human freedom: external possessions, inner capacities, relationships to family, friends, fellow-citizens and even fellow humans. These aspects substantiate various forms of respectful relations not only towards one's own self, but also towards other persons.

By analyzing some relevant passages of both Hegel's *Philosophy of Right* and part of the secondary literature on the topic, Laitinen attempts to clarify on which grounds Hegel's account of relations of recognition can be deemed "multi-dimensional", as is Hegel's view of personhood. Laitinen explains that, for Hegel, personal respect concerns relationships of mutual recognition in three spheres: (a) legal personhood, being identified with the agency of persons as "owners" in pre-moral and pre-institutional "abstract right"; (b) self-determining moral subjectivity, which is premised on the human possession of inner capacities; and (c) *Sittlichkeit* or *ethical life*, which concerns humans in particular concrete roles, for instance as members of family, civil society and the state.

One can therefore distinguish an *abstract* personal respect (one which resembles forms of respect in concrete market relations as realized by economic institutions) from other forms which Laitinen defines "thicker", such as esteem, love, or solidarity, and also other forms of recognition that contemporary thinkers like Honneth (2014) and Habermas (1996), following Hegel's lead, have stressed: respect for each other as democratic members in collective self-determination.

The idea of equal respect as something which we owe to each other underlies some of the most notable contemporary attempts to conceptualize respect in liberally-oriented political communities. One outstanding example is the work of John Stuart Mill. In his *John Stuart Mill: Individuality, Dignity, and Respect for Persons*, Loizides explores the idea of respect for persons in John Stuart Mill's moral and political thought as a concern with individuality and the sense of dignity. In the first part of the chapter, the author brings to light Mill's idea that respect for persons enables the addressees of respect to develop and strengthen a sense of their own worth. For this reason, he provides a preliminary discussion of the theory of individuality in Mill's *On Liberty* (1859), *The Subjection of Women* (1869) and *Principles of Political Economy* (1848); with reference to *Utilitarianism* (1861), he also tries to show that self-development and the pursuit of a worthwhile life create a sense of dignity, or self-respect. As Loizides points out, although Mill recognizes that this sense varies according to individual characters and aims, he lays special emphasis on the morally and intellectually best people, for whom self-respect combines a search for moral approbation with a just regard for the common good.

In the second part of the chapter, Loizides deals with a potential problem for Mill: can his utilitarian theory accommodate claims of *equal recognition respect?* As a way out of that potential conundrum, the author revisits the old debate concerning the consistency of Mill's moral and political thought, turning for answers to Mill's theory of an "Art of Life" as developed in the last pages of *A System of Logic* (1843). Here, Loizides argues, the sense of justice is informed by concern with the claims of others, and this concern appears to be precisely what makes that sense properly "moral". This becomes more evident if we consider that the importance of developing for its own sake a character unique to one's self directly connects with Mill's discussion of "Liberty and Necessity" in his *A System of Logic*. Although our character is formed – for us – during our childhood, it is possible through *appraisal respect* to initiate self-culture in maturity; and self-culture, as Mill argued in his essays on Jeremy Bentham and on aesthetics in the 1830s, makes for the very possibility of virtue. This takes us full circle back to Mill's *On Liberty* and the idea that "[a]mong the works of man, which human life is rightly employed in perfecting and beautifying, the first in importance surely is man himself".

Respect and, perhaps even more crucially, self-respect, play a pivotal role also in John Rawls' *A Theory of Justice*, arguably one of the most influential works in political philosophy of the 20th century. For Rawls, self-respect is "perhaps the most important primary good" (§ 67), one whose social bases are to be distributed equally according to the well-known two principles that make up his general conception of justice. John Rawls claims that self-respect and respect for persons are mutually interrelated, in that receiving respect from others leads to self-respect and "those who respect themselves are more likely to respect each other and conversely" (Rawls 1971, p. 179, § 29). What is more, every conception of justice should express men's respect for one another *publicly* (Rawls 1971, p. 179, § 29).

However, it has hardly been noticed that these notions are also central for Michael Walzer's *Spheres of Justice*. Knoll's essay *The Cardinal Role of Respect and Self-Respect for Rawls's and Walzer's Theories of Justice* provides a comparative analysis of both philosophers which aims to sustain Walzer's theory of justice. Knoll stresses the idea that, while Rawls uses the terms "self-respect" and "self-esteem" as synonyms, Walzer clearly distinguishes the two notions. As Knoll argues, despite Rawls's and Walzer's shared focus on the equal respect that is due to citizens of a democracy, their theories of justice are the result of different approaches to political philosophy. While Rawls's theory revolves around the ideal of a well-ordered society, Walzer interprets the world we live in and its normative order. Through an analysis of Walzer's theory of distributive justice emerging in his *Spheres of Justice* and, more specifically, in his chapter *Recognition*, Knoll lays special emphasis on Walzer's concept of public honor and individual desert as ideals that distributive justice ought to address to make self-respect possible.

The essays included in this volume do not aim to provide conclusive answers regarding the role played by the issue of respect for persons in ancient, modern and contemporary philosophy. Rather, they simply mean to offer some plausible suggestions on knowledge, morality and politics which the reader might find profitable for his or her own reconstruction of the notion of respect throughout the history of philosophy. Nevertheless, we hope to bring out two main ideas: (1) that respect for persons retains an original entanglement with self-respect; (2) that the evolutions undergone by these notions from ancient to contemporary times do not feature elements of rupture, but continuity. What ancient, modern and contemporary positions on respect have in common is concern for the fact that every form of respect requires distinctive kinds of recognition of oneself and others. Bringing respect into actuality, then, requires careful thought on the possibilities and limits of human cognition and interaction.

References

Bird, C. (2004): "Status, Identity, and Respect", *Political Theory* 32, pp. 207–232.
Brownsword, R. (2014): "Human Dignity from a Legal Perspective", in Düwell, M., Braarvig, J., Brownsword, R. and Mieth, D. (Eds.): *The Cambridge Handbook of Human Dignity. Interdisciplinary Perspectives*, Cambridge: Cambridge University Press, pp. 1–22.
Carter, I., Galeotti, A.E. and Ottonelli, V. (Eds.) (2008): *Eguale Rispetto*, Milano: Mondadori.
Carter, I. (2009). "Respect for Persons and the Interest in Freedom". In de Wijze, S.A., Kramer, M.H. Carter, I. (Eds.): *Hillel Steiner and The Anatomy of Justice*, New York: Routledge, pp. 167–184.
Carter, I. (2011): "Respect and the Basis of Equality", *Ethics* 121 (3), pp. 538–571.
Cranor, C. (1975): "Toward a Theory of Respect for Persons", *American Philosophical Quarterly* 12 (4), pp. 309–319.

Darwall, S. (1977): "Two Kinds of Respect", *Ethics* (88), pp. 36–49.
Darwall, S. (2006): *The Second Person Standpoint: Morality, Respect, and Accountability*, Cambridge (Mass.): Harvard University Press.
Dillon, R.S. (1992): "Respect and Care: Toward Moral Integration", *Canadian Journal of Philosophy* (22), pp. 105–132.
Dillon, R. (2007): "Respect: A Philosophical Perspective", *Gruppendynamik und Organisationsberatung* 38 (2), pp. 201–212.
Dworkin, R. (1977): *Taking Rights Seriously*, Cambridge (Mass.): Harvard University Press.
Dworkin, R. (1985): *A Matter of Principle*, Cambridge (Mass.) and London: Harvard University Press.
Galeotti, A.E. (2010): *La politica del rispetto. I fondamenti etici della democrazia*, Roma-Bari.
Geiger, I. (2007): *The Founding Act of Modern Ethical Life: Hegel's Critique of Kant's Moral*, Stanford: Stanford University Press.
Green, L. (2010): "Two Worries about Respect for Persons", *Ethics* 120 (2), pp. 212–231.
Hill, Th.E. (2000): *Respect, Pluralism, and Justice. Kantian Perspectives*, Oxford: Oxford University Press.
Honneth, A. (1996): *The Struggle for Recognition: The Moral Grammar of Social Conflict*, Cambridge: MIT Press.
Hudson, S.D. (1980): "The Nature of Respect", *Social Theory and Practice* 6 (1), pp. 69–90.
Kateb, G. (2011): *Human Dignity*, Cambridge (Mass.) and London: Harvard University Press.
Mordacci, R. (2012): *Rispetto*, Milano: Raffaello Cortina.
Neumann, M. (2000): "Did Kant Respect Persons?", *Res Publica* (6), pp. 285–299.
Nussbaum, M.C. (2011): *Creating Capabilities: The Human Development Approach*, Cambridge (Mass.) and London: Belknap Press of Harvard University Press.
Raz, J. (1979): *The Authority of Law. Essays on Law and Morality*, Oxford: Clarendon Press.
Raz, J. (1986): *The Morality of Freedom*, Oxford: Clarendon Press.
Raz, J. (2001): *Value, Respect, and Attachment*, Cambridge: Cambridge University Press.
Sennett, R. (2002): *Respect in a World of Inequality*, London: Penguin.
Sennett, R. (2003): *Respect: The Formation of Character in an Age of Equality*, London: Allen Lane.
Honneth, A. and Fraser, N. (Eds.) (2003): *Redistribution or Recognition?: A Political-philosophical Exchange* (translated by Joel Golb, James Ingram and Christiane Wilke), London and New York: Verso.
Priest (Ed.) (1987): *Hegel's Critique of Kant*, Oxford: Oxford University Press.
Rawls, J. (1971): *A Theory of Justice*, Cambridge (MA) and London: Harvard University Press;
Taylor, Ch. (1992): *Multiculturalism and the Politics of Recognition: An Essay*, Princeton: Princeton University Press.
Timmons, M. and Johnson R.N. (Eds.) (2015): *Reason, Value, and Respect. Kantian Themes from the Philosophy of Thomas E. Hill, Jr.*, Oxford: Oxford University Press.
Walzer, M. (1983): *Spheres of Justice: A Defence of Pluralism and Equality*, Oxford: Robertson.
Wallace, R.M. (1995): "Reformulation of the Kantian Argument for the Rationality of Morality", *American Philosophical Quarterly* 32 (3), pp. 263–270.

Giovanni Giorgini and Elena Irrera
Recognition: A Philosophical Problem

A philosophical enquiry into the ideal of respect and its primary conceptual components requires a preliminary understanding of the nature and inner mechanics of recognition. Due to the impossibility of an exhaustive discussion of the philosophical issue of recognition across the history of philosophy, this chapter will confine itself to proposing paths of analysis which touch upon just a few among the most significant positions that have been proposed on this matter. The approach we will adopt combines analytical aspects with historic-philosophical insights. First, we will propose that a pre-philosophical form of recognition may be found in the ethics of ancient Greek aristocracy. Then, we will suggest that a study of recognition can be pursued in two directions: a cognitive one, which shows the role played by recognition in epistemic processes aimed at truth, and a practical one, which leads to revised forms of human communication and coexistence.

1 Introduction

The principle of recognition plays a pivotal role not only in clarifying the notion of respect and the forms in which this notion finds expression (such as esteem, honor, trust, equal regard and concern), but also in actualizing respect in concrete circumstances. Every act of recognition requires by definition (a) a subject who recognizes, (b) a subject (animate or inanimate) who is recognized, (c) a figure which the recognized subject can be identified with, and (d) a relevant criterion for the identification of (b) with (c). Being recognized, then, amounts to *being recognized as* someone or something, *in virtue of* one's possession of one or more properties which the recognizing subject considers relevant to the process of recognition.

Not every form of recognition leads to respectful and benevolent ways of handling a certain subject. For instance, recognizing a certain person as guilty of a crime may prompt public reactions such as stigmatization and hatred towards that person. On the other hand, when the properties through which recognition takes place are considered positive values by those who express recognition, recognition produces appreciation, and the recognized subjects are deemed worthy of respect in the eyes of those who recognize them. Whether or not recognition is a precondition of respect and benevolence, it can be conceived of as a cognitive act (often accompanied by emotional expressions) that provides occasion for practically relevant forms of human interaction, in private relationships as well as in the public sphere. Recognition, for instance, encourages attitudes like admiration for people endowed with a certain type of excellence, or the expression of reverential feelings towards established institutional authorities. Most crucially, it prompts equal respect and a sense of mutual accountability.

Recognition of persons as equally entitled to rights and the pursuit of individual life plans has been widely regarded as a promising way of coping with issues of social justice, that is, one which any strategic approach based on mere appeal to principles of distribution of income, wealth and social positions would be unable to frame.[1] Hence, the need for a successful implementation of equal respect in contemporary societies elicits urgency to think of recognition as a distinctively philosophical problem.

Providing an exhaustive discussion of the philosophical issue of recognition within the scope of a short introduction is an impracticable task. Due to this impracticability, we will confine ourselves to proposing a perspective of investigation which touches upon just a few among the most significant positions that have been proposed on this matter throughout the history of philosophy. The approach we will adopt combines analytical aspects with historic-philosophical insights.

Beforehand, though, we should mention that we believe in the existence of a pre-philosophical form of recognition which may be found in the ethics of ancient Greek aristocracy. Greek aristocrats elaborated an ideology, in the sense of a set of consistent beliefs, of recognition of the equal value of the fellow-aristocrat. They considered, and described, themselves as the possessors of outstanding moral value, "the best", "the happy", "the well-born" and so on. Moreover, they viewed themselves as being on an equal footing, "peers", when considered together against "the other" – the commoners, "the bad", "the wretched". Inside this world-view, to respect and be respected by the fellow-aristocrat was considered the appropriate behavior, what a gentleman owed to the other and expected from him: recognition of the value inherent in being born into a noble family, which transmitted to the descendants an outstanding moral capacity. It is interesting to note that the historical development of Greek aristocracy had a consis-

---

[1] While several philosophers have focused on redistribution of economic resources and social positions as an appropriate strategy for addressing unjustified inequalities in liberal societies (see for instance Rawls' theory of "justice as fairness" in Rawls 1971 and Dworkin's theory of "equality of resources" in Dworkin 1981), others have suggested that social justice cannot be attained without addressing issues of recognition (cf. Galeotti 2002, Young 1996 and Kymlicka 2007). See in particular Nancy Frazer (Frazer 2003), who treats redistribution and recognition as two conceptually different, although deeply related analytical perspectives.

tent impact on the notion of recognition, for when democracy was established in Athens following Cleisthenes' reforms in 508 BCE, the new democratic ideology appropriated the aristocratic notion of recognition on the basis of equal value and extended it to the entire citizenry. What became important then was Athenian citizenship, which amounted to an aristocratic status and was based on the laws. This dramatic change paved the way to the subsequent elaboration of a vision of recognition based on the law, civil, natural or divine.

Although the notion of "recognition" is widely used in a range of important philosophical works, it has rarely been the object of systematic research. A notable exception is presented by Paul Ricoeur's *Parcours de la reconnaissance* (2005; French ed. 2004), a book whose main task is attempting to trace some meanings of the word "recognition" and reconstructing their development throughout the history of philosophy. By addressing authors like Homer, Aristotle, Descartes, Hobbes, Kant and Hegel, Ricoeur aims to elicit a view of recognition as a response to claims for equal treatment generally advanced by the members of a given community (for instance, those who feel themselves treated unfairly). His view is that throughout the history of philosophy, the "passive" aspect of recognition (that is, the image of recognition as the object of a specific demand) assumes an increasingly prevailing role over the image of recognition as "activity".

It is worth noting that, as Ricoeur himself suggests in the introductory chapter of his work, the word "recognition" presents a wide variety of meanings. What seems to be lacking in the relevant scholarship is an investigation of a unitarian framework in relation to which this multiplicity of meanings can be understood. Finding it impossible to provide a univocal definition of the word "recognition", Ricoeur identifies three semantic points of focus from which other meanings of this word can be derived. On the one hand, recognition can be thought of as activity of the human mind that prompts acquisition of knowledge, and allows every human being to view a multiplicity of images as representing one and the same subject (Ricoeur 2005, pp. 12–13).

In Ricoeur's view, a second way of looking at recognition can be traced back to the philosophy of Henry Bergson. Bergson takes issue with recognition in relation to the past images and their persistence in an individual's memory. As Bergson argues for instance in the second chapter of *Matter and Memory* (Bergson 1991, pp. 86–88), recognition consists in a concrete act through which we reaffirm the past in the present. In Ricoeur's view, Bergson takes up the Platonic notion of *anamnêsis*, according to which learning to know oneself and others consists in rediscovering pre-existing knowledge within us (Ricoeur 2005, pp. 17–18). For Bergson, then, it is recognition of memories that leads to self-knowledge. A third meaning of recognition regards the Hegelian notion of *Aner-*

kennung (Ricoeur 2005, pp. 18–20). In Hegel's philosophy, the issue of recognition plays a fundamental role not only in clarifying the nature of freedom, but also in explaining its effectual actualization in the domain of history and human interactions. In this light, recognition appears to have a practical worth.

In this chapter we will not reproduce Ricoeur's reconstruction of recognition throughout the history of philosophy. Nevertheless, his reflections suggest that a study of recognition can be pursued in two directions: a cognitive one, which shows the role played by recognition in epistemic processes aimed at truth; and a practical one, which leads to revised forms of human communication and coexistence.

2 Recognition as a Path to Knowledge. From Homer to Kant

In certain cases, recognizing someone (or something) means identifying a given subject as someone (or something) that one has already encountered in the past. In that case, the activity of recognition is premised on the capacity of the recognizing subject to recall that subject to mind; this presupposes an existing knowledge of that subject, the possession of a corresponding mental image, and the capacity to distinguish the featuring traits of that image as properties which define the known subject. Provided that a certain person (or thing) *Y* is recognized by *R*, when *R* sees in *Y* the same unique properties which he or she has ascribed in the past to a given person (or thing) *X*, *R* recognizes *Y* and *X* as one and the same subject (Ricoeur 2005, p. 6).

A notable example of this process is provided in Homer's epic poem, the *Odyssey* (circa 8th century BCE), which narrates the vicissitudes experienced by the king of Ithaca, Odysseus, throughout his ten-year journey home after the Trojan War. Homer describes the kingdom of Ithaca during Odysseus' absence as threatened by a number of unmarried men, called "the suitors", who have taken residence in Odysseus' home, trying to court his wife Penelope and demanding that she choose one among them as husband. Odysseus, landed in Ithaca after twenty years, is disguised as a wandering beggar by the goddess Athena. As we read in Book XXIII, Penelope, being informed about Odysseus' return by the nurse Eurycleia, appears initially reticent to believe that the beggar is truly her husband. Being reproached by her son Telemachus for such an attitude, she answers him:

> My child, the heart in my breast is lost in wonder, and I have no power to speak at all, nor to ask a question, nor to look him in the face. But if in very truth he is Odysseus, and has come home, we two shall surely know one another (*gnôsometh'allêlôn*) more certainly; for we have signs (*sêmatha*) which we two alone know, signs hidden from others. (*Od.* XXIII, 105–111)

Odysseus himself is well aware that, in order to recognize him as her husband and king of Ithaca, Penelope needs to overcome perplexity and reticence. As he tells Telemachus,

> Telemachus, suffer now thy mother to test me in the halls; presently shall she win more certain knowledge. But now because I am foul, and am clad about my body in mean clothing, she scorns me, and will not yet admit that I am he. (*Od.* XXIII, 114–119)

To assure herself that the beggar is her husband, Penelope puts him to the test by asking Eurycleia to move the wedding bed that Odysseus himself carved out of an olive tree. As the only person who (besides Penelope) knows that the bed cannot be moved out of the chamber, the beggar expresses his worry about Penelope's request. This is how Penelope *admits*[2] that the beggar is speaking the truth and thus *recognizes* him as Odysseus.

This piece of information, being used as a "sign of recognition", is not publicly known; nevertheless, by being known and shared by the subjects involved in the relation of recognition, Odysseus and Penelope, it makes recognition itself successful. Penelope's recognition of Odysseus, then, is the outcome of a successful correspondence: the one between her memory and mental image of Odysseus and the (previously unknown) figure of the beggar. The beggar, in that case, is *re-cognized*, that is, seen in a different light, and so is the king of Ithaka and husband of Penelope. Once discovered, this truth has the power to promote an active change in the story and the lives of the characters.

The idea of recognition as a path directed at the truth is central in the pursuit of human knowledge. As a way of "getting to know" something, recognition implies an activity of exploration and progression towards an established goal, which requires confrontation with unknown items. Confronting experienced items with mental images is a task not immune from doubt and error. This is for example what emerges in Plato's *Theaetetus* (probably written between 386 and 367 BCE), where the author, by staging a discussion between Socrates and the young Theaetetus, takes issue with the notion of "knowledge" (*epistêmê*)

---

[2] On the meaning of recognition as "acceptance/admission that something is true" see Bergson 2005, p. 7.

and the possibility of defining it. After rejecting the idea that knowledge is to be identified with sensation (*aisthêsis*; *Theaet.* 151d–187a), Socrates encourages Theaetetus to agree with him on the idea that sensory organs by themselves are just tools through which knowledge can be attained. What enables every human being to get knowledge of something is only the soul (*hê psychê*) (*Theaet.* 184c–185e). As a source of knowledge, the soul has a double function: on the one hand, it examines some immaterial objects by itself, such as being and not being, similarity and dissimilarity, identity and difference, unity and number (185c–d); on the other, it makes use of sensory faculties to elaborate a number of empirical inputs (*Theaet.* 185e) and turn them into a single image (*idea*; *Theaet.* 184d).

The idea that being and truth can be grasped by human beings only by way of a reasoning activity rather than by way of pure sense-perception (*Theaet.* 186d) is premised on the second definition of knowledge provided by Theaetetus: knowledge is true opinion (*hê alethê doxa*). Before ultimately rejecting this definition, Socrates sustains Theaetetus' suggestion by crafting a theoretical model in the light of which not only true opinion, but also and especially the creation of false opinions can be understood as a logical possibility.

The conceptual image outlined by Socrates consists in a wax tablet in our mind where several images are stored (*Theaet.* 191a–196c). The wax tablet contains both copies of past perceptions and imprints that represent our knowledge of general terms (e.g. 'man' and 'horse'). However, Socrates focuses on the copies of a perception of some object and argues that, if one has a sufficiently clear copy in one's mind, then it can be said that one remembers that object and knows it (cf. Bostock 1988, p. 178). False opinion might be a case of "false recognition", which arises when something that is currently perceived is forced to match an already existing imprint. As it seems, to incautiously fit a perception into the wrong imprint gives rise to the false belief that the object perceived is the same as the object that is remembered (Bostock 1988, p. 178).

The mismatch between memory and perception is expressed by Socrates as follows:

> [T]he possibility of forming false opinion remains in the following case: when, for example, knowing you and Theodorus [i.e. Theaetetus' teacher], and having on that block of wax the imprint of both of you, as if you were signet-rings, but seeing you both at a distance and indistinctly, I hasten to assign the proper imprint of each of you to the proper vision, and to make it fit, as it were, its own footprint, with the purpose of causing recognition; but I may fail in this by interchanging them, and put the vision of one upon the imprint of the other, as people put a shoe on the wrong foot; or, again, I may be affected as the sight is affected when we use a mirror and the sight as it flows makes a change from

right to left, and thus make a mistake; it is in such cases, then, that interchanged opinion occurs and the forming of false opinion arises. (*Theaet*. 193b – d)

The idea of false opinion as a failed correspondence between memory and perception will be subsequently rejected by Socrates, on the ground that to have a clear perception cannot lead to the consequence that a person fails to know what he knows (*Theaet*. 196c). Nevertheless, Plato does not reject the idea that the human mind contains some imprints independent of sense-perception. This idea will be at the foundation of the Platonic model of knowledge as "recollection" (*anamnêsis*) developed in dialogues like the *Meno*, the *Phaedo*, and the *Phaedrus*. Understood as re-collection, knowledge involves recognizing realities already present in the human mind; in that case, *re-cognition* is itself a form of *cognition*.

The view that recognition is an activity of the mind through which knowledge is achieved is also at the basis of René Descartes' philosophy (1596 – 1650). Just like Plato, Descartes believes that knowledge is a conquest that can be attained through introspection. Being committed to an exploration of the limits and possibilities of human knowledge, Descartes throws light not only on the roots of epistemic processes, but also on the nature of the subject committed to the search for knowledge. In his *Discourse on Method*, Descartes maintains that acquiring knowledge entails learning to discern the true from the false, so as to achieve incontrovertibility, clarity, and distinctness (Descartes 2006, II, 19, p. 17). Recognition of what is true occurs through discernment and, as Descartes also suggests in his *Meditations on First Philosophy*, provides "a reliable building-block for further deductions" (Descartes 2006, p. 70, note 17). In the *Meditations* Descartes' thinking activity requires not only understanding, but also mental activities like doubting, affirming and denying (Descartes 2006, XLVII).

While the first three *Meditations* provide valuable insights on the existence of human subjects as finite thinking substances and the existence of god as an infinite substance, in the fourth meditation Descartes copes with the paradox of a finite substance that, although being the creation of an infinite, perfect substance, is prone to making errors and producing false thoughts (Brandhorst 2010, pp. 134 – 137). Descartes suggests that the paradox is just an apparent one, on the ground that human faculties such as judgment, will, reason, the senses and imagination, are not by themselves flawed. It rather seems that God-given capacities can be put to bad use by human beings.

Getting to know something or someone, then, amounts to learning how to avoid errors and to use one's faculties in the most appropriate way. In order to achieve self-understanding, the thinking substance must set the relationships correctly. This task, as Descartes argues in the fourth meditation, is premised on an activity of recognition of the nature of God as a source of truth:

> ... first of all, I recognize [Latin *agnosco*] it to be impossible that He should ever deceive me; for in all fraud and deception some imperfection is to be found. (*Meditation* IV, Descartes 2003, p. 94)

Recognition of God's perfection represents a fundamental step for a proper understanding of the responsibilities of human beings in their epistemic experiences:

> From all this I recognize [Latin *percipio*] that the power of will which I have received from God is not of itself the source of my errors – for it is very ample and very perfect of its kind – any more than is the power of understanding [...] errors come from the fact that since the will is much wider in its range and compass than the understanding, I do not restrain it within the same bounds. (Descartes 2003, p. 97)

A clear experience of what is given by God leads people to admit that God is not responsible for the mistakes they freely commit. This form of recognition finds expression in the attitude and feelings of gratitude:[3]

> I have every reason to render thanks to God who owes me nothing and who has given me all the perfections I possess, and I should be far from charging Him with injustice. (Descartes 2003, p. 99)

To conclude, for Descartes the individual search for clear and distinct knowledge is premised on the capacity to conceptualize the difference between the self, God and the external world, which requires a "first-person" perspective (Rudder Baker 1998). Being able to think of oneself as a "self" distinct from others is the necessary condition for the use of the intellective faculty and the possibility of representing external reality. This capacity lies also at the basis of Kant's epistemology. Kant speaks of recognition (*Rekognition*) as a principle that, being involved in the activity of knowledge, relates empirical items to universal concepts possessed *a priori* by the human mind. As he explains in his *Critique of Pure Reason*, the objects of our experience are particulars that, in order to become objects of knowledge, must be "constructed" by the mind. To do so, the mind performs three types of "synthesis" (or organization) of empirical information. First, it must "apprehend" in intuition, that is, it must settle sensible items into a spatial and temporal structure. Once properly located, the spatial-temporally informed

---

[3] The equation of recognition and "gratitude" is presented by Ricoeur in Ricoeur 2005, pp. 12–16.

items must be associated with others and "reproduced" in a faculty called "imagination". This enables the mind to go from one item to the other. Finally, the combined items are to be "recognized" by means of concepts. This process is named by Kant "synthesis of recognition in a concept" (A 97–105). While the "synthesis of apprehension" regards sensibility, i.e. the sphere of perceptual inputs, the "synthesis of reproduction in imagination" consists in setting up mental associations by retaining intuitions previously received. In this way, the mind can return to them even in the absence of any current representation of them (A 100). This process occurs in the faculty of imagination, which has the power to connect several empirical intuitions into the form of an image (A 120).

Recognition, on the other hand, is the job of a synthesis into an object which, although needing empirical material, requires the use of memory and *a priori* concepts. As Kant explains in the first edition of the *Critique of Pure Reason* (A 103, *Von der Synthesis der Rekognition im Begriffe*),

> Without our being conscious that what we are thinking now is the same as what we thought a moment before, all reproduction in the series of representations would be vain. Each representation would, in its present state, be a new one, and in no wise belonging to the act by which it was to be produced by degrees, and the manifold in it would never form a whole, because deprived of that unity which consciousness alone can impart to it.

Consciousness" (*Bewußtsein*), here, is presented by Kant as the primary condition for recognizing an object as the same as an object we were thinking of at another time. Although the activity of recognition implies the use of memory, to re-cognize is not equivalent to recalling something to mind. Rather, re-cognize is to "get to know".

3 The Prescriptive Worth of Recognition

As has been shown so far, recognition plays a central role in the promotion of both self-knowledge and knowledge of the external world. The epistemic relevance of this activity of the human mind emerges not only in scientific endeavors, but also in practical agency informed by reason. Indeed, recognition encourages examination of the thoughts and feelings we experience in everyday life, thus prompting a change in the view of ourselves and others.

The capacity of recognition to actively shape the personal values, perspectives and expectations of human beings in several dimensions of their life has successfully been stressed by Aristotle (384–322 BCE). In the first place, recognition of oneself and recognition of others are carried out in the composition and fruition of Greek dramatic art, particularly Greek tragedy. As Aristotle explains in the *Poetics*, recognition (or "discovery") (*anagnôrisis*) represents a key aspect of the plot (which he considers the "life and soul" of tragedy; *Poet*. 6.1450a36–37), and is generally identified as the moment in which the main character attains the truth about himself (or herself) and his (or her) relationship to others, generally as a result of vicissitudes and misunderstandings (*Poet*. 16.1454b19–1455a21). In general, recognition occurs when a peripethy (*peripeteia*) takes place, that is to say, a reversal of fortune by which the action turns around to its opposite, subject always to our rule of probability or necessity (*Poet*. 11.1452a22–24).

Tragedy, which Aristotle defines as "an imitation (*mimêsis*) not of persons but of action and life" (*Poet*. 6.1450a15–16; trans. Bywater), i.e. "an action that is complete in itself, as a whole of some magnitude" (7.1450b24–25), elicits in the spectators mechanisms of identification with its characters, thus arousing in the spectators themselves feelings of pity and fear (*Poet*. 9.1452a3–4). By virtue of this experience, the spectators are purified by such feelings, and are thus enabled to attain a deeper understanding of human reality and agency.

The reversal from ignorance to knowledge, on the one hand, commits people to think of their own responsibilities and, possibly, to change inappropriate attitudes and behavior. On the other hand, a sound self-cognition enhances the sense of one's own value (as a person or as an expert in a certain field); this prompts many to demand from others recognition of their worth. When a person A fails to recognize the worth of a person B, B is generally inclined to feel the emotion of anger (*orgê*). This is explained by Aristotle in the *Rhetoric*, where he analyzes (and sustains) some commonly held convictions on the reasons that prompt anger. It is interesting that, in *Rhet*. 2.2.1378a31–33, he explains that anger may be defined as a "desire accompanied by pain, for a conspicuous revenge for a conspicuous slight (*oligôria*) at the hands of men who have no call to slight oneself or one's friends".

Oligôria, which might be rendered as "lack of respect" or even "lack of recognition", is described as an "actively entertained opinion of something as obviously of no importance (*mêdenos axios*)" (*Rhet*. 2.2.1378b10–11). A type of *oligôria*, i.e. contempt, derives from lack of recognition of the worth of something or someone (*Rhet*. 2.2.1378b14–16), whereas a second kind, spite, consists in preventing others from getting what they wish for no particular reason (*Rhet*. 2.2. 1378b16–17). Finally, insolence (*hybris*) is a lack of respect that consists in

> doing and saying things that cause shame to the victim, not in order that anything may happen to yourself, or because anything has happened to yourself, but simply for the pleasure involved. [...] The cause of the pleasure thus enjoyed by the insolent man is that he thinks himself greatly superior to others when ill-treating them. (*Rhet*. 2.2.1378b22–28)

In Aristotle's philosophy, neglecting the worth of someone or something does not necessarily amount to failing to recognize what makes persons entitled to equal respect as human beings. Aristotle rather refers to the recognition that people inferior by birth, power and virtue owe to those who are effectively superior. In one case, however, Aristotle speaks of forms of recognition shaping forms of mutual commitment and accountability: namely the case of friendship (*philia*). Aristotle identifies three forms of friendship: (a) friendship by utility, a relationship grounded on the search for mutual advantage (*NE* 8.3.1156a10–12; *EE* 7.2.1236a32–38); (b) friendship based on the pleasure of mutual companionship (*NE* 8.3.1156a31–35; *EE* 7.2.1236a39–41); (c) friendship based on recognition of virtue. This is the friendship which Aristotle names "primary" (*hê prôtê philia*; *EE* 7.2.1236a18, b12, 24; 1237a10, b8; 1238a30) or "perfect/complete" (*hê teleia philia*; *NE* 8.3.1156b7; 6.1158a11).

In virtue-based friendships, the subjects involved appear themselves as worthy of appreciation (and therefore of love) simply "because of what they are" (*dia to hautois*).[4] These friendships arise out of reciprocal recognition of *equality in virtue*, and not simply of *virtue*, as emerges for instance in *NE* 8.8.1159b2–3:

> it is equality and similarity that determine the bond of friendship, especially the similarity between friends according to virtue.[5] (*hê d'isotês kai homoiotês philotês, kai malista men hê tôn kat'aretên homoiotês.*) (cf. *EE* 7.3.1238b16–17)

To explain recognition of one another as "similar" or "equal" in virtue Aristotle resorts to the theoretical image of the friend as the "other self". This is a conceptual pattern which Aristotle employs in his ethical works by means of the linguistic expressions *allos autos* (*NE* 9.4.1166a31–32; *EE* 7.12.1245a30) and *heteros autos* (*NE* 9.8.1169a6–7; 1170a6–7; cf. *heteros egô* in *MM* 2, 15.1213a23–24). Starting from the assumption that the Aristotelian notion of "self" is rooted in a distinctively human rational faculty, intellect, Aristotle seems to imply that treating the friend as "another self" indicates a path of virtuous behavior towards one's friends that ought to be followed. In that case, recognition of a friend as "another self" would have a "prescriptive" worth (Annas 1988), and it is plausible to suppose that being able to observe the virtue of one's friend enables the observer to reflect on his own virtue and the possibilities of preserving (or even improving) it.

---

4 This is what may be indirectly inferred from *NE* 8, 3.1156a14–15, where Aristotle claims that friends who love each other for the sake of utility do not love each other for what they are.
5 Elena Irrera's translation.

The need to ground the sense of one's own worth in recognition of one's capacity for agency and interaction with one's fellows is also one among the most significant concerns of modern philosophy. As we will see in this volume (cf. Irrera's essay), a notable example of this tendency is represented by the thought of Thomas Hobbes (1588–1679). Indeed, Hobbes grounds self-respect and reverential respect for other people on recognition of the specific powers possessed by the addressees of respect. This activity is performed through the empirical observation of one's limits and possibilities, and it may occur not only in conditions of human coexistence ruled by juridical norms, but also in a state where no rule of reciprocal conduct is publicly established, such as the Hobbesian state of nature. In that state, knowledge of one's own powers proceeds alongside recognition of a power which human beings possess to an equal extent: the power to harm other people. Recognizing that each and every human being represents a potential threat to both individual freedom and peaceful coexistence is a preliminary step towards the theoretical elaboration (and subsequent implementation) of strategies for the promotion of reciprocal respect and equality of treatment. This, Hobbes maintains, is what leads people to activate a transition from the state of nature to the creation of a civil state.

A similar concern is expressed by Jean-Jacques Rousseau (1712–1778), whose investigation into the pre-political foundations of human life sheds light not only on the causes of interpersonal conflict, but also on the possibility of a respectful human coexistence in relations of equality and freedom (Bertram 2012). Although Rousseau does not employ the French word "reconnaissance" in the specific sense with which Hegel will later use the term "Anerkennung", it might be fairly stated that Rousseau is the first modern thinker who offered a proper theorization of the notion of recognition, placing it at the very center of his social, moral and political philosophy (Neuhouser 2008). Rousseau wonders how human freedom and equality of treatment can be preserved when people are accorded differential treatment, depending on their supposed superiority or inferiority concerning talents and virtues. This lack of equal treatment, which makes its first appearance in human societies, is not a trait of Rousseau's state of nature.

Unlike the Hobbesian state of nature, the one elaborated by Rousseau is portrayed as an ancestral condition of peace and satisfaction (perhaps one which never existed in real life) to which human beings cannot revert. On Rousseau's reconstruction of the origins of mankind, before progress and civilization, human beings did not feel the need to entertain social interactions. In the state of nature, people appear driven by nature towards their self-preservation, feeling a form of self-love (*amour de soi*) which, although helping them to pursue their immediate needs, cannot be identified with a selfish attitude harming others. In one of Rousseau's most famous works, *Emile*, *amour de soi* is introduced as a feeling which, if properly cultivated (that is, cultivated in conformity with a co-operative reason), suggests routes of correct other-regarding behavior. Indeed, the mechanisms of self-love can be extended so as to cover the sphere of love for close friends and family members (Rousseau 2013, pp. 340, 376), and they can even lead persons to develop a true sense of justice (which in Rousseau 2013, p. 343 is defined not as an abstract term, but as an affection of the heart enlightened by reason).

In this original state, human beings live a relatively autonomous life, free from external influences. Only with the development of a distinctively human society does the satisfaction of individual needs require increasingly more sophisticated forms of reciprocal inter-independence.

In his *Discourse on the Sciences and Arts* (conventionally known as *The First Discourse* and published in 1750) Rousseau argues that social development, including arts and sciences, ends up corroding both civic virtue and individual moral character. If, on the one hand, technical and scientific progress enhances several human potentialities, on the other it contributes to depriving persons of their own authenticity. Within an established society, human relationships are flawed by an inclination to hypocrisy, and an external attitude becomes often disjoined from a sincere disposition of the heart. This is what Rousseau explains for instance in sections 12–14 of the *First Discourse*. In section 12, he speaks of the state of nature as a condition of original purity and mutual transparency:

> before art had fashioned our manners and taught our passions to speak in ready-made terms, our morals were rustic but natural; and differences in conduct conveyed differences of character at first glance. Human nature was, at bottom, no better; but men found their security in how easily they saw through one another, and this advantage, to the value of which we are no longer sensible, spared them a good many vices. (Rousseau 1997, pp. 7–8)

In sections 13–14, in contrast, he emphasizes how social and technical development leads to "inauthentic" habits.

> Today, when subtler inquiries and a more refined taste have reduced the Art of pleasing to principles, a vile and deceiving uniformity prevails in our morals, and all minds seem to have been cast in the same mold: constantly politeness demands, propriety commands: constantly one follows custom, never one's own genius. One no longer dares to appear what one is; and under this perpetual constraint, the men who make up the herd that is called society will, when placed in similar circumstances, all act in similar ways unless more powerful motives incline them differently. One will thus never really know with whom one is dealing [...] what a train of vices must attend upon such uncertainty. No more sincere friendships; no more real esteem; no more well founded trust. (Rousseau 1997, p. 8)

If, in the *First Discourse*, Rousseau argues that the corruption of habits increases in proportion to the development of talents and competences, it is only in the *Second Discourse* (*Discourse on the Origin and Basis of Inequality Among Men*) that he brings the issue of recognition into sharp focus. As he explains here, desire for good recognition, being a passion which each and every human being is inclined to feel in societies, makes up the bulk of a form of self-love which Rousseau names *amour propre*.

The search for personal recognition, by proceeding parallel to the development of talents in the sphere of techniques and sciences, fosters not only reciprocal competitiveness, but also a search for support and confirmation from external observers. This creates a strong, harmful inter-dependency among human beings. Indeed, the sense that a person has of herself is naturally affected by her achievements as well as her failures (these being generally certified by others). Unlike the *amour de soi*, *amour propre* requires constant confrontation of the agent who feels it with external observers, thus leading him or her to lose his or her authenticity and to shape desires and expectations according to their preferences. This is how Rousseau frames the issue in the *Second Discourse*:

> Young people of the opposite sex live in adjoining Huts, the transient dealings demanded by Nature soon lead to others, no less sweet and more permanent as a result of mutual visits. They grow accustomed to attend to different objects and to make comparisons; imperceptibly they acquire ideas of merit and of beauty which produce sentiments of preference. *The more they see one another, the less they can do without seeing one another more* (my italics). A tender and sweet sentiment steals into the soul, and at the least obstacle becomes an impetuous frenzy; jealousy awakens together with love; discord triumphs, and the gentlest of all passions receives sacrifices of human blood. (Rousseau 1997, II, 15; p. 165)

Thus, Rousseau goes on to say,

> [A]s soon as men had begun to appreciate one another and the idea of consideration had taken shape in their mind, everyone claimed a right to it, and one could no longer deprive anyone of it with impunity.

As a desire to achieve recognition for outstanding talents and behavior, the *amour propre* experienced by each member of the developed society encourages the pursuit of targets which, once attained, generate inequality of assessment and of treatment. The notion of *amour propre*, then, seems to have a "diagnostic" role in Rousseau's theory of the evolution of the human society. This form of love contributes to social inequalities and the loss of human freedom, especially when the search for recognition leads human beings to conformity with the opinions and expectations of those who are called to assess them.

It is primarily with a view to contrasting such inequalities that Rousseau elaborates his contractarian theory. Unlike the Hobbesian view of a *pactum subjectionis* consisting in transferring individual rights and liberties, Rousseau's civil state aims at the creation of an agreement in which the reciprocal dependence of the citizens should not be a constraint, but the basis for a condition of independence of each one with respect to the others. The political pact so structured takes every political right back to the principle of the general will, a will which, rather than transcending the citizens, is a new dimension in which each of the citizens can express his own will and reasons.

As Neuhouser (2008) has noticed, it is interesting that, in Rousseau's theory of the civil state, recognition is not held to be a fundamental interest or a right to protect, as, in contrast, self-preservation is; nor is desire for recognition an inclination which might be put to good use. On the contrary, in *Emile* Rousseau himself seems to acknowledge that desire for recognition can have positive effects in the education of human beings, by developing their rational capacities and their sense of themselves as social creatures among others (Rousseau 2013, p. 395).

Rousseau's need to work out efficient strategies of actualization of freedom and pacific co-operation in the civil state reveals the relevance that the ideal of equal respect holds in his philosophy. His appreciation of the idea that all human beings ought to treat others and be treated by others as equal was noticed by Kant in his *Observations on the Feeling of the Beautiful and Sublime* (AK 20: 44). Like Rousseau (Sensen, p. 102), Kant considers respect for persons a foundational requirement of morality. According to several scholars, his original contribution to the modern theorization of respect is to be traced primarily in his well-known image of humanity as an end-in-itself conceptualized in the *Groundwork for the Metaphysics of Morals*. The formula of the Categorical Imperative

> So act that you use humanity, whether in your own person or in the person of any other, always at the same time as an end, never merely as a means (AK 4: 429)

suggests that respect for oneself and others, being derived from recognition of humanity, operates as a supreme limiting condition of individual freedom (AK 4: 429). As Kant implies in the *Metaphysics of Morals* (1797), what encourages respect is recognition of human beings as "persons", that is as self-legislating subjects endowed with pure practical reason. This reason, being structurally unaffected by subjective inclinations and desires, operates as the ground of a universal, objective will, which Kant considers the determining cause of decisions and actions. As he explains, man, being endowed with such a will,

> possesses a *dignity* (an absolute inner worth) by which he exacts *respect* for himself from all other rational beings in the world. He can measure himself with every other being of this kind and value himself on a footing of equality with them. (AK 6: 434–435)

What confers to a person the authority to be treated with respect (or, to put it differently, what constitutes the source of the inner worth of human beings) is a matter of debate. For example, it may be supposed that humans are worthy of respect by virtue of their capacity to act in accordance with laws that can be represented in their mind, whatever their content or sources are (see AK 4: 412, where such a capacity is defined as the "will"); alternatively, one might identify the basis of respect with agency stemming exclusively from a morally good will, one which suggests other-regarding, and not simply selfish courses of actions.[6] On the other hand, it is uncontroversial that each person, *qua* rational being, is able to recognize and, consequently, appreciate, the universal, rational nature of the moral law within him or her. More specifically, contemplating humanity in oneself and others is possible through a foundational act of recognition: the recognition of moral law and its distinctive sublimity. As Kant makes clear both in the *Groundwork for the Metaphysics of Morals* and in the *Critique of Practical Reason*, the moral law proves to be higher and more authoritative than those principles for action that, resting on subjective inclinations and empirical influences, fail to convey the sense of a duty-based morality.

Far from signifying a simple obligation or a necessity which human beings passively accept, the Kantian notion of "duty" refers to a "practical unconditional necessity of action", which holds for all rational beings *qua* rational beings (AK 4: 425). This necessity is the straightforward consequence of respect for the moral law and the reason that informs such a law (AK 4: 400). Mere conformity to the universal moral law is not sufficient to produce an authentic morally good volition. Only action "from respect" for the law (*aus Achtung fürs Gesetz*) can successfully determine it.

As Kant goes on to explain in the *Groundwork*, human beings ask themselves what they have to do in order that their volition be morally good. When the principles they choose are recognized as possible grounds for a universal law, for these principles "lawgiving reason forces from us immediate respect" (AK 4: 403). As he says,

---

6 For a list of different scholarly positions on this matter see Sensen 2009. Sensen mentions for instance a "pre-moral" capacity to set ends, but also a morally good will. His own position is that what makes a person worthy of respect is the Categorical Imperative itself, which would command respect for persons without rooting it on a supposed set of human capacities.

> Although I do not yet see what this respect is based upon [...] I at least understand this much: that it is an estimation of a worth that far outweighs any worth of what is recommended by inclination, and that the necessity of my action from *pure* respect for the practical law is what constitutes duty, to which every other motive must give way because it is the condition of a will good *in itself*, the worth of which surpasses all else. (AK 4: 403)

The undiscussed superiority of the moral law, then, being recognized and appreciated for its rational grounds, confers "sublimity and dignity in the person who fulfills all his duties" (AK 4: 440) and sets laws for himself or herself "with respect only for the reason" (AK 4: 440).

As Kant explains in the *Critique of Practical Reason*, the kind of respect he is referring to here is a reverential feeling which, unlike others, does not arise from pathological impulses and empirical factors (AK 5: 75). What is more, respect for the law is not to be considered a simple "incentive to morality"; rather, "it is morality itself regarded subjectively as an incentive inasmuch as pure practical reason" (AK 5: 76). Respect, in other words, is the way in which the moral law manifests itself to human beings, enabling them to recognize and accept it as an a priori principle of determination of human agency.

This is for Kant the only condition for authentic freedom.

It is interesting that, in the *Critique of Practical Reason*, Kant speaks of a form of recognition (*Anerkennung*) of the moral law by human beings in terms of "consciousness" (*Bewusstsein*):

> However, acknowledgment of the moral law is the consciousness of an activity of practical reason [engaged in] from objective bases, an activity that fails to express its effect in actions only because subjective (pathological) causes hinder it. (AK 5: 79)

The activity of recognition mentioned by Kant proves to be central for the process through which the moral law becomes a moral incentive (*Triebfeder*) for rational beings. In the *Critique of Practical Reason*, he explains that the moral law and its authoritativeness, being the object of a respect as "esteem" (*Schätzung*), causes the rational subject to "restrict" the subjective inclinations, and even the sense of personal worth that hinges on such inclinations (AK 5: 78). Kant speaks of this activity of pure practical reason in terms of "humiliation" (*Demütigung*). Recognizing the power and superiority of the moral law, on the one hand, initially causes rational beings to comply with the prescription of pure rationality. Conformity to the law is gradually replaced by an authentic respect, which occurs when rational beings understand that the law itself can be adopted as the ground for a more stable form of self-respect. This is how a "boundless esteem" (AK 5: 79) for the moral law, being grounded in previous rational recognition of it, demolishes an *Eigenliebe* (self-love) based on a consideration of personal talents or ambitions.

In Kant's view, the possibility of authentically righteous human agency is premised on recognition of a universal reason, one that abstracts from the contingencies and particulars that contribute to shape the individual history of persons. A different route of investigation is taken by Hegel (1770–1831). Although sharing with Kant the idea that recognition (*Anerkennung*) has normative implications, Hegel rejects the idea that individuals are to be recognized as "abstract equals" (Neuhouser 2013). Not only does Hegel consider recognition a sort of "freedom in the making"; he suggests that, in recognizing other persons and their relationships with us, we constitute ourselves as people endowed with a determinate, specific identity (Neuhouser 2013).

Against Kant, Hegel denies that a single formal rule of practical rationality is able to determine a priori a truly free agency. In Hegel's view, human freedom finds an opportunity for expression and realization in a series of concrete relationships of recognition, that is, in inter-subjective encounters that shape various dimensions of individual life, ranging from pre-political to properly political ones. Hegel works out a complex reconstruction of the conditions and the steps which every individual ought to undertake so as to recognize himself or herself as "reason" and to attain knowledge of the absolute truth.[7]

This is not the place to pursue an in-depth investigation of the Hegelian theory.[8] For our purposes, what is interesting to acknowledge here is that achieving freedom involves a complex process of mutual recognition, which cannot simply present people as individuals entitled to produce, acquire and exchange goods. Instead, human beings recognize each other as individuals capable of self-determination in the sphere of interpersonal relationships and, to the highest degree, in civil society (Pippin 2000, p. 164).

"Recognizing" a person implies according that person the authority to limit the sphere of action of the one who recognizes. This emerges, for instance, in the case of friendship and love. Here, as Hegel clarifies,

> we are not one-sidedly within ourselves, but willingly limit ourselves with reference to an other, even while knowing ourselves within this limitation as ourselves. (PR § 7 A)

---

[7] As Pippin explains (2000, p. 155), many Hegelian scholars have suggested that this route is to be understood primarily as a "manifestation of a grand metaphysical process, an Absolute Subject's manifestation of itself, or a Divine Mind's coming to self-consciousness". Like Pippin, we believe that it is easier to explain Hegel's theory of this process (and, especially, his view of Hegel's 'ethical life theory'as an account of successful recognition by human beings.

[8] We refer the reader to the essay of Laitinen included in this volume.

It is interesting that, although a given person, *qua* recognized, limits the will of the subject who recognizes, the activity of recognition does not imply a renunciation to freedom; on the contrary, self-limitation is a form of self-determination, and thus a clear expression of freedom.

> In this determinacy, the human being should not feel determined; on the contrary he attains his self-awareness only by regarding the other as other. (PR § 7)

Even recognition of some form of inferiority (for instance, social or economical) with respect to others is a mark of freedom and self-determination. Human intersubjective relationships, after all, are ultimately grounded in forms of mutual dependency. At PR § 192, for instance, Hegel states,

> Needs and means, as existing in reality, become a being (*Sein*) for *others* by whose needs and work their satisfaction is mutually conditioned. That abstraction which becomes a quality of both needs and means also becomes a determination of the mutual relations (*Beziehung*) between individuals. This universality, as *the quality of being recognized* (*Anerkannt-sein*), is the moment which makes isolated and abstract needs, means, and modes of satisfaction into *concrete*, i.e. *social* ones.

Recognition of one's individual nature finds its full expression in the state, which Hegel describes in terms of "actuality of concrete freedom". As he explains,

> [P]ersonal individuality (*Einzelheit*) and its particular interests should reach their full *development* and gain *recognition* (*Anerkennung*) of their right for itself (within the system of the family and civil society) and also that they should, on the one hand, pass over of their own accord into the interest of the universal, and on the other knowingly and willingly recognize (*anerkennen*) this universal interest even as their own substantial spirit, and actively pursue it as their ultimate end (PR § 260).

As has been suggested by Axel Honneth with reference to Hegel (Honneth 2011, p. 86), the mutual independence of people makes them recognize each other as "the other part of oneself". The otherness at stake, however, is not to be understood in terms of an abstract similarity or equality (as Aristotle, in contrast, does while referring to the concept of the "other self"). On the contrary, it is recognition of diversity and reciprocal complementarity which enables each subject to acquire a feeling of himself or herself as an individual with specific traits (Neuhouser 2013).

The dialectical character of activities of recognition (as opposed to the idea of recognition as a purely "intra-psychic" process) shapesa number of well-known contemporary theorizations of self-respect and respect for persons which we do not illustrate in this chapter (being addressed by Knoll's essay contained in this volume). Authors like John Rawls, Michael Walzer, Charles Taylor, Jürgen Habermas and Axel Honneth discuss and defend an idea of recognition which, being (both conceptually and practically) related to the regard that others display or fail to display towards a certain person, contributes significantly to shape that person's sense of his or her own worth. Political institutions themselves will be assessed on the basis of their capacity to promote and ensure recognition as one of the primary social conditions of self-respect.

As Charles Taylor for instance clarifies in his essay *The Politics of Recognition* (1994), politics aiming to ensure equal respect and dignity for each member of the community can be declined either in terms of recognition of specific identity-traits or as recognition of the equal worth of human beings with no concern for their individual differences. Whatever direction political theorists and actors undertake, they are called to understand a fundamental fact: whether understood as a pure epistemic principle or as a normative guide for human interaction, recognition qualifies itself as a vital human need.

Bibliography

Annas, J. (1988): "Self-Love in Aristotle", *The Southern Journal of Philosophy* 27, pp. 1–18.
Aristotle (1984a): *The Complete Works of Aristotle*, ed. by J. Barnes, Princeton: Princeton University Press.
Aristotle (1984b) *Poetics*, trans. by I. Bywater. In *The Complete Works of Aristotle*, ed. by J. Barnes, Princeton: Princeton University Press. Vol. 1.
Aristotle (1984c) *Rhetoric*, trans. by W. Rhys Roberts. In *The Complete Works of Aristotle*, ed. by J. Barnes, Princeton: Princeton University Press. Vol. 2.
Bergson, H. (1991): *Matter and Memory*, trans. by N.M. Paul and W.S. Palmer, New York: Zone.
Bertram, Ch. (2012): "Jean Jacques Rousseau". In *The Stanford Encyclopedia of Philosophy* (Winter 2012 Edition), http://plato.stanford.edu/archives/win2012/entries/rousseau/. Date of last access 31/08/2016.
Bostock, D. (1988): *Plato's Theaetetus*, Oxford: Clarendon Press.
Brandhorst, K. (2010): *Descartes' Meditations on First Philosophy. An Edinburgh Philosophical Guide*, Edinburgh: Edinburgh University Press.
Descartes, R. (2003): *Discourse on Method and Meditations*, trans. by E.S. Haldane and G.R.T. Ross, Mineola: Dover (reprint of the 1911 Cambridge University Press first edition).
Descartes, R. (2006): *A Discourse on the Method of Correctly Conducting One's Reason and Seeking Truth in the Sciences*, ed. and trans. by I. Maclean, Oxford: Oxford University Press.
Dworkin, R. (1981): "What is Equality? Part 2: Equality of Resources", *Philosophy and Public Affairs* 10, pp. 283–345 (reprinted in: Dworkin, Ronald (2000): *Sovereign Virtue. The Theory and Practice of Equality*, Cambridge: Harvard University Press, pp. 65–119).

Fraser, N. (2003): "Social Justice in the Age of Identity Politics: Redistribution, Recognition, and Participation". In N. Fraser and A. Honneth (Eds.): *Redistribution or Recognition? A Political-Philosophical Exchange* (original title *Umverteilung oder Anerkennung?*, trans. by J. Golb, J. Ingram and Ch. Wilke), London/New York: Verso, pp. 7–109.

Galeotti, A.E. (2002): *Toleration as Recognition*, Cambridge: Cambridge University Press.

Hegel, G.W.F. (2003): *Elements of the Philosophy of Right*, ed. by A.W. Wood, Cambridge: Cambridge University Press (first pub. 1991).

Homer (1919): *The Odyssey*, ed. and trans. by A.T. Murray, London: Heinemann, 1919.

Honneth, A. (2011): *Das Recht der Freiheit: Grundriss einer demokratischen Sittlichkeit*, Frankfurt a.M.: Suhrkamp.

Kant, I. (1922): *Immanuel Kant's Critique of Pure Reason. In Commemoration of the Centenary of its First Publication*, ed. and trans. by F. Max Mueller, 2nd revised ed., New York: Macmillan.

Kant, I. (1991): *The Metaphysics of Morals*, trans. by M. Gregor, Cambridge: Cambridge University Press.

Kant, I. (1998): *Groundwork of the Metaphysics of Morals*, trans. by M. Gregor, 2nd ed., Cambridge: Cambridge University Press.

Kant, I. (2002): *Kant. Critique of Practical Reason*, trans. by S.W. Pluhar, with an introduction by S. Engstrom, Indianapolis/Cambridge: Hackett Publishing Company.

Kymlicka, W. (2007): *Multicultural Odysseys: Navigating the New International Politics of Diversity*. Oxford: Oxford University Press.

Neuhouser, F. (2008): *Rousseau's Theodicy of Self-Love: Evil, Rationality, and the Drive for Recognition*, Oxford: Oxford University Press.

Neuhouser, F. (2013): "Rousseau e Hegel: due concetti di riconoscimento", *Consecutio Temporum. Hegeliana, Marxiana, Freudiana* 5, http://www.consecutio.org/2013/04/rousseau-e-hegel-due-concetti-di-riconoscimento/ (Date of last access 31/08/2016).

Pippin, R.B. (2000): "What is the Question for Which Hegel's 'Theory of Recognition' is the Answer?", *The European Journal of Philosophy* 8 (2), pp. 155–172.

Plato (1921): *Theaetetus*, trans. by H.N. Fowler, London: William Heinemann Ltd.

Rawls, J. (1999): *A Theory of Justice*, revised edition, Oxford: Oxford University Press (first published in 1971, Cambridge, MA: Belknap Press of Harvard University Press).

Ricoeur, P. (2005): *The Course of Recognition* (original title *Parcours de la reconnaissance*, 2004), trans. by D. Pellauer, Cambridge, MA/London: Harvard University Press.

Rousseau, J.-J. (1997): *"The Discourses" and Other Early Political Writings*, ed. and trans. by V. Gourevitch, Cambridge: Cambridge University Press.

Rousseau, J.-J. (2013): *Emile*, trans. by B. Foxtley, Topbooks (e-book).

Rudder Baker, L. (1998): "The First Person Perspective. A Test for Naturalism", *American Philosophical Quarterly* 35 (4), pp. 327–348.

Sensen, O. (2009): Dignity and the Formula of Humanity. In Timmermann (2009), pp. 102–118.

Taylor, Ch. (1994): "The Politics of Recognition". In A. Gutmann (Ed.): *Multiculturalism: Examining the Politics of Recognition*, Princeton: Princeton University Press, pp. 25–73.

Timmermann, J. (Ed.) (2009): *Kant's Groundwork of the Metaphysics of Morals: A Critical Guide*, Cambridge: Cambridge University Press.

Young, I.M. (1996): *Justice and the Politics of Difference*. Princeton: Princeton University Press.

Part I: **Respect in Ancient Philosophy**

Giovanni Giorgini
The Notion of Respect in Ancient Greek Poetry

Abstract: This essay contends that the idea of respect for persons finds its roots in the culture and history of Archaic Greece. I suggest that the idea of respect retains an aristocratic flavor, even when the historic-political evolutions leading to the creation of Greek democracy appear to set the basis for equality of treatment before the law (*isonomia*). I initially examine the notion of *aidôs* in Homer's poems, and suggest that this can be viewed as an embryonic form of self-respect nurtured (or threatened) by external observers. Then, I proceed to examine how the idea of respect for persons in Solon betrays adherence to a form of respect as honor, i.e., one that is founded on recognition of status. Subsequently, I examine some of Theognis' poems and show that equal recognition is premised on possession of outstanding moral excellence. Finally, lack of excellence and capacity for righteous behavior spark institutional responses such as the infliction of *atimia*.

1 Prelude

Every time the historian of ideas investigates the presence and the meaning of a concept in a certain age and in a certain society, he must be aware of the methodological requirements of the enterprise. As far as the current investigation is concerned these entail issues which fall under two headings. A first cluster of problems revolves around the difference between word and concept. The concept – the 'fact' assumed in the mind, issuing in a definition – may be present in an epoch or in a society without the corresponding word. John Milton, one of the strongest advocates of religious toleration in the 17th century, never used the word 'toleration' in his writings: the word was not available to him while the concept obviously was. On the other hand, the same word may acquire different meanings, and therefore refer to different concepts, in different ages and societies: Aristotle's notion of democracy (the rule of the poor to their sole advantage) is very different from Schumpeter's (the institutional arrangement which enables the people to make decisions for the common good) although the word used by them is the same. Isaiah Berlin's and Hans Kelsen's disparaging judgments on 'Soviet democracy' reveal their outrage for the Communist use of the word, which obviously did not correspond to what they thought to be the essence of democracy. '*Esprit de finesse*' and context-sensitivity are therefore all-important to counter these problems and to arrive at correct results. Secondly, the historian of ideas must be aware of, and alert to, the fact that the answers he finds depend on the questions he poses; he must therefore have a clear image of the object he is looking for. In the present case, searching for the roots of respect in ancient Greece, we must have a viable definition of 'respect' as our guiding light. In so doing, we must avoid the mistake of projecting our own notion of 'respect' onto Greek society and civilization; we should, rather, inquire whether the Greeks had the notion of 'respect' and whether there was a word to identify it; i.e., we have to examine what they meant by 'respect', how they defined and practiced it. We should interpret them as they interpreted themselves, aware that it is culture that molds the standards of behavior and even the emotions of people in a society.[1]

2 What Is Respect and Who Is Worthy of It?

Nowadays, when we speak of respect in morality and politics, we typically think of something we owe to each other simply qua human beings. From Kant onwards, all the elaborate, analytical definitions of respect share the basic tenet that, properly speaking, respect is due to every human being because each of them is an absolute center of value. This element of value is all-important in this perspective because it is intrinsic, is part of the very essence of being human. This marks a difference from the view of the unity of mankind which we find in ancient Greece, for instance in sophists like Hippias and Antiphon and subsequently in the Stoic philosophers. Realizing that "we all breathe out into the air by the mouth and the nose" and eat with the hands (to quote Hippias) and we are therefore kin by nature, does not mean that we are all valuable persons; asserting that the "wise man" discovers a "familiarity" (*oikeiôsis*) with other human beings around the world does not mean that we are morally equal.[2] The identification of a common, physical human nature may enable us to see beyond the difference between aristocrat and commoner, or even between Greek and 'barbarian'; but this does not immediately translate into equal respect for the above-mentioned categories, or for freeman and slave, friend and enemy, *kalokagathos* and *ponêros*. The modern notion of 'respect' entails moral equality,

---

[1] On the methodological problems highlighted here, I wish to refer to the Introduction to Giorgini 1993. On the difference between the emotions of the ancient Greeks and our own see Konstan 2006.
[2] See Hippias DK87 B44. Cooper 2012, chapter 4.

not just physical resemblance. My first stipulation is thus that in ancient Greek culture 'respect' (whatever we will find this to mean) is not due to every human being per se but is contingent to merit and status: you don't deserve respect because you are human but because you merited it for your actions or for who you are.[3] This, in my view, already marks an enormous difference from the current usage of the concept and the *Weltanschauung* that underpins it.

In fact, what distinguishes the two notions of respect is the completely different vision of human nature which lies at their foundation. For the modern, Western liberal view of mankind conceives human beings as naturally equal qua human beings, irrespective of their gender, status, religion and so on. We only need to look at two foundational documents of contemporary politics to find exemplifications. In the very first line of the Preamble to the 1948 *Universal Declaration of Human Rights* it is stated that "recognition of the inherent dignity and of the equal and inalienable rights of all members of the human family is the foundation of freedom, justice and peace in the world"; and article 1 reads that "all human beings are born free and equal in dignity and rights". Even more interesting is perhaps the Grundgesetz für die Bundesrepublik Deutschland (1949). Here article 1 reads: "Die Würde des Menschen ist unantastbar" – human dignity is inviolable; and it adds: "To respect and protect it shall be the duty of all State authority". There is only one "Menschlichkeit", which is composed of individuals equal in dignity. Not even the most daring ancient Greek thinker arrived at such a conclusion (and it is not that they lacked imagination); regardless of the fact that already in the 5th century BCE the physicians of the Hippocratic school had maintained that all human beings share a common nature (*physis*), uniformly responding to the same stimuli and drugs, which is the foundation of the physician's art. But sameness in bodily features never translated into equal dignity and respect: Greek thinkers were always convinced that human beings are born unequal in dignity and therefore deserved unequal treatment. In addition, Greek political thought never elaborated a language of 'rights', legal or natural, of citizens or human beings in abstract. Finally, respect also depended on the relationship one had with 'the other': friends and enemies, for instance, deserved different treatments. One of the basic maxims of ancient Greek ethics was the injunction to "help friends and harm enemies".[4] In one of his poems

---

3 Even a refined thinker like Aristotle believes that a 'human being' properly speaking is not just any new-born human but rather a man who has realized his natural potentialities; in this line of reasoning women appear to be defective men and the 'barbarians' are slave by nature. See *Pol.* I.
4 We only need to look at Plato's *Republic* I. Polemarchus gives a definition of justice which – he believes – will be accepted by everybody for being so traditional, obvious and widespread: justice, giving each person their due, means "helping friends and harming enemies" (*Rep.* I, 332a–

Solon, one of the traditional Seven Wise Men, asks the Muses to be sweet to his friends and bitter to his enemies, that is to say "viewed with respect by the former and with dread by the latter": he hopes and expects to be an object of respect (*aidoion*) for his friends and of fear for his personal enemies, literally the persons who hate him (*echthrois*).[5] The vital change – we may conclude – happened in the image of 'the other'.

Next, we may ask what is 'respect' in ancient Greek culture and who is worthy of respect (and who is not)? When we look for the Greek words which most closely approximate the meaning of 'respect', the likeliest candidates are *aidôs* and *timê*. *Aidôs*, which is usually translated as 'respect' or 'shame', identifies modesty and propriety in one's attitude and due respect for gods and men. It goes together with *sôphrosynê*, self-restraint or sound-mindedness, and it brings just measure.[6] The latter makes man recognize the consequences of his actions and thus represents the opposite of *hybris*, the arrogant refusal to remain within one's (human) limits. *Aidôs* brings restraint and is a social virtue because it identifies the fear of disgrace which comes from improper behavior. With reference to Homer, James Redfield remarked: "*Aidôs* is the most pervasive ethical emotion in Homeric society; it is basically a responsiveness to social situations and to the judgments of others".[7] Also, "the feeling of *aidôs*, entailing concentration on the self and one's own status, is prompted by and focuses on consideration of the status of the other" (Cairns 1993, p. 3); thus, "*aidôs* is inextricably tied to the respect one can expect for oneself" (Atwill 1998, p. 211). We experience *aidôs* when we feel that a certain conduct or circumstance could deprive us of our reputation (*doxa*). We may conclude that we act according to *aidôs* when we behave according to the standards of our society in our interactions with men and gods: we tribute them the respect they deserve according to their status; and from other men we expect the same. Two examples are illuminating. In the *Iliad* 24 Apollo upbraids Achilles for his behavior towards Hector after his defeat: he acted with a cruel heart, "like a lion", without pity or *aidôs* (44): *aidôs* distinguishes a

---

336a). We usually fail to recognize how revolutionary is Socrates' ethics, which commands that the just person never harm anyone.
5 Solon fr. 13, vv. 5–6.
6 See Plato, *Laws* VI, 771e–772a: the just measure of *aidôs* in religious festivals is exemplified by the sober modesty a person shows when looking at the naked bodies of young men and girls.
7 Redfield 1994, p. 115. Redfield adds that *aidôs* is "a vulnerability to the expressed ideal norm of the society" (p. 116). He can thus conclude that "*aidôs* is in general an emotion provoked by the perception of one's place in the social structure and of the obligations which accompany that place"; therefore "it is generally felt towards persons in the exercise of their social roles or when they are perceived as having a social relation to oneself" (p. 118).

human being from an animal.[8] In his wrath Achilles did not pay the customary, due respect to the body of his adversary, who had always acted honorably. In Herodotus, on the other hand, we find the amusing and telling story of Gyges and Candaules. Asked by his king Candaules to see the queen naked in order to admire her beauty, Gyges replies "together with the dress a woman also sheds her *aidôs*" – which is not her modesty or decency but rather the respect due to her as a woman (and a queen).[9] Candaules, "doomed to misfortune" in Herodotus' revealing comment (Hdt. I, 8, 2), acts against the social norms which uphold the respectability of a woman while Gyges entreats his lord not to commit him to something lawless (*anomon*: Hdt. I, 8, 4).[10]

The other important word in this semantic context is *timê*, honor, value, reverence. *Timê* identifies both the value of a person and his rank. Especially in the plural, *timai*, it may also indicate the 'honors', namely the positions, offices, that a man occupies in his city. *Timê* can be institutionalized in a regime (*timokratia*) and the same is true for its opposite, *atimia*. Plato, who uses the word *timokratia* for the first time, described it literally as the regime in which the ruling class is driven by love of honor. It represents the first degeneration of the perfect city (*kallipolis*): although its ruling class is not driven by love of knowledge anymore, its object of desire is represented by moral, immaterial things such as honor and glory. Already in Aristotle however, *timokratia* designates more generally a regime where offices are distributed according to value, namely property. And here we can make the first significant observation for our investigation. When we explore the ideas and values of ancient Greek civilization, we realize that we are dealing with an aristocratic society; namely a hierarchical society whose values are molded by the nobles. Nietzsche already observed (with satisfaction) that the Greek aristocrats described themselves as "the good" (*agathoi*), "the best" (*aristoi*), "the fortunate" (*ghennaioi*), "the prosperous" (*esthloi*); they accordingly described 'the other', the common people, as "the bad" (*kakoi*), "the miserable" (*deiloi*), "the poor" (*ponêroi*).[11] Difference of status entailed different

---

8 *Il.* 24, 39–55. Cf. Heller 1984, p. 222. See also *Od.* 9, 265 ff., where Polyphemus (a Cyclops who does not know justice or law – *oute dikas oute themistas*) is reproached by Odysseus for not following the traditional laws of hospitality set by Zeus: Odysseus' party acted as suppliants but Polyphemus did not heed their pledge and acted against the *aidôs* due to *xenioi* (271).
9 Hdt. I, 8. See Plato's version in *Rep.* II; cf. Cicero, *Off.* III, 38–39.
10 Indeed, Herodotus displays the entire array of words appropriate to the social conventions of the case and takes for granted that his readers know the complex associations between exposure and *aidôs:* Candaules did not show any *aidôs*, restraint, in his behavior and acted against the social conventions, thus depriving the queen of her *aidôs*, respectability: feeling "shamed" (*aischyntheisa, aischynê*), she recurs to *nemesis*, revenge: Hdt. I, 8–11.
11 F. Nietzsche, *On the Genealogy of Morals* (1887/2008), First Dissertation, chapters 2 and 5.

moral, social and economic characterization. A typical attitude of aristocrats all over the world consists in considering themselves, the nobles, as equals, on the same footing: a good contemporary example is English aristocracy, where the nobles are known as "the Peers" of England – they are "the Equals" *par excellence*.[12] In the ancient world this is very well exemplified by the Spartan regime, ruled by a small group of aristocratic families who considered themselves "peers" (*homoioi*), sharing the ideal of enjoying an exactly equal lifestyle (*isodiaitoi*).[13] Moreover, Greek aristocrats claimed to be such not only at home but everywhere; they wanted to be respected and their *timê* to be recognized everywhere for fear of being enslaved after an unsuccessful war. Aristotle mentions this fact, already with some skepticism, in his treatment of slavery, because the Athenian democratic revolution had already changed the perception of aristocracy dramatically. The notion at stake here is that of *eugeneia*, nobility, being "well-born", which goes together with being free (*eleutheria*): Aristotle observes that the Greeks maintain that such notions exist "absolutely" (*haplôs*) in their case and "non-absolutely" in the case of the barbarians, which is tantamount to identifying good with free and noble, and bad with slave and ignoble.[14]

The root of respect in Greek ethics and politics lies exactly in the aristocratic recognition of the equal value of the fellow-aristocrat. It is very interesting to note how the vicissitudes of aristocracy brought about an evolution and enlargement of this notion. It is possible to observe at least two important turning-points in the history of ancient Greek aristocracy (and therefore of respect). The first occurred in the 7th–6th century BCE when the rule of the most ancient nobility – the Eupatrids – was challenged by aristocrats of more recent date and by commoners of distinction (because of their wealth). The old aristocracy proved unable to find a solution to social turmoil and most Greek cities assigned to a single person the task of pacifying the conflict and giving new laws (*aisymnêtês, diallaktês, nomothetês*); in other cases, a man of the aristocracy himself grabbed sole power, thus incurring the hatred of his peers (*tyrannos*). The other, slower and less dramatic turning-point occurred with the establishment of democratic regimes, first in Athens (508 BCE) and then in other Greek cities. The ideological foundation of democracy was the equality of all citizens before the law (*isono-*

---

[12] This is valid for aristocracy considered as a stand or a class, in an "Us and Them" opposition. There are obviously differences of rank inside aristocracy, and there have always been. On the other hand, it is as Peers that the barons at Runnymede obtained the Magna Charta from king John, granting to every Freeman "the lawful judgment of his Peers" (1215).
[13] See Thucydides I, 65 and Cartledge 2009, pp. 9–10.
[14] Aristotle, *Pol.* 1, 6. 1255a33–36.

mia),¹⁵ notwithstanding the permanence of differences in status and wealth. I am inclined to think that the notion of *isonomia* too originated in an aristocratic context.¹⁶ Its first occurrence, the adjective *isonomikos*, is in a convivial song composed around the year 511 BCE to celebrate the "tyrant-slayers", Harmodius and Aristogeiton who had killed Hipparchus, the brother of the tyrant Hippias, and were celebrated in songs sung by aristocrats in their banquets.¹⁷ It is this idea of equality among peers that Cleisthenes appropriated in an operation well caught by Herodotus: Cleisthenes, "finding himself in a weak position (*essomenos*), associated the people to his aristocratic faction". The expression "*ton demon prosetairizetai*" renders perfectly this idea since the *hetaireiai* were aristocratic clubs; it was so peculiar, however, that when Aristotle, evidently using Herodotus as a source, recounts the story, he changes the verb and explains: "Cleisthenes having been worsted by the comradeships enlisted the people on his side" (*AP* 20). Democracy appropriated the aristocratic vision of equality among peers and gave rise to a new ideology of equality (*isotês*) which envisioned all citizens as equal in dignity and also as equally noble, in a way.¹⁸ In this new vision, respect was due to each citizen for his being an Athenian citizen and not for belonging to a noble family. The foundation of respect changed dramatically, for it now lay in public recognition and not in private possession.¹⁹

---

15 For an overview of the issues connected to this concept and a comparison with *eunomia* see Lombardini 2013.
16 This idea is debated. For a classic statement of the two opposite positions see Ehrenberg 1958; Vlastos 1953. For a recent sensible evaluation see Ober 1996.
17 On this event see Thucydides' insistence in setting the record straight: I, 20 and VI, 56–59; cf. Meyer 2008.
18 I am referring to the oft-repeated discourse of the collective 'nobility' of the Athenian people that we find in our literary sources of the 5th and 4th century BCE. The Athenian *demos* claims collective nobility because of its "autochthony" – the fact that they have lived for centuries on the same land. They thus claim common old ancestry, just like the nobles do individually. See for instance Thucydides I, 2, where this is stated as a fact, and II, 36 where it is a feature of Pericles' eulogy of Athens. It is interesting to note that *isotimia*, equality of consideration and respect, is not certainly attested in Greek before the 3rd century BCE.
19 This change is very well caught by Josh Ober, *The Athenian Revolution*, who remarks that the distinction between citizen dignity and personal honour shows the pragmatic consequences of democracy at Athens; for citizen dignity was protected by the ongoing and collective actions of the *demos* whereas honour was an affair of individuals or of families: Ober 1996, p. 87. Ober concludes that the elite individual's most precious possession was his honour; the most precious possession of the ordinary Athenian was the dignity he enjoyed as a citizen. On Cleisthenes' reforms, their consequences and legacy see the classic Leveque and Vidal-Naquet 1996; also the important contribution of Raaflaub, Ober and Wallace 2007.

We may add that it is only in the context of Athenian democracy that ability and competence in a certain field acquire dignity and prestige: the arts, *technai*, are conceived as self-contained and complete forms of knowledge.²⁰ This new status of the *technitês*, the person who has knowledge of an art, marks an enormous change in the notion of respect. Against the old aristocratic view that lineage guaranteed the judgment, discernment (*gnômê*) of the well-born person, we now find that art (*technê*) and virtue (*aretê*) can be taught and acquired: it is exactly on this terrain that the confrontation between Socrates and Protagoras will take place.²¹ Against Socrates' view of politics based on the analogy with the arts (only the specialist, who possesses political science, is entitled to rule) Protagoras maintains the political equality of mankind, based on the common possession of the two fundamental political virtues: respect (*aidôs*) and justice (*dikê*), which epitomize political science and the art of politics. This political equality makes democracy not only the best but also the most natural form of government for mankind.

For the scope of this essay it is worthwhile focusing on the first turning-point in the history of Greek aristocracy and the corresponding notion of respect. The figure that immediately stands out for his undisputed significance is the Athenian poet and statesman Solon.

3 Solon

Solon (c. 648–c. 560) lived in a time of great social turmoil.²² Athens was plagued by a conflict of factions and faced an economic problem of the utmost gravity which had become also a political issue: many Athenian citizens, sharecroppers and small landowners, who had not been able to repay their debts, had become *atimoi* (which meant 'disenfranchised' at this stage) and had been reduced to slavery and even sold abroad. In one of his poems, Solon remarks that many of these people were sold out of Attika *dikaios*, namely "legal-

---

20 The arts are many: *mantikê, iatrikê, nautikê, mousikê* and so on. In the 5th century BCE these arts become the subject of special treatises.
21 See the 'Great Speech' in Plato, *Prot.* 320c–328d.
22 The Athenians kept the list of archons from the year 594/3 BCE, when Solon was elected: a sign of the turning-point his reforms represented (Plato, *Hipp. Ma.* 285e). See Develin 1989. On Solon see the valuable recent work by Noussia-Fantuzzi 2010. On the significance of Solon's political action see Ober 1989; Balot 2006, pp. 41–47. Interesting observations can be found in Owens 2010.

ly" or "rightly", according to the laws of the land.²³ The old aristocrats, the Eupatrids ("the descendants of good fathers"), proved to be unable to find a solution within their circle and through the ordinary institutions of the polis. Plutarch informs us that Solon was thus elected archon with the task of pacifying the conflict between the factions (*diallaktes*) and of giving new laws to the city (*nomothetês*).²⁴ The fact that he was accepted both by the rich and by the poor testifies to his being not too involved in the factional strife as well as to his personal qualities: his reputation recommended him as umpire in the conflict. Solon enacted a number of very significant measures: his first reform, called *seisachtheia* or the "shaking-off of burdens", consisted in the cancellation of all existing debts and the legal abolition of slavery caused by debts for the future; it also included an amnesty for the rehabilitation of the *atimoi*.²⁵ We must here remark that behind Solon's provision there is an innovative image of the citizen and his *timê:* no man can use his body as a pawn for an economic transaction; and nobody can be deprived of his *timê* and made *atimos* for economic reasons. In this context, the curious provision (actually a law) cited by Aristotle and Plutarch to make *atimos* the citizen who did not take side during a civil strife (*stasis*) makes more sense; behind it there is a high consideration of politics: those who don't feel attachment to any side have no interest in politics and the common good, and therefore don't deserve to have political rights; they do not belong to the polis.²⁶

Although I believe we should credit Solon with a new and revolutionary anthropological view, there is no idea of equal dignity or respect in his works. Solon's policy was informed by an ideal of moderation of Delphic ascendancy, inspired by the Delphic motto "nothing to excess" (*mêden agan*). The notion of *dikê*, justice, features prominently in his thought and in his poems. It is *dikê* that commands self restraint to all parties in the city and fairness in the allocation of offices and economic resources. It is to be noted that for Solon fairness meant that unequal people receive different treatment, but in a harmonious political arrangement. In one of his poems, Solon attributes to himself the merit of

---

23 Solon fr. 36. See Valdes-Guia 2007.
24 Plutarch, *Life of Solon* 14, 2.
25 Plutarch, *Life of Solon* 19.
26 Aristotle, *AP* 9, 5. Aristotle comments that Solon's target were those citizens who, "through slackness, were content to let things slide (*to automaton*)": things do not happen 'automatically' in politics, active participation of the citizens is required. Cf. Plutarch, *Life of Solon* 20; *De sera numinis vindicta* 4. As Plutarch remarks, Solon probably wanted to ensure that no citizen be insensible or indifferent to the common good (*to koinon*). On the significance of this law see Kalyvas 2014.

giving to the *dêmos* exactly the honor and esteem, the recognition (*timê*) it deserved, neither more nor less:

> I gave the common folk such recognition (*timês*) as is sufficient for them, neither adding nor taking away. And as for those who had power and were envied for their wealth, I saw to it that they too should suffer no indignity.[27]

Solon praises himself for restraining the *dêmos* while at the same time keeping at bay "the greater and stronger". And in another poem, fr. 4 (the so-called "Eunomia"), Solon blames "the leaders of the people" for being unjust. Aristotle comments that Solon thus showed how the masses should be treated, without giving them too much freedom or oppressing them.[28] We may add that Solon had a clear view of the unequal status of Athenian citizens, which asked for a proportional recognition. An anecdote cited by Plutarch is very telling. Soon after his election, Solon was hailed both by the rich and the poor, for previously he had stated something to the effect that "equality (*to ison*) breeds no war"; the rich expected this equality to be based on "worth and excellence" (*axia kai aretê*), the poor on "measure and count".[29]

In his political measures Solon revealed himself to be closer to the aristocratic vision of 'equality'. In fact, in order to pacify the civil strife, Solon enacted a constitutional reform which shows his moderation as well as his aristocratic belief in the unequal dignity of citizens. Its most interesting feature for our purposes is the division of the citizenry in four classes based on their different *timê*; this was identified by the wealth of the citizens calculated according to the number of bushels (*medimnai*) of wheat that their properties could produce yearly. It is immediately evident that behind this reform there also lay an ideological assumption: *timê* is not a matter of blood and ancestry but rather of capacity and wealth; the former pair obviously could not be acquired whereas the latter could. The rigid criterion of birth ceases to be the discriminating factor for political participation; instead it is the law (*nomos*) that establishes the timocratic arrangement of society, based on different *timê*. We should note, however, that Solon was convinced that wealth had to be acquired without exploiting other people and without greed and not to an excess: excess breeds *hybris* and destroys virtue. Wealth should not therefore be immediately identified with status:

---

[27] Solon fr. 5.
[28] Aristotle, *AP* 12. Incidentally, the fact that Aristotle quotes so many Solonian poems in his little work on the Athenian constitution shows that he attributed a high historical value to them. This was noted by Linforth 1919, p. 182.
[29] Plutarch, *Life of Solon* 14, 2.

"Many bad men are rich and many good men poor; but we will not take their wealth in exchange for virtue since this is always secure, while wealth belongs now to one man, now to another" (fr. 15). Interestingly enough, this poem made its way also into the *Theognidea*, surely on account of its gnomic value.

Solon's reforms destroyed the Eupatrids' monopoly on Athenian politics and consequently their claim to the sole possession of *gnômê*, political judgment. This fact brought to a sudden end the old aristocracy's view that political capacity was inherited and opened the door to the new ideal of civic education: its highest instantiation (and idealization) was the Athenian citizen depicted by Pericles in Thucydides' Funeral Oration.[30] We may safely state that Solon's reforms were not democratic, but they paved the way to democracy and to its novel vision of citizen equality, *isonomia* (which entailed equal access to public speech, *isêgoria*, and the possibility to speak up one's mind, *parrhêsia*). Solon called his view of the perfect political arrangement *eunomia*, "good order", because in it the 'good' and the 'bad', namely the aristocrats and the commoners, lived harmoniously together: we should notice, however, that there are no good or bad citizens according to the democratic ideology of *isonomia*, but only equals, *isoi*. It is the same sentiment that informs another poem:

> I wrote laws for the good and the bad alike, providing straightforward justice (*dikê*) for each person.[31]

Here, it is the importance of the laws, which guarantee justice to all citizens regardless of their differences, that is exalted. Again, in another poem Solon prides himself to have denied *isomoiria* – an equal share of the fatherland – to the nobles and the commoners. In his words,

> [I]t gives me no pleasure to act with the violence of tyranny or to share the country's rich land equally between the good and the bad.[32]

Isomoiria, redistribution of land on an equal basis, was a drastic demagogic measure which received very strong popular support but also had unforeseeable destabilizing consequences. It was strongly associated with the extraordinary action of a tyrant. Solon thought that the principle of property should be defended,

---

30 Thucydides II, 35–46.
31 Solon fr. 36, vv. 18–20.
32 Solon fr. 34 = Aristotle, *AP* 12, 3. On this fragment see Rosivach 1992. Solon, however, was considered the father of the Athenian democratic constitution already in the late 5th century BCE; also the moderate political ideal of the *patrios politeia* vaguely refers to an imagined 'Solonian democracy'.

not because it favored the noble but because it furnished an ethical and social foundation for community life. Once shattered, property was open to the prevailing faction of the moment. It is in this context that we may examine Solon's use of the word *aidôs*. For he rejects the mockery and accusations of those citizens who thought he had been unwise not to try to exploit the situation to become sole ruler of Athens:

> If I spared my country, and did not defile and disfigure my fame by undertaking tyranny and brutal violence, I feel no shame (*aideumai*); for in this way I think I shall excel over all men.[33]

Solon is convinced that tyranny and violence never bring glory; and the honor that is attached to power comes only from positions acquired honorably and not basely, and exercised for the common good and not for one's own profit. The lure of absolute power must have been very strong in most Athenian citizens since Solon feels compelled to ironically give voice to one of them:

> Solon is not deep-thinking nor sage, for god offered him a great good and he declined it. [...] Now had I the power, I would have been only too glad to be flayed for a wineskin and my posterity wiped out, if only I might first have abundant wealth and be the tyrant of Athens for just one day.[34]

It appears evident that in his poems Solon retained the aristocratic language which associated moral goodness to political status, thus disclosing his aristocratic leanings. In his vision of good order, harmony exists because the laws fairly regulate the relation between rich and poor, aristocrats and commoners. These are conceived by Solon as people of unequal value and therefore deserving the appropriate proportional honor and respect. However, we should not blame Solon for not anticipating the future and not being a democrat. This is a futile exercise, for statesmen necessarily have to take into account the situation at hand: they think of the present circumstances and of the foreseeable consequences of their actions in the near future. The distant future is in the hands of chance because the result of human actions consists in their encounter with the singular, specific circumstances of the case. On the contrary, we should observe again Solon's innovative political vision, which emphasized the dignity that every citizen had simply as a citizen and the prerogatives that citizen status gave to everyone.

---

[33] Solon fr. 32.
[34] Solon fr. 33.

4 Theognis and the Theognidea

The *Theognidea*, the collection of poems that has come down to us under the name of Theognis, contains material from different authors and from a period of time comprised between the late 7th and the early 5th century BCE.[35] T.J. Figueira neatly summarizes the question thus: "Theognis was the poetic *persona* assumed by a number of Megarian poets active from the late seventh or early sixth century down to the early 470s".[36] Theognis himself was a citizen of Megara, on the isthmus between Attica and the Peloponnese;[37] his *floruit* according to Suda is in the 59th Olympiad, namely 544–541. The background of his political and poetical activity was the harsh civil strife, *stasis*, in Megara which paved the way to the tyranny of Theagenes.[38] The poems were composed to be sung at aristocratic parties, the symposia, where drinking and flute-playing were accompanied by the reading of such poetry. The purpose of this kind of compositions was thus moral and political – to assert certain values and infuse them into the young. The gnomic appearance of many of his poems made them suitable to be included in collection of epigrams for the instruction of the young, although this was not their original purpose; as Douglas Cairns correctly remarked in his analysis of *aidôs* in Theognis: "Certainly, all the passages which we shall consider emerge in a clearer light when seen against that background; several of the passages in which our terms occur deal directly with behaviour at the symposium."[39] Indeed, in the materials that compose the *Theognidea* we still find 'snapshots' of many ancient banquets. These collections of epigrams were among the primary means of transmission of the elite values from one generation to the

---

35 *For an introduction to Theognis and his context see Figueira and Nagy 1985.*
36 T.J. Figueira 1995, p. 42. Here Figueira also remarks how "Theognidean poetry was particularly favored by late 5th- and early 4th-century Athenian opponents of imperial democracy", which may explain the selection for preservation of poems most evocative of social tensions and civil war.
37 Not in Sicily, as wrongly reported by Suda II, 692.13 Adler and confirmed by Plato, *Laws* I, 630a.
38 For the ancient sources on Megara see Aristotle, *Pol.* 4, 15.1300a17; 5, 3.1302b30; 5, 5.1304b35; add "5, 5. 1305a24. Plutarch, *Quaestiones Graecae* 18; on the tyrant Theagenes see Thucydides I, 126.
39 Cairns 1993, p. 168. E. Irwin, *Solon and Early Greek Poetry* (2005) remarks: "when performed in the aristocratic symposium martial exhortation poetry represents a type of heroic self-fashioning, an attempt to claim for its singers a status within a wider community equivalent to that of epic heroes" (p. 62). Irwin also correctly stresses the 'international' circulation of these poems.

other.⁴⁰ Honor featured prominently in them, sometimes in a very clear and basic way: for instance, "Honor the gods, respect your parents" are typical precepts in collections of dicta down to the Roman times (Morgan 2007).

Theognis' poems were composed at a time when aristocratic privileges were challenged by the new rich who claimed more participation in power; this request caused social turmoil and civil strife and the tone of his poems reflects partisan affiliation as well as nostalgia for 'the old ways'. Theognis' verses transmit this sense of epoch-change, the disappearance of the old aristocratic order and system of values superseded by a 'materialistic' culture which places wealth at the top of values. We can still subscribe to Werner Jaeger's judgment: "Their [Pindar's and Theognis'] poetry did not commence a renaissance of the aristocracy in political and social life; still, it eternalized the aristocratic ideal at the moment when it was most gravely endangered by new forces [...]" (Jaeger 1939–1945: I, p. 186). Theognis declares, for instance, "I will order my homeland, a shining city, neither turning it over to the populace (*dêmos*) nor giving it to unjust men" (I, 947–948). To the poets' aristocratic eye these *nouveaux riches* could not appear but to be interlopers and, as a consequence, one of Theognis' constant messages to his audience is that wealth and *kalokagathia* do not go together anymore. By this word Theognis means both moral quality and political status, in the typical aristocratic coupling of beauty and virtue. He remarks that virtue and beauty are possessed by few human beings. These people will not be harmed by anyone either in honor (*aidous*) or in right (I, 933–938). We can concur with Ernest Harrison's observation that the poet "Tyrtaeus makes respect the reward of valour: Theognis makes it the homage paid to him who combines excellence with beauty" (Harrison 1902, p. 103).

Theognis dedicates his poems to a young aristocrat, Cyrnus, so that he can learn from them the sound aristocratic values in an age of change; for social and political change brings about upheaval in moral values. The ideals and values of the old aristocracy mean nothing to the new powerful people who now rule the city. This fact is also reflected in language, for the old *aristoi* are not "the best" anymore and the bewildered poet has to face this 'revolution' in the use of words:

> Cyrnus, this city is still a city, but the people are different, people who formerly knew neither justice nor laws, but wore tattered goatskins about their sides and lived outside this

---

40 Plato, *Laws* VII, 811a, already testifies to the existence of such collections. The fact that Theognis himself felt the need to place a 'seal' on his poems shows that verses from different sources were freely quoted and put together in these compilations. This is confirmed by the presence of other poets' verses in the *Theognidea*, including Mimnermus, Solon and Tyrteus.

city like deer. And now they are good (*agathoi*), Polypaides, while those who were prosperous (*esthloi*) before are now miserable (*deiloi*). Who can endure the sight of this? They deceive one another and mock one another, knowing neither the distinctive marks of the bad nor of the good. (I, 53–60; cf. I, 1109–14)

Theognis displays in a few lines the moral vocabulary of the old aristocracy and its impasse before the new power arrangement. Before, being well-born meant also being deservedly wealthy,[41] morally good and politically suited to rule: discernment (*gnômê*) in politics was believed to be a prerogative of the noble. Indeed, as Theognis states, "discernment (*gnômê*) and respect (*aidôs*) are appropriate to good men".[42] Political change has shattered this simple equation: now "the good" are not powerful anymore. To remark the ferocity of the new powerful, Theognis complains that the new citizens are "men who formerly knew neither *dikas* nor *nomous*" (I, 54; cf. I, 1135–50). The sentence easily reminded his listeners and readers of Homer's characterization of Polyphemus and the Cyclops, who have no understanding or respect of *dikai or themistes* (*Od.* IX, 215). The disappearance of an entire world of values is lamented also in another line:

> Order (*kosmos*) disappeared and no longer is there an equal distribution *(isos dasmos)*[43] in the common interest (I, 677–678).

Bewilderment is the poet's response to such spectacle:

> Many indeed have worthless brains but enjoy good fortune, and for them apparent failure turns into success. And there are those who labour wisely but suffer bad luck, and their efforts accomplish nothing.[44]

The only solution to this state of things seems to be pointing to God and fate as being responsible of man's condition: God dispenses good and bad fortune as he wishes and human beings must endure their lot.[45] But here again lies a difficulty; for the aristocrats claimed to have a certain vicinity to God, to be in a preferential relationship; and this obviously does not apply anymore. The Gods have

---

[41] See I, 525–526: "it seems appropriate that the good have riches and it is proper to a bad man to suffer poverty".
[42] I, 635. At I, 895–896, we read that the most precious possession for a man is discernment whereas lack of discernment (*agnômosynê*) is the most bitter. At I, 1171–72, Theognis states that *gnôme* is the best thing the gods give to mortal men, because "discernment has the ends of everything".
[43] On the political overtones of this expression see Cerri 1969.
[44] I, 161–164; cf. 865–866": God gives splendid prosperity to many worthless men.
[45] See for instance I, 441–446; 591–592; 1162 A–F.

abandoned them, to the point that the poet wonders who will trust the Gods seeing that the unjust man flourishes and the just is "worn out and consumed by grievous poverty" (I, 752). Theognis hints to an additional problem: since material fortune depends on the will of the Gods and is changeable, appraisal of a person should go beyond it. But this is not the custom of the day. Lionel Pearson commented that "Theognis says that *aretê* is not worth winning at the price of injustice, and that distinction and success deserve no respect if they are the result of chance" (Pearson 1962, p. 77). *Aretê* in the old ethics has the connotation of distinction and success; it will later be identified with true human excellence. *Aretê* is a *telos*, an end, and therefore the Socratic question whether it can be taught makes no sense until it becomes a means. Only the means can be taught. Aretê becomes a quality of mind and character, a mode of behavior. What, then, deserves respect? Theognis' answer is: justice, *dikaiosynê* (I, 147), which contains the sum of all virtue.

The same feeling of bewilderment prompts the poet to lament that "Hope is the only good god yet left among mankind; the rest have forsaken us and gone to Olympus." Honesty, self-restraint, piety, justice have all left the earth (I, 1135–50). It follows that in such a situation of upheaval and unrest it is difficult to discern what is good and what is bad, who the trustworthy people are and who should not be consorted with. Hence Theognis advice to his protégé:

> Be sensible and do not, at the cost of shameful or unjust acts, seize for yourself prestige, success or wealth. Know that this is so and do not seek the company of base men, but always cling to the good. [...] For from the noble you will learn noble things, but if you mingle with the base, you will lose even the sense you have. Knowing this, consort with the good, and one day you will say that I give good advice to my friends. (I, 29–38; cf. 69–72; 465–466)

Theognis foresees that social change and political turmoil will corrupt the city and will pave the way to "a corrector of our evil insolence" (*hybrios:* I, 39–40), himself an "insolent (*hybristên*) man, a leader of grievous strife" (I, 1081–82): a tyrant.[46] The man that elsewhere is described as "the tyrant who devours the people (*dêmophagon tyrannon*)" (I, 1180–82); such a man can be put down without causing any revenge from the gods and will go below ground not mourned by the poet (I, 1203–06). In such changing circumstances, the art of deception will prove to be of fundamental importance: Cyrnus must keep an apparently cheerful attitude and be friendly to everybody while in fact trusting no-

---

[46] Social unrest and civil strife are the typical background for the appearance of a tyrant on the political scene. On this theme see Giorgini 1993.

body. For the new elite has no idea of truth or of honor and respect and therefore cannot be trusted. Indeed, the poet admonishes, "You may wander around the entire world and you'll find people to fit barely in one boat who have respect (*aidôs*) on their tongues and on their eyes" (I, 83–86).

The new value, the new driving force in social relations is wealth:[47] "Wealth mixes stock" because aristocratic men or women prefer to marry someone rich rather than good; or sometimes are forced to do so by necessity (*anagkê*: I, 195). Indeed, Wealth is "the fairest and most desirable of all the gods", because with it "a man becomes good even if he is bad" (I, 1117–18) – where 'good' and 'bad' do not have moral connotations but rather are indicative of status. This situation brings about a complete reversal of values. Theognis laments that:

> Now what the noble consider vices are deemed virtues by the base, who rule with devious[48] laws; for all sense of respect (*aidôs*) died, and shamelessness and pride (*hybris*), having overcome justice, prevail in all the land (I, 289–292).

We may compare these verses with I, 647–648, where the poet reiterates that "all sense of respect died among men, while shamelessness roams the earth".

The reversal of values accompanies the reversal of fortune of people: the citizens who once were wealthy are now impoverished and unable to accomplish anything in line with their intrinsic excellence and distinction (*aretê*). For poverty casts men in a situation of powerlessness and perplexity, a condition summarized by the word *amêchaniê*.[49] In a sad genealogy "poverty is the mother of perplexity" (I, 384–385); which, in turn, confuses a man's mind and prompts him to commit base actions. A poor man cannot shine morally nor excel politically: "For in effect a man overwhelmed by poverty is powerless to say or accomplish anything and his tongue is bound fast" (I, 177–178). In addition, when someone finds himself in such a condition of powerlessness and perplexity he will discover that he has few true friends and comrades: everybody prefers to stay away from people saddled with poverty, powerlessness and perplexity.[50] In this context Solon's admonition is repeated:

---

47 I, 699–700. The conclusion of the poem is trenchant: "For all people wealth has the greatest power" (I, 718).
48 *Ektrapelos:* an unusual adjective, literally "turning away from the common way".
49 See for instance I, 619–620: "Often I toss about amid perplexities, distressed at heart, for we have not surmounted the crest of the wave of poverty".
50 I, 645–646; cf. 1075–78. Perplexity and poverty are coupled also at I, 1114.

> Many bad men are rich, and many good men poor; but we will not take their wealth in exchange for virtue, since this is always secure while wealth belongs now to one man, now to another (I, 315–318).

Discernment (*gnômê*: I, 319), on the contrary, like virtue, is always secure. And only the good men, the noble, possess it and therefore know how to observe due measure (*metron*) in every matter (I, 614). This statement goes together with the admonition to "Be not over-eager (*mêden agan*) in any matter; due measure (*kairos*) is best in all human works" (I, 401).

In this universe of values it is evident that respect is due only to peers, to those one can call friends and comrades (*hetairoi*: I, 399–400). Theognis admonishes thus Cyrnus and his audience in general:

> Respect (*aideisthai*) your friends and shun oaths that bring ruin to men carefully, avoiding the wrath of the Immortals.

And he adds:

> You will not leave your sons a better treasure, Cyrnus, than the respect (*aidous*) which accompanies the good men (*agathois*: I, 409–410).

In this context of aristocratic values, where respect is due to a noble both for his rank and for his moral value, Theognis laments that he has not been appropriately honored by his lover and protégé Cyrnus. With beautiful imagery Theognis complains that although by celebrating Cyrnus he gave him wings to fly over human affairs and go down in history, he received in exchange "scant respect" (*aidous*: I, 253). Indeed, Cyrnus tried to deceive the poet as if he were "a little child". Theognis concludes thus his complaint at Cyrnus:

> Boy, you paid back a bad exchange for kindness. No thanks from you for favours. You've never given me pleasure. And though I've often been kind to you, I never won your respect (*aidous*).[51]

We should, however, note that these complaints rather refer to the convivial setting of the poems and to private love matters. A subject on which Theognis feels ready to give counsel, be it the proper behavior with a boy-lover or the right measure in wine consuming. We thus read that a drunken person loses control over his mind and his tongue and has no shame in his actions (I, 475–476). Or, revealing a typical convivial attitude, the statement to the extent that "What

---

51 I, 1263–66. See Hubbard 2003.

worth is to me wealth and respect (*aidôs*)? Gaiety and good cheer together surpass all things" (I, 1066–68).

5 The Institutionalization of Respect: timê and atimia

Political institutions and social norms embody the ideology, namely the set of consistent beliefs, of a political entity. They reflect the values upon which a community is built. We can therefore shed more light on our object of study by examining the institutionalization of respect in ancient Greece. As we have seen, *timê* identified the personal honor of a citizen and the consequent respect it commanded, as well as an office or position that a person occupied. The same word had thus both personal and institutional connotations: the personal prestige of a person was increased when he was elected general or judge in a court, for instance. It is interesting to note that the same mix of public and private, of moral condemnation and political exclusion, applied to its opposite, the notion of *atimia*. In its original sense, *atimia* meant outlawry, loss of the protection of the law; therefore, a person who committed very serious crimes, such as high treason or attempting to become tyrant of a city, would lose legal protection: he could be killed or his property plundered or taken by anyone. This was tantamount to being cast out of the community: the *atimos* person would find himself defenseless, banned in a way similar to the *pharmakos*. In the case of Athens, this measure would have made it almost impossible for a person to live within Athenian territory and it can be considered equivalent to expulsion from Attica; this measure could accordingly be imposed also on aliens (MacDowell 1978, pp. 73–74).

Atimia "deprived an Athenian of the protection of the courts. Consequently, his enemies could harm him to any degree with impunity" (Sealy 1994, p. 12). This harsh punishment was the consequence of the loss of honor of a person incurred by committing a terrible crime: this reflected an aristocratic mentality, where honor is the most valuable possession of a noble person. It is therefore very interesting that in due course the notion of *atimia* became more lenient: it entailed milder penalties, although a citizen could incur such penalty by committing lesser crimes against the community. For instance, "a citizen who owed a financial debt to the state and did not pay it by the ninth prytany of the year became *atimos*. By the time of Dêmosthenes many of the *atimoi* were public debtors" (Sealy 1994, p. 13). This fact reflects the idea that a citizen who did not discharge his duties towards the community, of whatever kind, lost the right to have access to certain public spaces and ceremonies. One very good testimony is again that of Dêmosthenes. In his oration *Against Philip 3*, Dêmosthenes cites an old event and reminds his Athenian audience that "*atimia* in the past was a severe penalty, amounting to death without retribution, in contrast to *atimia* as his audience knows it, which concerns exclusion from participation in the Athenian *koina*".[52] The more the polis lost its aristocratic connotations the more crimes against the community were considered punishable; and the punishment consisted in exclusion from public life. It was the political, rather than the moral, aspect that was emphasized by this development, as it suits a democratic ideology which stresses the importance of political equality.

In fact, it was around 510/07 that this change took place in Athens. Interestingly enough, this change was not legally enacted but rather came about by practice around the time of Cleisthenes' reforms. *Atimia* took up the meaning of "disenfranchisement", loss of civic rights or, more generally, exclusion from the privileges of Athenian public life (Hansen 1976). Therefore, an *atimos* "was not allowed to enter temples or the Agora. He could not hold any public office, nor be a member of the Boule or a juror. He could not speak in the Ekklesia or in a law-court [...]" (Mac Dowell 1978, p. 74). We may add that there existed a, so to speak, automatic *atimia* and an *atimia* by sentence: the first applied to people guilty of certain offenses, not necessarily crimes, such as prostitution. In this case, the original meaning of *timê* is still reflected: by such behavior, these people lost their honor and respectability and therefore forfeited their civic rights. As Deborah Kamen correctly remarked: "The very word *atimos*, meaning both 'deprived of civic offices' (a + *timai*) and 'deprived of honor' (a + *timê*), encapsulates both the degraded political status and the degraded social status of such individuals".[53] It is my impression that in the course of time, with increasingly democratic institutions and a fully-fledged democratic ideology established in Athens, the emphasis shifted from the personal/moral to the public/political realm: what commanded more condemnation was the offense against the community; it dishonored the citizen and deprived him of his civic privileges. The fact that *atimia* was context-sensitive seems confirmed also by its different implications in such diverse political entities as Sparta and Athens. Plutarch, *Agesilaus* 30, informs us that at Sparta soldiers who fled the battlefield were labeled runaways and they were dishonored. In oligarchic Sparta, where honor com-

---

[52] Dêmosthenes IX, 44–47. See Evelyn van't Wout 2011.
[53] Kamen 2013, chapter 7; p. 78. Kamen also maintains that prostitutes and people who squandered their money were found guilty of a crime by analogy and therefore punished: for instance, someone who sold his own body would be ready to sell his city. Cf. Aeschynes, *Contra Tim.* I, 28–30.

mands equal respect from the peers, this is a state of infamy rather than real outlawry. To this testimony we may add that of Xenophon, who maintains that certain Spartans made *atimoi* for being cowards preferred actual death to the utter dishonor, entailing social death, deriving from such a "*atimos* and reproachful life".[54] An Athenian *atimos*, by contrast, incurred civil death, the loss of all civic prerogatives. This seems to be the sense of the Decree of Eukrates of 346 BCE, which made people who attempted to or actually subverted the democratic regime *atimoi*. I subscribe to David Teegarden's opinion: "To prescribe that an offender 'is to be *atimos*', is, I suggest, a quasi-magical speech act comparable to self-imprecation, intended to protect the interests of the community" (Teegarden 2014, p. 146). These are formulaic protections, entrenchment clauses, rather than actual penalties. Their purpose is coercing compliance, putting on an aura of untouchability, rather than punishing offenders; for it is not clear what government will punish those who overturn the government.

Another very interesting notion to examine in this connection is that of *hybris*, a word notoriously difficult to translate. This is due to the fact that it encapsulates both a disposition of presumption, an attitude of wanton insolence, and the ensuing actions towards actual people (or the gods). In the second respect, this made it difficult for the legislator to pin down the exact actions determined by wanton insolence although it was important, because *hybris* entailed dishonor (*atimia*) for the offended.[55] This fact was recognized by the Athenian penal code, which included a law against *hybris*. In fact, according to the Athenian laws it was possible to bring a law-suit for *hybris* and also for *atimia*. Since the precise borders of these crimes were blurred and undefined, the suitor had to appeal to the conventional knowledge and wisdom of the jurors, namely to a shared perception of what these terms entailed for the ordinary citizens. To restrain wanton suits penalties were fixed for bringing an unsuccessful suit. We must also note that often these law-suits had the purpose of outmaneuvering a political opponent, of excluding him from the public arena. Athenian democracy was a very agonistic political society. As Lene Rubinstein has remarked: "Athenian legal actions, public as well as private, can be characterized as 'zero-sum games' in which the prize for which the two opponents competed was recognition of status or honor (*timê*): in this game the successful litigant could add to his own prestige the prestige lost by his unsuccessful opponent [...]" (Rubinstein 2000, p. 29). Therefore, in most *atimia* cases the real purpose

---

54 Xenophon, *Resp. Lac.* IX, 6, 4–5.
55 See Aristotle, *Rhet.* 2.2.1378b 29–30: "Dishonour is part of *hybris*, for the one who dishonours slights". For a comprehensive discussion of the subject see Fisher 1992; for a detailed critical discussion see Cairns 1996.

of the prosecution was to discredit a political rival and to silence him: "citizens are defined by their *parrhêsia*, the right to speak publicly, and non-citizens, including the disenfranchised, are branded by their legal silence" (Wohl 2010, p. 51).

A very interesting case is the famous orator Dêmosthenes who, in his *Against Meidias*, trying to persuade the jurors that Meidias' behavior was insolent, wishes to distinguish between the actual damage caused by a punch and the dishonor that it brings about when it is done with "wanton insolence" (*hybris*). He recounts the story of Euaion, who at a dinner party killed Boiotos who had punched him, and comments: "It was not the blow that made him angry, but the dishonor (*atimia*); nor being hit is such a serious matter to free men (*eleutherois*), though it is serious, but rather being hit with *hybris*".[56] Dêmosthenes goes on to argue that, put in much worse circumstances by Meidias, who punched him at the Dionysian festivals of 348 in front of Greek citizens and foreigners, he restrained himself and now asks for satisfaction through the law and by the court. His point is clear:

> I think that you should set up a precedent for all to follow, that no one who wantonly assaults and outrages another should be punished by the victim himself in hot blood, but must be brought into your court, because it is you who confirm and uphold the protection granted by the laws to those who are injured.[57]

Dêmosthenes argues that a court and the laws of the city redress the hybristic act of injustice which dishonored him. The protection of a citizen's honor is now a political and legal matter and a person cannot take justice into one's own hands. It can be argued, however, that Dêmosthenes did not act merely in the name of the public interest but also in order to get rid of Meidias's presence in the public arena.

Finally, there is one more area we need to explore concerning the public perception of honor, dishonor and respectful behavior. This consists in what we could call the ritualistic aspect of *timê*, namely specific, deliberate behavior that causes dishonor. We already noted how Homer stigmatized Achilles' inhuman behavior towards Hector and his corpse. It is especially in tragedy that we find examples of acts of inhuman conduct, like maiming a body, performed with the intent to dishonor it. For instance, this is the case of *maschalismos*, severing parts of a corpse in order to dishonor the person: cutting off hands, feet, the nose or the genitals. This is the fate that Agamemnon meets on his return

---

[56] Dêmosthenes 21, 71–72.
[57] Dêmosthenes 21, 76.

from the Trojan War: killed by his wife Clytemnestra and her lover and then maimed. This event is recounted by Aeschylus, *Coeph.* 439–443, as well as by Sophocles *El.* 444–446. Both Aeschylus and Sophocles indicate that *maschalismos* made Agamemnon further dishonored (*atimos*) in death (Iles Johnston 1999, pp. 156–159). Again, in Aeschylus, *Eum.* 810, we find that the Furies describe themselves as *atimai*, dishounored, and "mourning over dishonor" (*atimopentheis*), and therefore seeking revenge. Since one of the many intents of the *Oresteia* trilogy is to show how the ancient custom of revenge is interrupted by the Gods and replaced by law and human courts, the message Aeschylus wants to convey is that the old idea of personal honor requiring taking justice in one's own hand is here superseded; a fixed law valid for everyone (not only the citizens but also the gods) and a public court will from now on judge and make legally binding decisions. For Aeschylus the institution of the tribunal of the Areopagus marks the beginning of a new era in Athens, in which *nomos basileus* reigns over mortals and immortals. And with it respect is due to every Athenian citizen simply qua citizen.

Bibliography

Aristotle (1984): *The Athenian Constitution*, ed. by P.J. Rhodes: London, Penguin.
Aristotle (2013): *Politics*, transl. by C. Lord, Chicago: Chicago University Press.
Aristotle (1992): *The Art of Rhetoric*, ed. by. H. Lawson-Tancred, London: Penguin.
Atwill, J.M. (1998): *Rhetoric Reclaimed. Aristotle and the Liberal Arts Tradition*, Ithaca: Cornell University Press.
Balot, R. (2006): *Greek Political Thought*, Oxford: Blackwell.
Cairns, D.L. (1993): *Aidôs. The Psychology and Ethics of Honour and Shame in Ancient Greek Literature*, Oxford: Clarendon Press.
Cairns, D.L. (1996): "Hybris, Dishonour, and Thinking Big", *Journal of Hellenic Studies* 116, pp. 1–32.
Cartledge, P. (2009): *Ancient Greek Political Thought in Practice*, Cambridge: Cambridge University Press.
Cerri, G. (1969): "*Isos dasmos* come equivalente di *isonomia* nella silloge teognidea", *Quaderni Urbinati di Cultura Classica* 8, pp. 97–104.
Cooper, J.M. (2012): *Pursuits of Wisdom: Six Ways of Life in Ancient Philosophy*, Princeton: Princeton University Press.
Demosthenes (2002): *Against Meidias*, ed. by D.M. MacDowell, Bristol: Bristol Classical Press.
Develin, R. (1989): *Athenian Officials 684–321 BC*, Cambridge: Cambridge University Press.
Ehrenberg, V. (1958): "Isonomia". In A.F. von Pauly and G. Wissowa, *Realencyclopaedie der classischen Altertumswissenschaft*, Stuttgart: Metzler, Suppl. VII, cc. 293–301.

Figueira, T.J. (1995): "*Khremata:* Acquisition and Possession in Archaic Greece". In K.D. Irani and M. Silver (Eds.): *Social Justice in the Ancient World*, Westport, CT: Greenwood, pp. 41–60.

Figueira, T.J. and Nagy, G. (1985): "Theognis of Megara". *Poetry and the Polis*, Baltimore: Johns Hopkins University Press.

Fisher, N.R.E. (1992): *Hybris. A Study in the Values of Honour and Shame in Ancient Greece*, Warminster: Aris & Phillips.

Giorgini, G. (1993): *La città e il tiranno*, Milan: Giuffrè.

Hansen, M.H. (1976): *Apagoge, Endeixis and Ephegesis against Kakourgoi, Atimoi and Pheugontes*, Odense: Odense University Press.

Harrison, E. (1902): *Studies in Theognis. Together with a Text of the Poems*, Cambridge: Cambridge University Press.

Heller, E. (1984): "Man Ashamed". In *In the Age of Prose. Literary and Philosophical Essays*, Cambridge: Cambridge University Press.

Herodotus (2008): *The Histories*, transl. by R. Waterfield, Oxford: Oxford University Press.

Hubbard, T.K. (Ed.) (2003): *Homosexuality in Greece and Rome*, Berkeley: University of California Press.

Iles Johnston, S. (1999): *Restless Dead. Encounters between the Living and the Dead in Ancient Greece*, Berkeley/Los Angeles: University of California Press.

Irwin, E. (2005): *Solon and Early Greek Poetry: The Politics of Exhortation*, Cambridge: Cambridge University Press.

Jaeger, W. (1939–1945): *Paideia: The Ideals of Greek Culture*, Oxford: Blackwell.

Kalyvas, A. (2014): "Solonian Citizenship: Democracy, Conflict, Participation". In P.M. Kitromilides (Ed.), *Athenian Legacies: European Debates on Citizenship*, Florence: Olschki, pp. 19–36.

Kamen, D. (2013): *Status in Classical Athens*, Princeton: Princeton University Press.

Konstan, D. (2006): *The Emotions of the Ancient Greeks*, Toronto: University of Toronto Press.

Leveque, P. and Vidal-Naquet, P. (1996): *Cleisthenes the Athenian. An Essay on the Representation of Space and Time in Greek Political Thought from the End of the Sixth Century to the Death of Plato*, Atlantic Highlands: Humanities Press International.

Linforth, I.M. (1919): *Solon the Athenian*, Berkeley: University of California Press.

Lombardini, J (2013): "*Isonomia* and the Public Sphere in Democratic Athens", *History of Political Thought* 34, pp. 393–420.

MacDowell, D.M. (1978): *The Law in Classical Athens*, Ithaca: Cornell University Press.

Meyer, E.A. (2008): "Thucydides on Harmodius and Aristogeiton, Tyranny, and History", *Classical Quarterly* 58, pp. 13–34.

Morgan, T. (2007): *Popular Morality in the Early Roman Empire*, Cambridge: Cambridge University Press.

Nietzsche, F. (1887/2008): *On the Genealogy of Morals*, Oxford: Oxford University Press.

Noussia-Fantuzzi, M. (2010): *Solon the Athenian, the Poetic Fragments*, Leiden: Brill.

Ober, J. (1989): *Mass and Elite in Democratic Athens*, Princeton: Princeton University Press.

Ober, J. (1996): *The Athenian Revolution*, Princeton: Princeton University Press.

Owens, R. (2010): Solon of Athens: *Poet, Philosopher, Soldier, Statesman*, Brighton: Sussex Academic Press.

Pearson, L. (1962): *Popular Ethics in Ancient Greece*, Stanford: Stanford University Press.

Plato (1982): *Hippias Major*, transl. by P. Woodruff, Indianapolis: Hackett.

Plato (2012): *The Republic*, ed. by C. Rowe, London: Penguin.
Plutarch (1914): *Lives*, ed. by B. Perrin, vol. 1, Harvard, Harvard University Press.
Plutarch (1927): *Moralia*, ed. by F. Cole Babbitt, Harvard: Harvard University Press.
Raaflaub, K.A., Ober, J. and Wallace, R. (2007): *Origins of Democracy in Ancient Greece*, Berkeley-Los Angeles/London: University of California Press.
Redfield, J. (1994): *Nature and Culture in the Iliad: The Tragedy of Hector*, Durham: Duke University Press.
Rosivach, V.J. (1992): "Redistribution of Land in Solon, Fragment 34 West", *Journal of Hellenic Studies* 112, pp. 153–157.
Rubinstein, L. (2000): *Litigation and Cooperation. Supporting Speakers in the Courts of Classical Athens*, Stuttgart: Franz Steiner.
Sealy, R (1994): *The Justice of the Greeks*, Ann Arbor, MI: University of Michigan Press.
Solon (1999): *Greek Elegiac Poetry*, ed. by D.E. Gerber, Harvard, Harvard University Press.
Suidae Lexicon (1928–1938), ed. by A. Adler, Leipzig: Teubner.
Teegarden, D.A. (2014): *Death to Tyrants*, Princeton: Princeton University Press.
Thucydides (2009): *The Peloponnesian War*, ed. by P.J. Rhodes, Oxford: Oxford University Press.
Tyrtaeus (1999): *Greek Elegiac Poetry*, ed. by D.E. Gerber, Harvard, Harvard University Press.
Valdes-Guia, M. (2007): "Peur et contrainte des dépendents ratifiées par des pratiques judiciaires et religieuses: les paysans *atimoi* de l'Attique archaique".
   In A. Serghidou (Ed.): *Fear of Slaves, Fear of Enslavement in the Ancient Mediterranean*, Besançon: Presses Universitaires de Franche-Comté, pp. 99–114.
Van't Wout, E. (2011): "From Oath-Swearing to Entrenchment Clause: The Introduction of Atimia-Terminology in Legal Inscriptions". In A. Lardinois, J. Blok and M.G.M. van der Poel (Eds.): *Sacred Words: Orality, Literacy and Religion*, Leiden: Brill, pp. 143–160.
Vlastos, G. (1953): "Isonomia", *American Journal of Philology* 74, pp. 337–366.
Wohl, V. (2010): *Law's Cosmos. Juridical Discourse in Athenian Forensic Oratory*, Cambridge: Cambridge University Press.

Christopher J. Rowe
Plato on Respect, and What "Belongs to" Oneself

Abstract: It is not clear whether we find anything much like the modern notion of 'respect' in Plato. But he certainly has plenty to say about things that might fall under this general heading. Thus he holds that we must not harm others, but always act justly towards them; he also attaches great value to love, and to friendship, devoting three whole dialogues to these subjects. But at the same time he also holds – in common with other Greek philosophers, at least until the advent of Christianity – that in all our actions each of us inevitably aims at his or her own good (that being the very nature of human desire). The difficulty is to understand how Plato thinks he can combine these two positions. The most important claim made in this chapter is that he effects the necessary combination by using the notion of what is 'ours', or 'belongs to' – is *oikeion* to – ourselves, so that it includes others and others' interests as well as our own. A second claim is that the resemblance of this approach to the Stoic idea of *oikeiôsis* is not accidental.

The modern notion of 'respect', as such, is probably not to be found in Plato; at any rate there is no word in his vocabulary that fully corresponds to it.[1] Strictly speaking, then, he might be said to fall outside the scope of the present volume. Nevertheless if 'respect' is understood more generally, in terms of what should govern our relationship to others, Plato has plenty to say that is relevant to the volume's concerns. He – or usually his Socrates – holds, for example, that we must not harm other people; we must always act justly towards them. Love and friendship are also quite central to what he regards as valuable in life, as can be judged from the fact that he devotes a major part of three whole dialogues (*Lysis*, *Symposium*, *Phaedrus*) to these subjects. But at the same time, in common with other Greek philosophers, at least until the advent of Christianity, he holds that in each and every one of our actions, without exception, the human agent inevitably aims at his or her own good; that, Plato claims,

---

1 The term *aidôs*, often translatable as 'respect', seems typically associated with fear and shame (which are not what chiefly concern the present volume). 'Respect' as such will be mentioned only once in what follows (in the final paragraph, in a parenthesis, and followed by a question mark).

is part of what it is to be human. The problem for the interpreter is to understand how Plato thinks he can combine these two positions. The central claim of this chapter is that he reconciles them by using the notion of what is 'ours', or what 'belongs to' – is *oikeion* to – ourselves, in such a way that it includes others and others' interests as well as our own. A second claim, made already by one ancient voice but hardly recognized in modern times, is that Plato's approach here has much in common with, although in some respects it sharply differs from, the Stoic idea of *oikeiôsis*. It is with this Stoic idea that I begin.

The Stoics are well-known for their doctrine of *oikeiôsis*, usually translated into English, unhelpfully, as 'appropriation'. The translation is unhelpful because *oikeiôsis* is properly the process by which we come to *recognize* the kinship, *oikeiotês*, of things and of people to ourselves; we do not *make* them *oikeia* (things) or *oikeioi* (people), for they are *oikeia/oi* already, if they are, by virtue of their and of our very nature.[2] The basic idea is explained in the following passage from Diogenes Laertius:

> They [the Stoics] say that an animal has self-preservation as the object of its first impulse, since nature from the beginning makes it [i.e., self-preservation] *oikeion*, as Chrysippus [3rd century BCE] says in his *On Ends* book I. The first thing that is *oikeion* to every animal, he says, is its own constitution and the consciousness of this. For nature was not likely either to alienate the animal from itself, or to make it and then neither alienate it from itself nor make it *oikeion* to itself. So it remains to say that in constituting the animal, nature made it *oikeion* to itself. This is why the animal rejects what is harmful and accepts what is *oikeion*. They hold it false to say, as some people do, that pleasure is the object of animals' first impulse. [86] For pleasure, they say, if it does occur, is a by-product which arises only when nature all by itself has searched out and adopted the proper requirements for a creature's constitution, just as animals [then] frolic and plants bloom. Nature, they say, makes no distinction between plants and animals, in that it [sometimes] directs animals as well as plants without impulse and sensation, and in us [too] certain processes of a vegetative kind take place. But since animals have the additional faculty of impulse, through the use of which they go in search of what is *oikeion* to them, what is natural for them is to be governed in accordance with their impulse. And since reason, by way of a more perfect management, has been bestowed on rational beings, to live correctly in accordance with reason comes to be natural for them. For reason supervenes as the craftsman of impulse. (Diogenes Laertius, *Lives of the Philosophers* 7.85–86, trans. Long and Sedley, modified).

What is evidently the same basic idea, though without explicit mention of the idea of *oikeiotês*, then comes to be applied much more broadly (the passage is

---

[2] Annas (1993, p. 148, 149 n. 3, etc.) prefers 'familiarization' over 'appropriation'. I shall adopt Annas's alternative, on the grounds that it is at least less unhelpful than 'appropriation'.

from the 5th-century compiler Stobaeus, some two centuries later than Diogenes, reporting Hierocles, a Stoic from the 1st century CE):

> Each one of us is as it were entirely encompassed by many circles, some smaller, others larger, the latter enclosing the former on the basis of their different and unequal dispositions relative to each other. The first and closest circle is the one which a person has drawn as though around a centre, his own mind. This circle encloses the body and anything taken for the sake of the body. For it is virtually the smallest circle, and almost touches the centre itself. Next, the second one further removed from the centre but enclosing the first circle; this contains parents, siblings, wife, and children. The third one has in it uncles and aunts, grandparents, nephews, nieces, and cousins. The next circle includes the other relatives, and this is followed by the circle of local residents, then the circle of fellow-tribesmen, next that of fellow-citizens, and then in the same way the circle of people from neighbouring towns, and the circle of fellow-countrymen. The outermost and largest circle, which encompasses all the rest, is that of the whole human race. Once these have all been surveyed, it is the task of a well tempered man, in his proper treatment of each group, to draw the circles together somehow towards the centre, and to keep zealously transferring those from the enclosing circles into the enclosed ones ... It is incumbent on us to respect people from the third circle as if they were those from the second, and again to respect our other relatives as if they were those from the third circle. For although the greater distance in blood will remove some affection, we must still try hard to assimilate them. The right point will be reached if, through our own initiative, we reduce the distance of the relationship with each person. The main procedure for this has been stated. But we should do more, in the terms of address we use, calling cousins brothers, and uncles and aunts, fathers and mothers ... For this mode of address would be no slight mark of our affection for them all, and it would also stimulate and intensify the indicated contraction of the circles ...[3] (Stobaeus 4.671,7–673, 11, trans. Long and Sedley)

In other words, it is not just our immediate family and friends that are *oikeioi* ('related', 'belonging') to us, and not just our fellow-citizens or countrymen, who might be thought of anyway, by anyone, as somehow 'ours': *all* human beings are *oikeioi* to us, simply by virtue of being human, and the rational, the wise thing to do will be to treat them accordingly, so far as we can. Scholars are divided about where to find the roots of this special, and characteristically Stoic, notion of *oikeiôsis:* in Theophrastus, perhaps, or in Aristotle – or in Plato.

---

3 Beautifully summed up by Cicero: "They [the Stoics] think it important to understand that it is by nature that children are loved by their parents; the shared community of the human race that we seek derives from this beginning" (Cicero, *De Fin*. III.62, my translation). Cicero's use of 'understand' here is important: in its extended version too, the Stoic notion of *oikeiôsis* is about recognizing what is already the case, namely that the whole human race does in fact form a single community; it is not about *coming to regard* it *as* forming such a community. In other words, this Stoic notion is all about the application of reason, not at all about what we *ought, sc.* 'morally', to do.

Terry Penner and I are among the few who have suggested the latter possibility, albeit in passing.⁴ But the suggestion is an old one, having been made already, towards or even before the beginning of the Christian era, by the Anonymous Commentator on Plato's *Theaetetus*.⁵ The commentator is skeptical about one particular use of the theory of *oikeiôsis*, for reasons that will be discussed later in this chapter, but he adds, almost casually, that anyway "this much talked-about *oikeiôsis* is brought in not only by Socrates but by the sophists in Plato".⁶ "Socrates" is of course "bringing it in", according to the Commentator, there in the *Theaetetus* passage that he is currently commenting on, but his pairing of Socrates with "the sophists in Plato" could suggest that he is also referring to Socrates in the dialogues more generally; certainly, that Socrates "brings it in" (more generally) would help to justify his own introduction of *oikeiôsis* into a context that does not itself mention it.⁷

G.B. Kerferd, in 1972, looking at the earlier history of the word *oikeiôsis*, found no instances of the noun in Plato but a single instance of the adjective *oikeiôtikos*, together with a number of instances of the verb *oikeioô*. He concluded that in all the passages listed for *oikeioô*⁸ "we are concerned not with mere acquisition or appropriation but with the establishment and recognition of a more intimate and fundamental relationship" (Kerferd 1972, p. 183). The most interesting of the instances of the adjective *oikeios* he discusses is "[i]n the important opposition between *oikeion agathon* and *allotrion agathon* developed by Thrasymachus in the first book of the *Republic*", where "*oikeion agathon* is not any good which is acquired, it is the good which belongs most intimately to oneself be-

---

4 Penner and Rowe 2002, p. 152 n. 142, 323. But see also Charlotte Murgier 2013, § 2 (and cf. McCabe 2007, p. 416 n. 17).
5 Cf. Bonazzi 2008.
6 *Commentarium in Platonis "Theaetetum"*, ed. Bastianini and Sedley (1995), col. VII, ll.20 – 25: *tê[n de] oikeiôsin tau[tên] poluthrulêton ou mo[no]n ho Sôkratês eis[ag]ei alla kai hoi para tôi Platôni sophist [ai.]*.
7 One cannot, of course, assume that he – the statistical probability is that it is a he – would have thought he needed such justification. (My colleague George Boys-Stones confirms that there is little or no evidence that a Platonist like the Anonymous Commentator would have read the *Lysis* in the first place.) It is nevertheless interesting that it – the justification for his introduction of the idea of *oikeiôsis* – actually exists.
8 The passages are: *Prot*. 326b2 (Protagoras himself is speaking, of the inculcation of rhythm and harmony in the souls of the young), *Parm*. 128a5, *Tim*. 45e4, *Letter III* 317e4, *Laws* V.738d7, *Letter VII* 330b2, *Rep*. 46[6]c1; *oikeiôtikos* in *Soph*. 223b2, on which see further below (the list is from Ast, but "an unpublished Platonic word list compiled by Dr L. Brandwood" confirms that it is complete).

cause it is rooted in one's very nature, and so is opposed to the good which is not so rooted".[9]

Kerferd's list is avowedly lexical rather than conceptual. Even so, it is surprising that it should omit any reference to the *Lysis*. The conclusion of the main argument of the dialogue, after all, gives a central role to what is *oikeion* ('belongs') to us, making it the object of "passion and friendship and desire" – that is, since the discussion is entirely general, of *all* "passion and friendship and desire":

> "So is it in fact the case, as we were saying just now, that desire is cause of friendship, and that what desires is friend to that thing it desires and at such time that it desires it, and that what we were previously saying being a friend was, was some kind of nonsense, like a poem that's been badly put together?"
> "Quite likely."
> "But", I said, "what desires, desires whatever it's lacking. Isn't that so?"
> "Yes."
> "And what is lacking, in that case, is friend of whatever it's lacking?"
> "It seems so to me."
> "And what becomes lacking is whatever has something taken away from it."
> "Of course."
> "It's what belongs to us (*to oikeion*), then, that's actually the object of passion (*erôs*) and friendship (*philia*) and desire (*epithumia*), as it appears, Menexenus and Lysis."
> The two of them assented.
> "The two of you, in that case, if you're friends to each other, in some way naturally belong the one to (are *oikeioi* to) the other."
> "No doubt about it," they said together.
> "And if, then, any one person desires any other," I said, "you boys,
> or feels passion for him, he wouldn't ever desire, or feel passion, or love, if he didn't actually in some way belong to (wasn't in some way *oikeios* to) the one he is feeling passion for, either in relation to the soul or in relation to some characteristic of the soul, or ways or form."
> "Absolutely so," said Menexenus; but Lysis said nothing.
> "Very well. What naturally belongs to us (what is by nature *oikeion* to us), then – it's become evident to us that it's necessary to love it."
> "It seems so," he [Menexenus?] said.
> "It's necessary, in that case, for the genuine lover, one who's not pretended, to be loved by his darling." (*Lys*. 221d2–222a7; translation from Penner and Rowe 2005)

According to this passage, whatever we feel passionate about, or love, or desire, will be something we lack, something that naturally belongs to us but which we

---

[9] But this, it has to be said, will be utterly different from the Stoic idea of *oikeiotês*, insofar as the 'good' Thrasymachus sees as *oikeion* to him and us is as narrow as the Stoics' is broad; his self-interest is just that, i.e., purely selfish.

do not have: something we need in order to complete our nature. Not long before, in 220d–220e, it has been agreed that the only true 'friend', i.e. the only thing truly loved, is the friend for which we love all the others – the *prôton philon*, or 'first friend'. The identity of the 'first friend' is not revealed, but let us suppose that it is the good, i.e., our own individual good, what is truly good for each of us: then the result will be (a) that we love, or desire, the good, and – presumably[10] – whatever may be a means to it, and (b) that this good is the completion of our nature. Add in the focus, from the early on in the dialogue, on the importance of *knowledge*, and we have a schema that is both recognizably Socratic (nothing is good without/apart from knowledge: what else will tell us what is and is not a 'friend' for the sake of the 'first friend'?), and also, I propose, bears more than a passing resemblance to the kinds of ideas we find in the two Stoic passages cited above, from Diogenes Laertius and Stobaeus/Hierocles. My thesis, in short, is that the *Lysis* is one text to which the Anonymous Commentator could certainly have looked to as justification for the claim that *oikeiôsis* "is brought in ... by Socrates";[11] although he could also have referred to numerous passages elsewhere in Plato. There are a significant number of contexts, stretching from the *Charmides* to the *Laws*, in which the good is identified with the *oikeion*, or what is 'ours': see, e.g., *Charm.* 163d2–6, *Symp.* 205e4–206a1, *Rep.* IX.586e1–2, *Laws* X.900d1–3. But the *Lysis* is the core text in this context, providing an extended argument for what is simply assumed, without argument, elsewhere; it is, I claim, what *allows* it to be so assumed.

Two things need to be stressed here: first, that the claim is not that what we find in the *Lysis* (and elsewhere in Plato) is actually the same as what we find in Stoicism; rather it is to say either that the two sets of ideas overlap enough to justify our seeing one (the Platonic) as the ancestor of the other, or at least that they overlap enough to allow a Platonist to claim that they do (or both). But secondly, what is at issue is much more than a resemblance in terminology; the similarity in terminology marks a deeper connection. As for the Commentator's reference to *oikeiôsis* being brought in by "the sophists in Plato", I for one find it hard to resist the temptation to connect this with the isolated use of *oikeiôtikos* in Plato's *Sophist*, in the summing up of the first account of what a sophist is:

---

10 I shall later justify this presumption (which a first reading of the relevant context might appear to contradict).
11 That is, were he is in fact intending this as a general claim, and not just one based on the text before him: see above.

Then according to what we are saying now, Theaetetus, it seems that if we take expertise in appropriation (*oikeiôtikê*), in hunting, in animal-hunting, in land-animal-hunting, in the hunting of humans, by persuasion, in private, involving selling for hard cash, offering a seeming education, the part of it that hunts rich and reputable young men is – to go by what we are saying now – what we should call the expertise of the sophist. (*Theaet.* 223b1–7, trans. Rowe[12])

Kerferd's comment here is that "the reference is to the acquiring of young men by the sophist in a way comparable with the acquisition of animals whether wild or tame. But there is probably included the sense of making the young men feel that they belong with the sophist" (Kerferd 1972, p. 184). This looks like over-interpretation: in the context of the summary Socrates is offering, *oikeiôtikê* merely stands in as a substitute for *ktêtikê*, of which hunting has been said to be one part.[13] In order for the Commentator, in a political context, to say that "the sophists in Plato" bring in *oikeiôsis*, it would perhaps be enough that Plato used an adjectival form of the term in a context describing what sophists – allegedly – do.[14]

The fact that modern scholarship has so rarely been inclined to connect Stoic *oikeiôsis* with Plato, whether in the *Lysis* or anywhere else, is attributable to a variety of reasons. What is perhaps the currently prevailing, or at any rate the most often repeated, view of the moral psychology endorsed by Plato's Socrates has him saying, not that what we desire is our real and true good (in brief, whatever really and truly completes our nature), but that the object of our desire is whatever we *believe* to contribute to our real good;[15] and this latter interpretation places him poles apart from the Stoics. But such an interpretation cannot, in my view, survive a joined-up reading of the *Lysis* (or, I think, of a large number of other dialogues). What we love and desire, according to the *Lysis*, is what is naturally *oikeion* to us, not what we think is *oikeion* but may or may not actually be so. But to see this, one must find one's way through the highly compressed, often thicket-like, endlessly surprising arguments of the dialogue, a task that most modern readers of Plato are apparently unready to undertake. Those who do give the *Lysis* any serious attention are for the most part content to see it as a somewhat peculiar, even perverse, exploration of the ordinary concept of *philia*. But it has to be more than that: if the focus of the dialogue really is on *philia*, and

---

12 Plato 2015.
13 Additionally, the "acquiring of young men", on the Visitor's account, must actually be a case of the hunting of tame animals, not just "in a way comparable" to it.
14 Or is the reference to Thrasymachus in *Rep.* I (see above), and/or Protagoras in the *Protagoras* (n. 8 above)?
15 See especially Brickhouse and Smith 2010 (discussed in Rowe 2012).

erôs, as narrowly understood, still in its later movements the dialogue incontrovertibly explores the general structure of human desire, and that exploration cannot avoid having implications beyond the immediate topic of *philia* (as narrowly understood). And in fact, by the end of that exploration, we seem to have arrived at a thoroughly radical and unfamiliar conception of friendship: one that extraordinarily makes it actually *necessary* for the beloved to love his lover, provided that the lover is true and not pretended.[16] Why so? Here is one explanation (taken from Penner and Rowe 2005, p. 169):

> Providing that we may suppose the "genuine" lover to be the one who loves in this way, i.e. wanting his beloved to be wise, and provided also that this "genuine" lover would in fact contribute towards the beloved's wisdom, the latter would *have* to love him; for according to Socrates' argument in the *Lysis*, what we love is what is good for us – what "naturally belongs to" us. But what else would the "genuine" lover be except the one who meets the requirements for loving other people, and who actually does have something to contribute to the development of the beloved (rather than having some general commitment to his development, without much idea of what *real* development would be)? A "pretended" lover, by contrast, would be someone who either had no real desire for the beloved's happiness, or who knew nothing about what it might consist in; or both.[17]

The conclusion of course delights Hippothales, Lysis' aspirant lover, and embarrasses Lysis and Menexenus.[18] But then Hippothales has no idea what the conclusion is actually saying; and for their part Lysis and Menexenus have a somewhat shaky hold on what Socrates is about, as is shown by their readiness to give up on it, and to allow themselves to be plunged back into aporia.

One recent reader of the *Lysis* has, however, fully recognized the potential connection between its deployment of the concept of the *oikeion* and Stoic *oi-*

---

16 See the long passage cited above from the end of the *Lysis*; the conclusion in question is actually the conclusion of the main argument of the dialogue, before the supposed *bouleversement* that leads to Socrates' familiar declaration that the discussion has got nowhere.

17 There is, of course, a ready-made pretext to hand for anyone who wishes to set aside the analysis of desire in the *Lysis:* namely that the dialogue officially ends in aporia, with the suggestion from Socrates that actually they have got nowhere. But this depends on our taking his objections to the foregoing argument seriously, in the way that his interlocutors (Lysis and Menexenus) do, and I believe that those objections are manufactured rather than genuine. In any case, the overlaps with what we find in non-aporetic dialogues are sufficient to show that the conclusions of the *Lysis* are to be taken more seriously than any apparent retraction by Socrates; and few would wish to suggest that no progress at all is made in aporetic dialogues. The chief point of formal aporia in such cases, I claim (at least as a working hypothesis), is to preserve Socrates' position as master of the ignorant.

18 "At that Lysis and Menexenus barely somehow nodded assent, but there was no mistaking Hippothales' pleasure, which made him go all sorts of colours" (*Lys.* 222b1–2).

keiôsis. This is Charlotte Murgier, who sets out specifically to discover whether "le lien entre *oikeion* et *oikeiosis* est-il simplement d'étymologie[19] ou bien la parenté lexicale recouvre-t-elle quelque chose de plus substantiel?" (Murgier 2013, § 2). Murgier examines two examples, one Platonic, one Aristotelian, her assumption being that while the fully worked-out theory of *oikeiôsis* will very likely have been a Stoic innovation, nonetheless "[e]n se saisissant du vocabulaire du propre pour construire le concept d'appropriation, les stoïciens reprennent un terme déjà doté d'une certaine épaisseur philosophique, dont il peut être fecond d'évaluer la contribution au concept qui en est dérivé" (Murgier 2013, § 20). The Platonic example is from the *Lysis*, the Aristotelian from the *Nicomachean* (and *Eudemian*) *Ethics;* it will plainly be the first that concerns me here.

Murgier's analysis gives pride of place to the discussion between Socrates and Lysis that opens the main part of the dialogue. Surely, Socrates says, your parents don't love you, if they don't allow you to do just what you want, like riding your father's chariot or messing with your mother's weaving? Only when you've acquired the necessary knowledge will they give you free rein – and the same goes for everyone: the neighbor, the Athenians, even the Great King himself will hand things over to you *if* you have the requisite knowledge, and not before. In short, "if you become wise, everyone will be friends to you and everyone will belong [will be *oikeioi*] to you, for you will be useful and good, but if you don't [become wise], neither anyone else nor your father will be friend to you, nor your mother nor those belonging to you [i.e. your *oikeioi*]" (*Lys.* 210d1–4).

> These lines,[20] playing as they do on the dialectical opposition *oikeion /allotrion*, confirm the enlargement of the circle of what 'belongs' ('l'appropriation') and the overturning of the very sense of the term: the natural belonging of family relationships gives way to a relationship founded on reason. Wisdom ... is revealed as the only source of relationship worth speaking of, rendering all things 'our own' (*hêmetera*)[21] that were alien (*allotria*)[22] in the absence of wisdom. Whether a thing belongs to us or is alien is a matter of whether it is beneficial for us or not, and whether it benefits or harms us is determined solely by whether or not we know how to use it . .... This correlation between belonging ('l'appropriation') and use makes wisdom the foundation of *oikeiotês* ('la propriété'), as the source of all benefit, whether for oneself or for others. (Murgier 2013, § 24)

---

[19] As perhaps Kerferd's inquiry might have suggested (see above).
[20] Murgier has cited a longer passage, from 210a9–d6.
[21] 210b5.
[22] 210c4.

Murgier recognizes that this is far from being the last word on the *oikeion* in the *Lysis*:

> Socrates will deepen the concept by showing that the *oikeion* founds desire itself; desire (whether for an object, for a friend, or for a lover) is at bottom desire for what belongs to us (221e), and what one looks for and finds in the other, in authentic friendship, is what belongs but is lacking to us. What binds true friends is the fact of their being *oikeioi* ('appropriés') by nature to one another (222a). The latter idea, however, emerges in the course of a discussion of the exact nature of this *oikeion*, in which it remains an open question whether it should be identified with what is like or with what is good.[23] The discussion here sets up the connection, even if in an aporetic context, between the *oikeion*, desire, nature, and the good that will be systematized in Stoic *oikeiôsis*. (Murgier 2013, § 24)

This analysis seems to me sound only up to a point. The problem lies in the sentence "What binds true friends is the fact of their being *oikeioi* by nature to one another (222a)". Nowhere is the *Lysis* concerned with *reciprocal* friendship.[24] Admittedly, there will be love on both sides in the case of the genuine lover in 222a. The lover loves the boy, and the boy will (necessarily!) love the lover. But the motivation of the lover is distinct from, though identical in kind to, the motivation of the beloved: that is, each will love the other, but as a means each to his own good. Friendship here is still a one-way relation, as it generally is in the *Lysis*; it is just that in this case the one-way relation '*x* loves *y*' coincides with another one-way relation, i.e. '*y* loves *x*'. Equally, the fact that Lysis will or would be a 'friend' to the Great King, if he had the knowledge to cure the King's son, no more makes the Great King Lysis's friend, i.e., loved by Lysis, than Lysis's being loved by his parents because he is useful to them makes him love *them*. This is somewhat obscured by the following passage of Murgier's:

> One then notices that if wisdom makes things 'ours', it not only has its effect in relation to things from which we will draw benefit, but by the same token makes us, too, *oikeioi* to others insofar as we will be useful to them and thus sought by them. The *oikeion* when founded in reason makes us in principle related to a limitless range of others, stretching as far as the Great King. Wisdom is thus what makes not only things be related to us but other people too, by causing their attachment to us. In this twofold effect of wisdom, at once towards oneself and towards others, we seem to be dealing with something that will be picked up by the Stoic concept of Stoic *oikeiôsis*, itself two-faced or two-directional ... (Murgier 2013, § 25)

---

[23] This is Murgier's interpretation; it is not the question Socrates actually raises in 221b–c.
[24] "[E]xcept as something that crops up and immediately disappears in the course of a dialectical argument" (Penner and Rowe 2015, p. 56; the claim is justified in the volume, *passim*); 222a is no exception, as I shall argue below.

Plato on Respect, and What "Belongs to" Oneself — 77

The effect of wisdom in relation to things, here, seems radically different from its effect in relation to other people; with things it is a matter of their usefulness to us, whereas with people it is our usefulness to them ("insofar as we will be useful to them and thus sought by them"). But unless Murgier supposes, wrongly, that others' wanting us involves our wanting or being in any sort of relationship with them, there seems little justification for the claim, at least as regards people, that the *Lysis* is at this precise point occupying the same sort of territory as the Stoics (if indeed they would claim it as theirs). So far as the argument of this part of the *Lysis* is concerned, we, and Lysis, may be *oikeioi* to limitless numbers of others, but they are not thereby rendered *oikeioi* to him or to us.

There is, in short, no evidence in the *Lysis* of any interest in, let alone a basis for, the claim that our *oikeioi* ultimately include the whole human race. After all, while it might be plausible to claim that *anyone* might be useful to us, as somehow completing our nature (especially by increasing our share of knowledge), it would be highly implausible to claim that *everyone* could be useful in this way, and so *oikeioi* all together. The idea of universal kinship is surely Stoic, not Platonic – just as the Anonymous Commentator said. At the same time – and here too the Anonymous Commentator was right – Plato clearly was interested in widening the notion of what is *oikeion* to us beyond the ordinary understanding of kinship and belonging, and in widening it in something like the kind of way the Stoics do so. It remains true, as Murgier says, that the *Lysis* ultimately "sets up the connection ... between the *oikeion*, desire, nature, and the good that will be systematized in Stoic *oikeiôsis*."

In fact, in one respect the connection is rather closer than Murgier proposes. On her account, the ordinary notion of *oikeiotês*, which sees it in terms of family and friends (as ordinarily understood) is *supplanted* by the new and broader one:[25]

> Everything makes it look as if a natural, relatedness (in the biological sense) is *supplanted* by another, *capable of eclipsing the force of familial relations* [i.e., the first sort of 'relatedness'], insofar as it reaches the very foundation of what attaches human beings to one another: wisdom, and the benefit that it procures. The conclusion that Socrates draws from this is intended to highlight the connection between wisdom, benefit and friendship. [Murgier then cites *Lys.* 210b–d, referred to and partly cited in this chapter, above]. These lines, playing as they do on the dialectical opposition *oikeion / allotrion*, confirm the enlargement of the circle of what 'belongs' ('l'appropriation') and the *overturning of the very sense of the*

---

25 Murgier refers to a similar proposal by Francisco Gonzalez (Gonzalez 2000, on which see n. 29 below).

term: the natural belonging of family relationships gives way to a relationship founded on reason. (Murgier 2013, § 23–24).[26]

The Stoics thought quite differently. The Stoic idea – as expressed, for example, in the passage from Stobaeus quoted at the beginning of this paper – is not that the new-found *oikeioi* will displace the old, but rather that the new will be increasingly regarded in the same way as the old.[27]

And that, I propose, is much what Socrates is saying in the *Lysis* too. His suggestion that Lysis' parents do not love him, because he is useless, is based on the argument that they do not want him to be happy – which they would, if they loved him – because they prevent him from doing what he wants to do. But of course they do want him to be happy, and they show that they do precisely by stopping him from doing things that he lacks the knowledge to handle.[28] The whole argument is designed to humble Lysis, and to provoke us, while simultaneously introducing the familiar Socratic connection between knowledge and the good, i.e., what is good for someone.[29] In short, the passage provides no clear evidence that the Plato of the *Lysis* denies the reality of parental love, any more than it provides any evidence that he denies the reality of

---

[26] The last sentence was already cited above, in a different context; the italics are mine.
[27] On which see further below.
[28] Which, I add, is precisely the kind of thing they should be doing, on Socrates' own view.
[29] For a completely different interpretation of this part of the *Lysis*, see Gonzalez 2002, § 3: "Socrates' first conversation with Lysis ... seems to be Plato's version of what was apparently a notorious 'paradox' of the historical Socrates [namely that he "refused to grant any value to family ties as such"], one that can be understood only against the background of the primacy granted kinship in the traditional conception of *philia*. Socrates' argument that Lysis' parents have no reason to love him if he is ignorant and useless, rather than being an ad hoc argument serving no more purpose than the humiliation of Lysis, was central enough to Socrates' thought to be threatening in the eyes of many Athenians and apparently influential among Socrates' followers" (Gonzalez 2002, p. 389). This can be seen as raising in an extreme form the fundamental issue around which this chapter ultimately turns: can we then love others at all, if we only love the good and useful? Gonzalez answers yes, relying on a proposal by W. Ziebis, *Der Begriff der Philia bei Platon* (1927), which he summarizes as follows: "the fact that the good by nature belongs to all of us is what enables us to belong by nature to each other. In other words, our shared kinship with the good provides the basis for our kinship with one another. This view of course makes all human beings akin, but it can also explain more local kinship: two people who explicitly recognize their mutual kinship with the good and therefore pursue the good together [*sc*. like Lysis and Menexenus] will be *oikeioi* in the strictest sense" (Gonzalez 2002, p. 395). The point about "more local kinship" seems well made; but the rest of Ziebis's 'solution', insofar as one can understand it without the fuller explanation no doubt provided by Ziebis himself, is surely liable to the same sort of objection raised above against Charlotte Murgier's discovery of universal kinship in the *Lysis*.

Lysis' love for Menexenus, or Menexenus' for Lysis, or his own for them.[30] When Socrates says that all but the 'first friend' are not '*really*' friends,[31] his point is to distinguish whatever it is for whose sake we love or desire other things (the 'first friend') from these other things we love for the sake of it. His point is not to say that we do not love or desire them at all.[32] Similarly, if the 'first friend' is the same as the *oikeion*, other things apart from this can also be *oikeia*. Suppose that the *oikeion* in this context is the good, or knowledge, or a rational life: there will be more than enough room in or beside these for our loving others – family, friends, teachers, fellow-citizens ... – as well as ourselves.[33]

Nonetheless, the idea that *everyone* is *oikeios* to us, however, is evidently a step too far for Plato; at any rate, I myself find no clear indication to the contrary anywhere in the corpus. The Anonymous Commentator, however, disagrees. It is worth quoting more from the relevant part of his commentary, which is on *Theaet.* 143d1–5:

> "If it had been people in Cyrene I cared about (the verb is *kêdesthai*) more, Theodorus, I would be asking you how things were there – whether there were any young people in Cyrene interested in geometry or philosophy of some sort; as it is, I'm less fond of the people there than I am of people here."[34] [There follows the commentary:] He [the speaker, Socrates] cares for the Cyrenaeans, but to the same degree as any other human beings. For we experience *oikeiôsis* towards those of the same kind as us (*homoeideis*), but he experiences *oikeiôsis* to a greater degree towards his own fellow-citizens. For *oikeiôsis* is more and less intense. So as for any who bring in justice from *oikeiôsis* [i.e. who derive justice from it – as Plato did not, deriving it rather from the idea of our becoming like god: col. VII.14–19], if

---

30 See 223b4–8 (the last few lines of the dialogue): "Now just look at us, Lysis and Menexenus! We've made ourselves ridiculous, I, an old man, and you too. For these people here will say as they leave that we think that we're friends of one another – for I count myself too as one of you – but haven't yet been able to find out what the friend *is*."
31 *Lys.* 220b, with context.
32 Thus in the analogy he uses in 219e–220a, that the father loves the son above all else not only does not rule out but actually makes it necessary that he also 'loves' the cup that contains the wine, and also 'loves' the wine he really thinks will counteract the hemlock he's seen his son taking (even if these are not the things he 'truly' loves, just things he loves for the sake of what he 'truly' loves).
33 A fuller justification for the interpretation of the *Lysis* contained in the foregoing paragraph, and elsewhere in the chapter, will be found in Penner and Rowe 2005. It goes without saying that Penner is not committed to anything in the chapter that does not square with the arguments and conclusions of the book.
34 It should be said that what is translated here is in part a (reasoned, and highly plausible) reconstruction of the original text, our manuscript evidence for which is not in the best condition.

they say an individual's *oikeiôsis* to oneself and to the farthest Mysian[35] is equal, well, their thesis preserves justice, but it is not agreed that the *oikeiôsis* is equal, because that is something that is contrary to what is obvious and to one's perception of oneself [*sunaisthêsis*]. For *oikeiôsis* towards oneself is natural and non-rational, while that towards one's neighbours is also natural, but not non-rational ... (col. V.3–42)

This much-talked-about (*poluthrulêtos*) *oikeiôsis* is introduced not only by Socrates, but also by the sophists in Plato. Of *oikeiôsis* itself, part, namely that in relation to oneself and to one's neighbours, has to do with caring (*kêdemonikê*), and treats them as if they [one's neighbours and oneself] were in a way equal; and part has to do with choice, namely [the process of *oikeiôsis*] by which we choose goods for ourselves, not because we care for them for themselves, but because we want to have them. It is clear that *oikeiôsis* towards oneself and those of the same kind (*homoeideis*) as oneself is not a matter of choice; for no one chooses himself, but rather that he should exist, and that he should have what is good, whereas he cares for himself and his neighbours. This is why he said "If it had been people in Cyrene I cared about more", showing that such *oikeiôsis* is "of the sort that has to do with caring". (col. VII.20–VIII.6)

Evidently, for the Commentator, and for his Socrates,[36] as for the (or some?) Stoics, we *are oikeioi* (*ôikeiômetha*: 'we are made akin to'?) any and every member of the human race, simply by virtue of the fact that we belong to the same kind. But they – the Commentator and his Socrates – diverge from what might be termed orthodox Stoic thinking by saying that there are degrees of *oikeiotês*. It is self-evident, and contrary to our experience, to suppose that we stand in the same relation to people at the end of the earth as we do to ourselves. An essential part of the Stoic conception of *oikeiôsis* is, one supposes,[37] that the fully rational person, the sage, will actually treat all members of the human race as if they were actually related to us, and indeed *as* related to us, thus effecting a transformation of the very notion of kinship;[38] plainly not so, says the Commentator. But interestingly, he chooses to frame this criticism as an attack on those who treat *oikeiôsis* as the basis for justice, and these unnamed opponents

---

[35] Cf. *Theaet.* 209b6–8: "Is there any way that this thought [*sc.* that "Theaetetus is the one who is a human being, and has a nose, eyes, a mouth", etc.] will make it Theaetetus I'm thinking of rather than of Theodorus, or of the most distant of the proverbial Mysians?"
[36] I.e., Socrates in the *Theaetetus*, and by implication – especially given the reference in the passage to Plato himself – in Plato.
[37] See Hierocles *ap.* Stobaeus as cited above.
[38] A transformation, in fact, of the sort that Charlotte Murgier (with Francisco Gonzalez: see nn. 25 and 29 above) sees as already occurring in Plato's *Lysis*, in my view mistakenly.

cannot be Stoics, or at any rate orthodox Stoics, for whom justice along with the other virtues derives from a rational requirement to live in harmony with nature, a position that is ultimately not so far removed from the account of justice that the Commentator attributes to Plato. (Plato derives it "from our becoming like god, as we shall show", col. VII.17–20.)[39] Justice presupposes equal treatment, whereas *oikeiôsis* only involves 'a *sort* of equality' of treatment.[40] At the same time it involves what the Commentator's language suggests is a real relationship: one of 'caring', however watered down such 'care' may be by the time it reaches the 'farthest Mysian'.

The net result of the argument of the Anonymous Commentator is what could perhaps be seen, from a modern perspective, as a clear advance on Plato's own thinking about relationships between ourselves and others. Adopting Stoic ideas,[41] but also adapting them,[42] the Commentator constructs, and fathers on Plato, a claim that we naturally owe *something* – whether we call it 'care' (or even 'respect'?) – to others, however remote they may from us, just in virtue of the fact that we and they belong to the same kind. Plato himself has a mechanism, plausibly seen as an ancestor of *oikeiôsis* as developed by the Stoics (and the Anonymous Commentator), for making love of others, and a concern for their interests, compatible with our natural and inevitable pursuit of our own good: in short, the happiness of others is bound up with our own.[43] They 'belong to' us as well as, perhaps even as much as, we 'belong to' ourselves.[44] But the range of 'others', in the original Platonic context, is strictly limited. It is the Commentator who, in effect, recognizes the full potential of the Platonic idea by extending it to the whole human race, while recognizing that it would – of course – be absurd not to suppose that there are degrees of 'belonging'. It seems altogether civi-

---

39 God, in a Platonic context, is purely rational; if becoming just is part, or a consequence, of becoming like god, then justice is a rational choice, independent of any considerations about our relationship to others.
40 Col. VII.31–32.
41 As may have been normal for his time: "By the first century B.C., ... the Stoics seem to have dominated ethical discussion, and it may be that even an author professing to give a straightforward account of another theory would find it congenial to do so in terms of *oikeiôsis*" (Annas 1993, p. 280, offering the Anonymous Commentator's description of *oikeiôsis* as "commonplace" – "much-talked-about", *poluthrulêtos* – as part of the evidence).
42 And, I think, doing better than them: that anyone should care as much for the 'farthest Mysian' as for his or her own children seems to me unreasonable (i.e., unworthy of anyone with a claim to sagehood) and, or possibly because, plainly undesirable.
43 See Penner and Rowe 2005, esp. ch. 12.
44 But see *Laws* IX, where the law endorses the commonplace that one "belongs most and is dearest" (is *oikeiotatos* and *philtatos*, 873c2) to oneself.

lized – humane – to suppose that what happens to someone the other side of the world will in some way touch us. But what happens to us, our family, our friends, our fellow-citizens ... must touch us more.[45]

Bibliography

Annas, Julia (1993): *The Morality of Happiness*, Oxford: Oxford University Press.
Bastianini, Guido and Sedley, David (eds.) (1995): "Commentarium in Platonis 'Theaetetum'". In *Corpus dei papiri filosofici greci e latini*, 4 volumes (Florence: Olschki): III.227–562.
Bonazzi, Mauro (2008): "The commentary as polemical tool: the Anonymous Commentator on the *Theaetetus* against the Stoics", *Laval théologique et philosophique* 64 (3), pp. 597–605.
Brickhouse, Thomas and Smith, Nicholas (2010): *Socratic Moral Psychology*, Cambridge: Cambridge University Press.
Gonzalez, Francisco (2002): "Socrates on loving one's own: a traditional conception of PHILIA radically transformed", *Classical Philology* 95, pp. 379–398.
Kerferd, George (1972): "The search for personal identity in Stoic thought", *Bulletin of the John Rylands University Library* 55, pp. 177–196.
Long, A. A., and Sedley, D. N. (1987): *The Hellenistic Philosophers*, Volume I: *Translations of the Principal Sources*, Cambridge: Cambridge University Press.
McCabe, Mary Margaret (2005): "Extend or identify: two Stoic accounts of altruism". In R. Salles (Ed.): *Metaphysics, Soul and Ethics. Themes from the work of Richard Sorabji*, Oxford: Oxford University Press, pp. 413–445.
Murgier, Charlotte (2013): "La part du proper (*oikeion*) dans la constitution du concept stoïcien d'appropriation (*oikeiosis*)", *Methodos: Savoirs et textes* 13 (Pratiques d'interprétation); open access at http://methodos.revues.org/.
Penner, Terry and Rowe, Christopher (2005): *Plato's* Lysis (Cambridge Studies in the Dialogues of Plato), Cambridge: Cambridge University Press.
Rowe, Christopher (2012): "Socrates on Reason, Appetite and Passion: A Response to Thomas C.Brickhouse and Nicholas D.Smith, *Socratic Moral Psychology*", *The Journal of Ethics* 16, pp. 305–324.
Plato (2015): *Theaetetus and Sophist*, ed. and trans. by Christopher Rowe (Cambridge Texts in the History of Philosophy), Cambridge: Cambridge University Press.

---

[45] Annas 1993 includes an extended discussion of "self-concern and other-concern" in ancient ethics; the discussion unfortunately omits any systematic treatment of Plato, on the grounds that this would be too problematical (a claim justified on [Annas 1993] pp. 17–20); Part III ("The Good Life and the Good Lives of Others") nevertheless raises many issues that are relevant to the present chapter. [My thanks to Terry Penner and to George Boys-Stones, both of whom read a draft of the chapter and made useful suggestions about how to improve it.]

Simon Weber
Aristotle and Respect for Persons

Abstract: The notion of respect for persons is usually regarded as a genuinely modern moral concept. According to the common doxography of the history of moral ideas, it was Immanuel Kant who in the late 18th century brought the concept of respect for persons to the very heart of morality. In this article, I will inquire whether or not, and if so, in what regard, Aristotle contributes in his moral and political philosophy to the history of the idea of respect for persons.

1 Respect for Persons

Does Aristotle have anything to say about the idea of respect for persons in his moral and political philosophy? To deal with this question, we need, first and foremost, a reasonable interpretative standard by reference to which we are able to evaluate contemplable doctrines in his *Ethics* and *Politics*. However, to determine such a standard entails a certain degree of arbitrariness, since there is no universally accepted definition of the idea of respect for persons.[1] In fact, recent advocates of this idea vary broadly in their formulations. For the purposes of the following inquiry into whether or not Aristotle contributes to the history of the idea of respect for persons, I will adopt Stephen Darwall's popular conception of this idea. According to Darwall, respect for persons is a special case of so-called 'recognition respect', or rather, 'moral recognition respect'. Darwall defines the latter as follows:

> One rather narrower notion of recognition respect conceives of it as essentially a moral attitude. That is, some fact or feature is an appropriate object of respect if inappropriate consideration or weighing of that fact or feature would result in behavior that is morally wrong. To respect something is thus to regard it as requiring restrictions on the moral acceptability of actions connected with it. And crucially, it is to regard such a restriction as not incidental, but arising because of the feature or fact itself. One is not free, from a moral point of view, to act as one pleases in matters which concern something which is an appropriate object of moral recognition respect. (Darwall 1977, p. 40; cf. *Ibid.*, p. 39)

In terms of respect for persons, the relevant fact of respect is of course the existence of another person. Giving inappropriate weight to the existence of another person in one's practical deliberation and corresponding action would, there-

---
[1] For several recent conceptions of the idea of respect see Dillon 2015, ch. 2.

fore, lead to a morally wrong behavior. The existence of another person, consequently, "restricts", as Kant famously says, "all arbitrary choice (*Willkür*)" (AK 4: 428), insofar we have a basic moral duty always to treat other persons "as ends in themselves, i.e. as something that may not be used merely as means" (AK 4: 428).

Three characteristics of 'recognition respect' are especially relevant if we consider respect for persons as a basic moral principle. In contrast to other, more ordinary, cases of respect which Darwall classifies under the notion of 'appraisal respect' – for example, the respect for a sportsman or an artist[2] – recognition respect for persons is: (1) *Categorical:* Recognition respect for persons is 'categorical' in the sense that every person is entitled to it. It is owed to all persons as such, i.e. simply because of the fact that they are beings of this kind, independent of any acquired excellence as person or within any specific practice she engages in. In opposite to this morally owed attitude to persons, I don't have to respect a tennis player just because she is a tennis player. I will only respect her "on the hypothesis" that she is a *good* tennis player, i.e. if she has some *merits* in the activity of playing tennis (Darwall 1977, p. 45). (2) *Non-Grading:* While I can respect a tennis player to a higher or lesser degree, depending on her excellence as a tennis player, the recognition respect for persons is of a non-grading nature. It does not admit of degrees, since the moral constraints on one's behavior that are imposed by the existence of another person are always one and the same and do not vary from person to person (i.e. the morally owed behavior towards another person does not depend on how good or bad the person is in the different situations in which we have dealings with them) (Darwall 1977, p. 44 and 45 ff.). (3) *Reciprocal:* Unlike appraisal respect which might only go in one direction – insofar as *I* respect a tennis player for her skills but *she* is under no obligation to respect me for my tennis skills in the same way – recognition respect for persons is defined by reciprocity. It is reciprocal since each person as the proper object of moral recognition respect is to be respected by all other persons and vice versa.

Nothing so far has been said about the concept of a person. Concerning the following discussion, I will not be arguing for any particular conception. I will simply adopt Frankena's "unloaded descriptive concept of a person" which is characteristic for ethics of respect for persons (Frankena 1986, pp. 152 ff.). According to this concept, a being is deemed a person if, and only if, it has such

---

[2] According to Darwall, the "exclusive objects" of appraisal respect "are persons or features which are held to manifest their excellence as persons or as engaged in some specific pursuit" (Darwall 1977, p. 38).

properties as practical reason, (rational) will, autonomy, rationality, sensibility etc. The advantage of Frankena's "unloaded descriptive concept of a person" is that it is broad and flexible enough to cover most of the historically significant conceptions of a person within an ethics of respect for persons. Consequently, if Aristotle has anything to say about the respect for *persons* in his practical philosophy, it is likely that this can be seen in light of this underlying concept.

Hence to inquire into the issue of whether or not Aristotle contributes to the idea of respect for persons in his moral and political philosophy, involves asking questions such as: Does Aristotle argue that beings, because they have practical reason, (rational) will, etc., are morally important and therefore restrict our arbitrary choice? Does he maintain that we have to give other rational beings proper weight in our practical deliberations, since otherwise it would result in morally bad behavior? Are there other beings, simply due to the fact that they are rational, who must always be treated as ends in themselves and not as mere means? Are all rational beings morally entitled to this kind of attitude? Do attitudes of respect admit of degrees? Are these kinds of attitudes towards rational beings independent of any acquired excellence as a person or within a particular occupation?

2 Four Major Objections

Off the cuff – if asked whether or not Aristotle contributes to the history of the idea of respect for persons – one is highly tempted to say "No!" Indeed, this snap verdict seems far from superficial, since there are at least four major objections to the idea of respect for persons in Aristotle's moral and political philosophy:

(1) The question, as stated, seems to involve linguistic confusion: like the ancient Greeks in general, Aristotle has no single (technical) term that equates with our notion of "respect" nor one that tallies with our notion of "person". The Greek word that probably comes closest to the notion of "respect" in Aristotle's writings is the verb "*timaô*" and the corresponding noun "*timê*". However, in Aristotle, "*timaô*" and "*timê*" relate – to make use of Darwall's distinction – either to a form of moral appraisal respect, i.e. the esteem for an agent's outstanding moral qualities, or to a form of appraisal respect such as honor which means the attitude and conduct owed to a good statesman and other virtuous officeholders. However, *timaô/timê* are definitely not related to recognition respect for persons, i.e. the recognition of the equal, inherent and absolute moral value of human beings qua persons, independently of their individual merit. Furthermore, the etymology of the word "person" putatively goes back to the Greek

word "*prosôpon*". But the notion of "*prosôpon*" does not play any significant part in Aristotelian ethics. Likewise the word "*anthrôpos*" – the generic Greek term for human beings – barely bears any moral significance in Aristotle's practical philosophy since "*anthrôpos*" also refers to natural slaves who exist as a mere instrument for someone else's needs (see below).[3]

(2) Talking of respect for persons in Aristotle also seems to imply an anachronistic fallacy: the notion of respect for persons is usually regarded as a genuinely modern moral concept. According to the common doxography of the history of moral ideas, it was Immanuel Kant who in the late 18th century brought the concept of respect for persons to the very heart of morality for the very first time (Green 1982, p. 1). Kant argues that human beings qua persons are ends in themselves (*Zwecke an sich*) which means that they are of an absolute and overriding moral value (dignity (*Würde*)), which is to be respected in all circumstances. According to Kant, the respect for persons – or rather, for the moral law which is autonomously enacted by persons – is thereby the source of all moral obligation.

(3) Attributing the idea of respect for persons to Aristotle also involves a major philosophical difficulty: While Aristotle advocates a teleological, eudaimonistic approach in moral philosophy, the concept of respect for persons seems to be an essentially deontological doctrine. Respect represents, as Birch puts it, a genuine "deontic experience" (Birch 1993, 312, 315), namely the experience that we owe another being a certain kind of behavior without reference to any egocentric interests or our own well-being. Respect is a responsive attitude towards another being's existence and, therefore, "object-generated", rather than "subject-generated" (Dillon 2015, chap. 1.1). But how a doctrine that places constraints on one's own interests and desires, and perhaps even on one's own well-being, for the sake of other persons can fit into a eudaimonistic approach in ethics demands at least further explanation.

(4) As the contemptuous theory of natural slavery in *Politics* 1 makes clear, Aristotle holds the view that there are human beings who exist as a mere ensouled tool (*empsychon organon*: *NE* 8.13, 1161b4) for another person. So, according to Aristotle, some human beings are not to be treated as ends in themselves and are, therefore, not proper objects of respect. A more direct conflict with the idea of respect for persons can hardly be imagined. A similar objection could be raised from Aristotle's statements about the natural inferiority of women and children in *Pol.* 1.

---

[3] I say *barely*, because there are a few passages in which *anthrôpos* seems to indicate a general moral worthiness of human beings. See, for example, the prohibition to kill human beings (*anthrôpoi*) for food and sacrifice (*Pol.* 7.2, 1324b39–41).

But, as so often, things are much more complex than a cursory survey may lead us to believe. Concerning objection (1), I think historians of ideas are methodically well-advised to differentiate between the history of an idea in a close or literal sense and in a broad or systematic sense. The former examines the philosophical meaning and significance of a certain concept or idea within a certain theory (or bundle of theories) by means of an already well-established technical term for this idea. For example, we can investigate the concept of matter (*hylê*) in Aristotle, since he was the first thinker who used the word "matter" in a technical sense (see Happ 1971, pp. 273–277). But we can also look into the idea of 'matter' in the Pre-Socratics and Plato, since they developed theorems that are in some respects similar to Aristotle's concept of matter and are intended to explain (at least some of the) phenomena which Aristotle tries to explain by reference to his concept of *hylê*. Therefore, the relevant doctrines of the Pre-Socratics and Plato could be considered genuine parts of the history of the idea of 'matter' in a broad sense in ancient Greek philosophy, even if they did not use the notion of "*hylê*" or other single technical terms for this idea. Indeed, Aristotle himself refers to the relevant ideas of his philosophical predecessors by the notion of "*hylê*" (see *Met.* A.3, 983b6 ff.). Consequently, Aristotle may have to say something about respect for persons in his ethics and politics in the broad sense of the history of ideas, even though he has no technical or standardized term for it.[4] (Granted, the broad sense of a history of ideas involves many conceptual difficulties, which I am not able to answer here. First and foremost, it would be necessary to identify the relevant criteria for similarity between two or more theorems within different theories so that they may legitimately be considered parts of the history of a single idea. However, for the purpose of this article I presume that we are able to find such criteria and that historians of ideas, from Aristotle on, are indeed engaged in this broad sense of the history of ideas.)

Having the distinction between a history of ideas in a narrow and a broad sense in mind, we could respond to objection (2) that Kant was probably the first thinker who used the concept of respect for persons in a technical way. This, however, does not rule out the possibility that other moral philosophers developed ideas that are sufficiently systematically related to this idea of respect and should therefore be considered as genuine parts of its history. Moreover, if we define respect for persons as giving appropriate weight to the existence of another person in one's behavior, then it is unlikely that a moral theory has noth-

---

[4] For a similar distinction between interpretative approaches to philosophical ideas, see Fred D. Miller who differentiates between the *literal exegesis* and the *philosophical reconstruction* of a text (Miller 1995, p. 21 ff.).

ing to say about this basic principle, since otherwise it would defend a kind of crude or maximizing egoism, i.e. the maximization of one's own interests and well-being without attributing any independent value to the interests and well-being of other persons.[5] However, even though there are such maximizing egoistic theories in the history of moral philosophy, they are certainly the exception.

In my view, objection (3) is based on a conceptual misbelief. As I have said, there may indeed be eudaimonistic theories that are forms of a maximizing egoism – for example, the ethical doctrine held by Thrasymachus in *Republic* 1. However, there are no necessary conceptual reasons why this always has to be so. In Aristotle's theory of the human good, for example, the moral virtue of justice as well as friendship plays a significant role. Now justice demands the fair distribution of goods between two or more individuals according to their justified claims to them. Thus, the virtuous man is not allowed to maximize his own well-being at the cost of another individual's justified claims, i.e. in an unjust manner. Similarly, according to Aristotle, one of friendship's central features is that friends reciprocally wish each other well for their own sake (*ekeinou heneka*) (*NE* 8.2, 1155b31; 8.4, 1156b10; 9.4, 1166a4; *Rhet.* 2.4, 1380b36). Again, if the good human life requires having friends, I have to take my friends' well-being into consideration as substantive reasons when deliberating what to do. Hence taking into account the interests and well-being of one's fellow citizens and friends seem to be an essential part of Aristotle's practical philosophy. There is, consequently, sufficient conceptual space to build something like the idea of respect for other human beings into a eudaimonistic theory. However, a substantive justificatory difference remains: in the deontological ethics of respect for persons, the idea of respect for persons functions as the most basic moral principle from which all other moral rights, duties, virtues, and so on are derived (see Frankena 1986, p. 150 ff.). This is obviously not true of eudaimonistic approaches in ethics in which happiness (*eudaimonia*) acts as the fundamental moral principle. Thus, in a eudaimonistic theory the moral obligation to take another beings' justified claims appropriately into account when deliberating what to do is ultimately not derived from the fact that the other being is a *person*. Rather, in it the moral obligation to respect another being is ultimately grounded on the fact that this other being is a *potential subject of happiness*. "Eudaimonistic respect" for other human beings refers, thereby, to the normative principle of impartiality, i.e. the supposition that there is no prima facie reason why another

---

[5] That Aristotle is not an egoist in this maximizing sense is one of the main points of Richard Kraut's *Aristotle on the Human Good* (Kraut 1991).

being's happiness should be of less value than my own one. Hence, her claims to certain goods are prima facie as justified as my claims. Consequently, giving inappropriate weight in one's practical deliberation to the existence of another being's happiness and her relevant claims to certain goods would result in morally wrong behavior. Thus, if we look for doctrines in Aristotle that are systematically related to the modern notion of respect for persons, we will at best find doctrines that restrict the morally allowed actions towards others because these beings are able by nature to lead a good life to which every rational being is equally entitled.

Objection (4) also has a significant impact on the inquiry in hand. Aristotle argues in his inhuman theory of natural slavery (*Pol.* 1.4–7) that there are slaves by nature.[6] According to Aristotle, a natural slave is a human being who does not exist for his own sake (*mê hautou esti*: *Pol.* 1.4, 1254a14 ff.), but exists for the sake of someone else (*allou esti*: *Pol.* 1.4, 1254a15). Therefore, slaves are nothing other than mere tools for the well-being of others. To be a natural slave, consequently, does not fit in anyway with the moral status of a person who is entitled to respect. Hence, in Aristotle, not all human beings are entitled to respect. So, if Aristotle has something to say about the idea of respect for persons in a broad sense, we nonetheless should not expect him to advocate a 'universal' conception of respect to which all human beings are entitled. At best, we can hope to find a 'non-universal', 'selective' theory of respect in his moral and political writings, according to which only some (or a few) human beings are proper objects of respect.

Seeking the roots of respect for persons in Aristotle – in the broad sense of the history of ideas – I will now (section 3) turn to the doctrine I consider the most promising candidate for the idea of respect for other human beings in Aristotle's political philosophy. In the last section, I will make a few closing remarks concerning whether or not, and if so, to what extent it makes sense to speak of "respect for persons" in Aristotle.

3 Aristotle's Doctrine of the Natural Free Man

After discussing the major objections to the idea of respect for persons in Aristotle, we can now tackle the question by thoughtful exegesis of several passages

---

[6] At the end of *Pol.* 1.5, Aristotle holds the existence of natural slaves (as well as the existence of natural unfree man) as adequately proved: "It is manifest therefore that there are cases of people of whom some are freemen and the others slaves by nature" (1254b39–55a2). Translations of Aristotle's *Ethics* and *Politics* by Horace Rackham (in a very few instances slightly modified).

in his *Ethics* and *Politics*. Let me start with some introductory, mainly negative, remarks.

In a recent article, Øyvind Rabbås argues that Aristotle's "ethics should [...] be seen as [...] some kind of deontological theory, which essentially includes a conception of normativity understood as something like the deontological notion of moral obligation to respect the status of persons" (Rabbås 2015, p. 621 ff.). Rabbås sees the deontological concept of respect for persons as somehow implied in Aristotle's theory of virtue, namely, in the "person parameter" of Aristotle's *"parameter doctrine"* in *NE* II.6 (Rabbås 2015, p. 626 ff.). However, as Rabbås himself points out, a person's worth, to be respected by a virtuous individual, is her *"axia"*, i.e. the person's moral desert or her good moral character. So, even if we follow Rabbås' interpretation, the kind of respect that is included in Aristotle's theory of virtue would at most be a kind of "moral appraisal respect", since the object of respect is the acquired excellence of an individual being as moral agent. Recognition respect for a person, however, as we saw above, morally requires us also to respect a morally bad character such as a murderer, just because he/she is a person. Yet, according to Aristotle, a murderer has no *axia* and is therefore no proper object of respect. So Rabbås' reconstruction of the concept of respect for human beings in Aristotle's theory of virtue does not seem to satisfy the categorical, the non-grading or the reciprocal criterion of moral recognition respect.[7]

Another doctrine that might be regarded as promisingly related to the idea of respect for persons in Aristotle's ethics is his theory of friendship (*NE* 8 and 9; *EE* 7). The feature that makes Aristotle's theory of friendship interesting with regard to the discussion at hand is that Aristotelian friendship consists in the ethical attitude of reciprocal benevolence[8] and, therefore, to many interpreters, it implies a genuine element of altruism.[9] Even more, Aristotle's theory of

---

[7] Rabbås, of course, sees this. The systematic point of his paper seems rather to be to show that "moral recognition respect" is not a *genuine moral concept*, but only a *special conception* of "moral appraisal respect" (see Rabbås 2015, pp. 640–642).

[8] As stated above, reciprocal benevolence – "to wish our friend well for his own sake" – is one of friendship's defining characteristics.

[9] For altruism in Aristotle's theory of friendship, see, for example John M. Cooper: "If this characterization is correct, it should be clear why Aristotle's theory of friendship must be considered a cardinal element in his ethical theory as a whole. For it is only here that he directly expresses himself on the nature, and importance to a flourishing human life, of taking an interest in other persons, merely as such and for their own sake." (Cooper 1977, p. 622) For alternative approaches to the kind of altruism included in Aristotle's theory of friendship, see Julia Annas (1977) and Charles Kahn (1981).

friendship seems to imply a certain kind of moral universalism.[10] However, as Aristotle makes unambiguously clear, friendship between two individuals is by its very own nature based on certain acquired goods (virtue, the useful, the pleasant) which one attributes to the other person. So, I am the friend of another person because I think that she is a virtuous, a pleasant or a useful individual. But if this is true, the ethical attitude towards another person which Aristotle identifies as friendship is obviously built on the possession of certain acquired skills – for example, virtues, strategic or rhetorical abilities, eloquence, humor, etc. With this in mind, we can see that friendship does not seem to fit either the categorical requirement or the non-grading criterion of moral recognition respect. To resume the example of the murderer: the respect for persons places on us the moral demand to respect a murderer, even if she/he is – most likely – neither a virtuous, nor a pleasant or useful individual. Further, Aristotelian friendship also seems to violate the non-grading criterion since it allows degrees (depending on the extent to which another person is useful, pleasant or virtuous).

In the rest of this section I will examine a widely neglected doctrine in *Politics* 1: Aristotle's doctrine of "the natural free man" (*physei eleutheros*). To my mind, it is this doctrine that comes closest to the idea of respect for persons in Aristotle's philosophical writings. This conjecture is prompted by the fact that Aristotle's depiction of the natural free man acts systematically to oppose the most inhuman part of his moral and political philosophy, his portrayal of the slave by nature in *Politics* 1.[11] Taken together, the two doctrines of the natural

---

10 For the universal dimension of Aristotle's theory of friendship, see especially, *NE* 8.1, 1155a21 ff.: "Even when travelling abroad one can observe that a natural affinity and friendship exist between man and man universally." See also Aristotle's statement about a possible friendship between slave and master: "Therefore there can be no friendship with a slave as slave, though there can be as human being: for there seems to be some room for justice in the relations of every human being with every other that is capable of participating in law and contract, and hence friendship also is possible with everyone so far as he is a human being." (*NE* 8.13, 1161b5–8) As Kahn points out, this universal attitude is not an essential feature of Aristotle's theory of friendship (Kahn 1981, p. 20 n. 2).

11 One may speculate that Aristotle's doctrine of the free man is neglected in secondary literature, *because* it is formulated in the vicinity of his doctrine of natural slavery. Due to its moral depravity, most interpreters try to cope with Aristotle's repulsive doctrine of natural slavery by arguing for its *philosophical* irrelevance: they either try to point out its incoherence and inconsistency with other well documented theorems of Aristotle's philosophy and/or try to discredit it as a purely *ideological* doctrine (see, for example, Smith 1991; Garnsey 1996, pp. 107, 125). Since both doctrines contribute to Aristotle's theory of rulership, the suspicion of ideology concerning Aristotle's doctrine of slavery might disable philosophical discussion of its correlative doctrine, that of the natural free man. In contrast, I take Aristotle's statements in *Politics* 1 seriously as a philosophical theory. In this, I follow Schofield 2005.

free man and the natural unfree man set up what we might call Aristotle's "theory of rulership".

Aristotle's overall project in *Politics* 1 is to justify different forms (*eidê*) of rule (*archê*) over human beings.[12] Aristotle argues against some of his philosophical predecessors who held the view that there is only one single form of rulership which is essentially the same in all human communities (households, poleis). According to Aristotle's opponents, these communities differ only quantitatively, i.e. with regard to the number of their members, whereas the behavior which the head of a household is obliged to adopt in relation to his household dependents does not differ from the behavior that a statesman owes to his citizens. The wording of *Pol.* 1.1, 1252a7–18, thereby suggests that Aristotle refers to the position of the Eleatic stranger in Plato's *Statesman* (258e–259b).[13]

Very roughly sketched, Aristotle's argument against the identity theory of his opponents runs as follows:
(1) Men live by nature in several communities ('natural communities').
(2) A community is a compound entity consisting of a ruling and a ruled part.
(3) The natural communities among human beings differ with regard to the nature of their related members, i.e., the ruling and ruled part.
(4) Every human being is to be ruled in a way that corresponds to his nature.
(5) There are different kinds of rule over human beings in the natural communities, depending on the particular nature of the ruled part.

In this subsection, I will very briefly elucidate each step of this Aristotelian argument. I will focus on a presentation of its basic structure and not address the serious exegetical problems of Aristotle's theory of rulership.[14]

Ad (1): One of the basic insights of Aristotle's political philosophy is that human individuals are not by themselves self-sufficient beings. It is only by means of manifold cooperative work with his fellows that men are able to survive and flourish. This is why, by their very nature, human beings spend their lives in several communities. Aristotle calls a community on which human beings depend insofar as it provides a good that is essential to the fulfillment of human nature a "natural communities" (*koinônia kata physin*: *Pol.* 1.2, 1252b13). More specifically, in *Pol.* 1.2 Aristotle lists five of these natural communities. He starts with the most elementary forms of a natural community which meets the most

---

[12] By identifying the main philosophical project of *Politics* 1 with the differentiation of several kinds of rule, I follow the interpretation of Charles Kahn (1990) and Marguerite Deslauriers (2006).
[13] Deslauriers (2006) also refers to Xenophon's Socrates (*Mem.* 3.4.6; 3.4.12; 3.6.14; *Oec.* 13.5).
[14] For a more detailed discussion of this argument, see Weber 2015.

basic human needs and goes on to more complex forms which exist for the sake of higher needs: (i) the community of man and woman which exists for the sake of sexual reproduction (*genesis: Pol.* 1.2, 1252a28). (ii) The community of master and slave in which men cooperate for the sake of material preservation (*sôtêria: Pol.* 1.2, 1252a31). (iii) The amalgamation of these two elementary communities sets up the first complex natural community, the household (*oikia*), which exists for the sake of "the satisfaction of the needs of every day" (*Pol.* 1.2, 1252b12–14). (iv) The "village" (*kômê*) – the association of several households – is the next, more complex natural community. The outcome of social cooperation on the village level is such that it provides the villagers with goods that serve the "satisfaction of not mere daily [i.e. higher] needs" (*Pol.* 1.2, 1252b15 ff.). (v) Finally, the union of several villages sets up a polis which is the "perfect community" (*koinônia teleia: Pol.* 1.2, 1252b28) insofar as it exists for the sake of the final and perfect human good, the good human life (*eu zên: Pol.* 1.2, 1252b30). By means of the polis, human striving comes to fulfillment, since the polis provides its inhabitants with all the goods that are necessary for the fulfillment of their nature. Consequently, there is no further, more complex, community on which human beings depend by nature. Aristotle therefore considers the polis and its citizens as completely self-sufficient (*autarkês/autarkeia: Pol.* 1.2, 1252b29; 1253a1). (vi) In *Pol.* 1.3 Aristotle adds a sixth natural community, the community of father and child, which represents the third elementary community of the household. This community results from the successful satisfaction of the reproductive drive in the community of husband and wife. As Aristotle's genetic analysis of the polis in *Pol.* 1.2 makes clear, the polis ultimately consists of households, and the household can again be broken down into three sub-communities. These three elementary domestic communities are, correspondingly, the most basic elements into which the polis can be analyzed. So, if we learn something about the elementary communities of the household, we will also learn something about the polis, since – according to Aristotle – some of the characteristics of the polis are to be explained by reference to the characteristics of its elements (*Pol.* 1.1, 1252a17–23).

Ad (2): According to Aristotle, every community is a compound whole, consisting of a "ruling element" and "ruled element". This hierarchical internal structure, however, does not only apply to communities within the realm of human social behavior but also to communities of other animals and even to communities of non-organic entities such as, for example, tones forming a harmony (*Pol.* 1.5, 1254b32 ff.). Therefore, this principle of the internal structure of a community seems to be more of a metaphysical than genuine practical kind. Aristotle states this principle which could be called Aristotle's "principle of the necessity of rulership" in *Pol.* 1.5: "because in every composite thing, where a plurality of parts [...] is combined to make a single common whole, there is always found a ruling (*to archon*) and a ruled element (*to archomenon*) [...]" (1254a28– 31). Now, if we apply this structural principle to Aristotle's natural communities, we can infer that these communities are ruling associations, insofar as all of them have a ruling and a ruled part. With regard to the household and its sub-communities which are the main object of inquiry in *Pol.* 1, the ruling part is the *oikonomos* in his threefold function of (i) husband, (ii) master, and (iii) father. The corresponding ruled parts are his related dependents, namely, (i) his wife, (ii) his slave, and (iii) his child. Aristotle depicts the household as a complex monocratic ruling association with the (Greek) adult male at its head.

Ad (3): According to Aristotle, the ruled elements of natural communities differ in their nature. The most fundamental distinction concerning the ruled individuals in the three elementary communities of the household (and, qua elementary analysis in *Pol.* 1.2, also concerning the more complex forms of natural human communities) is whether one is by nature a free (*physei eleutheros*) or an unfree human being, i.e. a natural slave (*physei doulos*). Accordingly, at the beginning of *Pol.* 1.3 Aristotle separates the members of the household and the inhabitants of the polis into two camps:

> And now that it is clear what are the component parts of the polis, we have first of all to discuss household management; for every polis is composed of households. Household management falls into departments corresponding to the parts of which the household in its turn is composed; and the household in its perfect form consists of slaves and freemen. (*Pol.* 1.3, 1253b1–4; cf. *Pol.* 1.13, 1259b21)

Hence, with regard to Aristotle's theory of different forms of rule, the distinction between a natural free man and a natural unfree man turns out to be the most crucial category. But what does it mean exactly to be a "free" or "unfree man by nature"? Aristotle answers this question with recourse to his moral psychology.[15] Simplistically speaking, to be a "natural free man" means to participate in practical reason, insofar as one has the deliberative faculty (*bouleutikon*). By way of contrast, the "natural unfree man" does not have the deliberative faculty by his own, but participates in practical reason only by means of the directions of another practical rational being.

> For the free rules the slave, the male the female, and the man the child in a different way. And all possess the various parts of the soul, but possess them in different ways; for the slave has not got the deliberative part (*bouleutikon*) at all (*holôs ouk echein*), and the female

---

[15] For Aristotle's moral psychology, see especially *NE* 1.13, 1102a26–1103a3; see also *NE* 1.6, 1097b33–1098a37; *Pol.* 7.14, 1333a16–30.

has it (*echein*), but without full authority (*akyron*), while the child has it (*echein*), but in an undeveloped form (*atelês*). (*Pol.* 1.13, 1260a10–14; see also *Pol.* 1.5, 1254b16–26)

Since children and women "have the deliberative part" – even if not in the fullest sense, but each in a particular deficient way –[16] like adult males, they are free by nature (*Pol.* 1.12, 1259a40 ff.). In contrast, the natural slave is by nature unfree since he is only able to participate in practical reason via the directions of his (natural free) master: "For he is by nature a slave [...] who participates in reason so far as to apprehend it but not to possess it" (*Pol.* 1.5, 1254b20–23; see *Pol.* 1.2, 1252a31–34). Whether one is a free or unfree human being is, according to Aristotle, a question of one's status as an independent practical rational being.

But why should it be so important, whether or not someone is an independent practical rational being, when we get on to the question of how an individual should be treated by another person who exercises power (*archê*) over her? This is where Aristotle's eudaimonism comes into play. For it is the possession of the *bouleutikon* that determines whether or not someone is able to acquire the moral virtues and, consequently, to lead a good human life. This is so, because a moral virtue, according to Aristotle, equates with a *hexis prohairetikê*, a stable disposition to make choices of a certain kind. To make choices (*prohaireseis*) an individual must have the deliberative faculty, since a choice must be preceded by deliberation (*bouleusis*) (see *NE* 3.5). Thus, an unfree human being, without deliberative faculty, is not able to acquire moral virtues and, consequently, is not able to lead a good human life, which is the activity of one's soul in accordance with these virtues (cf. *NE* 1.6, 1098a16 f.). It follows that the natural slave's level of happiness is equal, or at least close to 'zero' and, therefore, cannot be significantly diminished or increased by other persons' behavior towards him.[17] In contrast, the happiness of a natural free human being who is

---

16 The natural deficiency of the child's practical rationality (*atelês*) obviously consists in not being fully developed. The natural deficiency of women's practical reason is much more dubious. For example, according to William Fortenbaugh, the female and male deliberative faculty do principally not differ. Nevertheless, women possess a natural tendency towards the weakness of will (*akrasia*), i.e. they do not always act in accordance with the decisions of the deliberative faculty (Fortenbaugh 1977, p. 138 ff.). Whereas Kraut takes Aristotle to be saying that the female deliberative faculty is by nature of a lesser degree. According to Kraut, women are by nature able to deliberate about the less complex matters of the household, not the more complex matters of political life (Kraut 2002, p. 286 fn. 22).
17 See *Pol.* 3.9, 1280a31–34: "[...] but if [...] the state was formed not for the sake of life (*zên*) only but rather for the good life (*eu zên*) (for otherwise a collection of slaves or of lower animals would be a state, but as it is, it is not a state, because slaves and animals have no share in well-

by definition able to acquire the moral virtues, can obviously be affected by the ruler's treatment, depending on whether he uses power to promote his dependents' virtuous activity or to impede it. And this fact, whether or not a person's happiness can be increased and diminished by how they are treated by authorities, is clearly of prime importance within a eudaimonistic framework.

Since the natural unfree man is on the one hand able to carry out the directions of a natural free being, insofar as he is able to listen to practical reason, and suffers on the other hand no loss of happiness by being instrumentalized, Aristotle depicts the slave's nature as a mere, albeit animated, tool (*empsychon organon*: *NE* 8.13, 1161b4) for another person's well-being. Quite similarly, he states in *Pol.* 1.4 that the natural unfree men, due to his rational deficiency, is nothing more than an instrument for the *praxis* of his master and his master's children and wife (*organon praktikon*: 1254a17). Finally, Aristotle summarizes his description of the unfree man's nature by the formula that he – due to his lack of rationality – does not exist for himself (*mê hautou esti*) but for another person (*allou esti*).

> These considerations therefore make clear the nature of the slave (*physis tou doulou*) and his essential quality: one who is a human being (*anthrôpos*) belonging by nature not to himself (*mê hautou physei*) but to another (*allou ôn*) is by nature a slave (*physei doulos estin*) [...]. (*Pol.* 1.4, 1254a13–15)

It stands to reason that the natural free man, unlike the natural unfree man, does exist for his own sake (*hautou esti*) and not for the sake of another person (*mê allou esti*). This is so because the life of the natural free man as an independent rational being could become *eudaimonia*, the final and intrinsic good. Consequently, the free man does not exist by nature as the mere animated tool for someone else's well-being, but rather his well-being is the ultimate practical value. This conclusion is confirmed by a passage in the *Metaphysics*. In *Metaphysics* 1.2 Aristotle defines the nature of the free man exactly by the *allou esti/hautou esti*-distinction. According to this passage, the free man's existence can serve as an analogy for the intrinsically valuable and autotelic activity of the First Science, *sophia*, Aristotle is looking for in the *Metaphysics*.

> Clearly then it is for no extrinsic advantage that we seek this knowledge; for just as we call a human free (*anthrôpos* [...] *eleutheros*) who exists for himself (*hautou heneka*) and not for

---

being (*eudaimonia*) or in purposive life (*kata prohairesin*))". For Aristotle's doctrine that slaves do not partake in happiness, see also *Pol.* 7.13, 1331b39–41; *NE* 10.6, 1177a6–11.

another (*mê allou ôn*), so we call this the only free (*eleuthera*) science, since it alone exists for itself (*hautês heneken estin*). (*Met.* 1.2, 982b25–27)[18]

So, what Aristotle implies in *Pol.* 1.4 *ex negativo* by contrasting the status of the natural free man to that of the natural unfree man, he claims explicitly in the *Metaphysics:* the freedom of a human being qua rational being consists in existing for his own and not for someone else's sake; to be free by nature means that one's life is the proper subject of *eudaimonia* and is of a non-instrumental, intrinsic and ultimate value.

By the adverbial adjective "*physei*" Aristotle emphasizes that the difference between *natural* free and *natural* unfree men exists by birth.[19] This means, to be free or unfree by nature is, in Aristotle's view, not an acquired characteristic of men[20] and not earned by individual conduct. Neither is it a question of positive law or convention. It simply depends on an individual's natural endowment with practical reason. This kind of naturalness is, indeed, emphasized by Aristotle in *Pol.* 1 several times:

> Yet when they say this, they are merely seeking for the principles of natural slavery of which we spoke at the outset; for they are compelled to say that there exist certain persons who are essentially slaves everywhere (*pantachou*) and certain others who are so nowhere (*oudamou*) (*Pol.* 1.6, 1255a29–32).
>
> [...] things are marked out from the moment of birth (*ek genetês*) to rule (*epi to archein*) or to be ruled (*epi to archesthai*). (*Pol.* 1.5, 1254a23 ff.)

The status of a free and unfree human being is, therefore, to be regarded as innate and extra-positive.

Ad (4): In light of the categorical difference between natural free and natural unfree human beings, Aristotle argues that each human being is to be ruled in a way that answers her particular nature. As Aristotle puts it: "it is proper for the one party to be governed (*archesthai*) and for the other to govern (*archein*) by the

---

18 Translation of the *Metaphysics* by Hugh Tredennick, slightly modified.
19 The relevant concept of nature (*physis*) in Aristotle's theory of rulership in *Pol.* 1 is found, in my view, in *NE* 2.1, 1103a19–23: "[...] for no natural property can be altered by habit. For instance, it is the nature of a stone to move downwards, and it cannot be trained to move upwards, even though you should try to train it to do so by throwing it up into the air ten thousand times; nor can fire be trained to move downwards, nor can anything else that naturally behaves in one way be trained into a habit of behaving in another way".
20 For an alternative interpretation, see Jill Frank (2004). According to her, the status of the natural slave is not based on an innate lack of nature, but on the deforming activities a slave is required to perform. In this reading, in principle, the status of the natural slave is revisable. A similar view is held by Darrell Dobbs (1994).

form of government for which they are by nature fitted" (*Pol.* 1.6, 1255b7 ff.; cf. 1.7, 1255b16–20; 1.13, 1260a8–10; 7.3, 1325a27–30).

Ad (5): The last step of Aristotle's argument for his own theory of rulership and against the identity theory of his philosophical opponents consists in describing the different forms of rule for which the natural free and unfree man are fit. Accordingly, Aristotle differentiates between two principle forms of rule: "political rule" (*archê politikê*) in a broad sense[21] which is the appropriate kind of rule over natural free human beings and "despotic rule" (*archê despotikê, despoteia*) which is the appropriate kind of rule over natural unfree human beings.

> And even from these considerations it is clear that the rule of a master over slaves (*despoteia*) is not the same as political rule (*politikê*), nor are all forms of rule (*archai*) the same, as some assert. Political rule controls men who are by nature free (*eleutherôn physei*), despotic rule men who are by nature slaves (*doulôn*); [...]. (*Pol.* 1.7, 1255b16–18; cf. *Pol.* 1.13, 1260a8–10; *NE* 8, 1160b31 ff.)

Hence, Aristotle makes the distinction between unfree and free human beings the most important category in his theory of rulership, i.e. the most important category with regard to the normative question how an individual is rightfully treated by authorities.[22]

Since despotic rule is the kind of power to be exercised over an unfree human being it is not committed to the advantage of both parties in the cooperation but only to the advantage of the master. This is so because there is no injustice in treating a mere tool as a tool and to instrumentalize a human being who exists by nature for the sake of another person (cf. *NE* 8.12, 1160b29–31; 8.13, 1161a32–b5).

> The rule of a master over a slave (*despoteia*), although in truth when both master and slave are designed by nature for their positions their advantage is the same (*tauton*), nevertheless governs in the greater degree with a view to the interest of the master, but incidentally with

---

[21] The qualification *in a broad sense* is necessary here. Political rule in a broad sense means the kind of rule for which free human beings in general are fit by nature. Political rule in a narrow sense denotes the kind of rule characterized by the political regime of a polity. Political rule in the broad sense is like a genus of which political rule in the narrow sense is a species. This differentiation equates with Aristotle's use of the word *"politeia"*: *politeia* in the broad sense is the generic term for all forms of constitutions, and designates in the narrow sense a particular form of constitution, i.e. a "polity", the proper form of constitutions among *free and equal* citizens.
[22] It is worth noticing that Roman private law follows Aristotle's theory of different forms of rule, insofar as it conceives the *status libertatis* as the most basic criterion for the legal status of family members. For the legal status of family members in the Roman private law, see, for example, Max Kaser (1992, pp. 68–70).

a view to that of the slave, for if the slave deteriorates the position of the master cannot be saved from injury. (*Pol.* 3.6, 1278b32–37)

Moreover, since the slave is not able to lead a good human life, he helps to realize the highest and most final human good by his instrumentalization, at least in an indirect manner (the only way in which he is able to realize *eudaimonia*), namely, insofar as he carries out physically the work which is necessary to provide the material conditions for the flourishing of free household members.

There is also another form of rule, namely political rule. In contrast with despotic rule, political rule in the broad sense, the kind of rule that is to be exercised by the *oikonomos* over his wife and his child, is committed to the advantage and well-being of its subjects, since they exist as natural free human beings for their own sake, since their lives are of an intrinsic and ultimate value.

> [...] and rule (*archê*), as has been said in the first discourses [*Pol.* 1.], is of two sorts, one carried on for the sake of the ruler (*archôn*) and the other for the sake of the ruled (*archomenon*); of these the former is what we call the rule of a master (*despotikê*), the latter is the rule of free men (*tôn eleutherôn*) [...]. (*Pol.* 7.14, 1333a3–6)
>
> Rule over children and wife [...] is exercised either in the interest of those ruled or for some common interest of both parties, – essentially, in the interest of the ruled [...]. (*Pol.* 3.6, 1278b37–40)

The adult man is morally obliged to rule his children and wife as free human beings in their interest, because a 'non-political' treatment would significantly impede the possible realization of *eudaimonia* within the household. Indeed, the *oikonomos* realizes the greatest extent of human happiness for which he is responsible qua head of the household only if he uses his power to create the conditions that enable his wife and children to flourish. Most importantly, he is responsible for their suitable education, helping them to acquire the kind of virtues of which they are capable (see *Pol.* 1.12).[23] And since there are (at least) two different forms of rule over human beings, Aristotle believes that the identity theory of his philosophical predecessors is to be rejected.

---

23 As Aristotle states in *Pol.* 1.13, 1260b3–7, in a certain way, this is also true of the master's rule over the slave: the master must admonish the slave and lead him to the kind of virtue of which he is capable by his nature. However, the virtues of the slave are not *constitutive* for *eudaimonia*. The slave's virtues only make him a better instrument for securing the material needs of free household members. So, in the end, this kind of "slave education" is not in the interests of the slave, but in the interests of the master and his family, because they now possess a better instrument for their own flourishing (and, thereby, the *oikonomos* realizes *eudaimonia* to a higher degree than without "educating" the slave).

However, the scope of Aristotle's doctrine of the natural free man is not limited to the household. It also acts as the normative framework for Aristotle's constitutional theory in his *Politics*, especially for his famous constitutional scheme in *Pol.* 3.7. Hence, I conclude this sketch of Aristotle's theory of rulership by suggesting the relevance of the doctrine of the natural free man for this scheme. As the sixfold scheme of constitutions in *Pol.* 3.7 shows, it is precisely the intrinsic and ultimate value of the natural free man's life that becomes the main directive for the rightful exercise of power in the polis. Accordingly, Aristotle defines the dividing line between the right and just constitutions, on the one side, and wrong and unjust constitutions, on the other, by the qualitative criterion whether the constitutional and political order complies with citizens' natural status as free men who exist for their own sake. Consequently, in *Pol.* 3.6, 1279a17ff., Aristotle calls only those forms of constitution correct (*orthai*) in accordance with the absolute right (*to haplôs dikaion*) that aim at the common advantage (*to koinê sympheron*), i.e. the advantage and well-being of each and every citizen.

> It is clear then that those constitutions (*politeiai*) that aim at the common advantage (*to koinê sympheron*) are in effect rightly (*orthai*) framed in accordance with absolute justice (*kata to haplôs dikaion*), while those that aim at the rulers' own advantage only are faulty (*hêmartêmenai*), and are all of them deviations (*parekbaseis*) from the right constitutions (*tôn orthôn politeiôn*); for they have an element of despotism (*despotikai*), whereas a city is a community of free men (*koinônia tôn eleutherôn*). (*Pol.* 3.6, 1279a17–21)

So, citizens are not to be ruled in an arbitrary or exploitative way. The latter would pervert political rule into despotism, i.e. the kind of rule that is rightfully exercised over a natural unfree man. In fact, the only kind of rule citizens qua natural free man are rightfully subjected to is the kind of power that is directed to their well-being. And, by now, it should be obvious why this must be the case within Aristotle's eudaimonistic framework of political philosophy: if the many natural free citizens were instrumentalized for the sake of the interests of a small political elite or a single ruler, this kind of despotic power would violate Aristotle's highest practical principle – to realize *eudaimonia* to the greatest possible account. This is so, because by instrumentalizing Greek citizens the ruler, or rather the ruling class, would 'waste' the most capable subjects of *eudaimonia*. Consequently, Aristotle assesses regimes that aim at the particular interests of the ruling class as "degeneration" (*parkebasis*, cf. *hêmartêmenê*) and as the highest form of injustice.

4 Conclusion

Let us now take up again the initial question of this paper and draw some conclusions. Does Aristotle in his moral and political philosophy contribute to the history of the idea of respect for persons, in the broad sense? The standard by which we have to decide this question (see section 1) is whether or not Aristotle argues in his *Ethics* and *Politics* that beings, because they have practical reason, (rational) will, etc., are morally important and thereby restrict our arbitrary choices, insofar as not giving proper weight to them in our practical deliberation would result in morally bad behavior. Further, we said that this moral attitude towards other individuals must – unlike the attitude of appraisal respect – be *categorical*, *non-grading*, and *reciprocal*.

Judged by these standards, I think, we can justifiably say that Aristotle develops within his theory of rulership a concept of morally required attitudes towards other persons that are systematically linked to the modern idea of respect for persons. As we have seen, in *Pol.* 1 Aristotle argues that there are practical rational beings whose lives – due to their rational nature – are the proper subject of happiness. The head of a household, as well as political regimes and statesmen are therefore morally forbidden from instrumentalizing free human beings and have the moral obligation to rule them for their advantage, i.e. in a political manner. Consequently, each ruler has the moral obligation to create conditions which enable his free dependents to flourish. Hence, not to give the existence of other free human beings appropriate weight in practical deliberations would result in morally wrong behavior. Correspondingly, natural free human beings have a justified claim against their authorities not to be instrumentalized but always to be treated for their own sake. Thereby, the existence of natural free men restricts the arbitrary choices of others simply because they are beings of that kind.

Furthermore, as we have seen, being a natural free man is for Aristotle solely a question of one's natural endowment, namely, whether or not one has the deliberative faculty. Being free by nature does not depend on an individual's acquired skill, her excellence as a person or in a particular business she engages in. In this sense, the morally required attitude towards natural free men is also *categorical*. It is owed to *all* natural free human beings just because they are beings of this kind. Consequently, Aristotle argues in *Pol.* 1 that the head of the household owes it to his free household dependents (child, wife). In *Pol.* 3 he argues that political regimes and statesmen owe it to natural free citizens, and, finally, he argues in *Pol.* 7.2, 1324b22–36, that this attitude of respect is also owed to citizens of foreign poleis, in the event of conquering other cities by which one becomes responsible for the realization of their citizens' happiness.[24]

However, in addition to the conceptual problems mentioned in section 2, there are also essential differences between the morally required attitude towards natural free human beings in Aristotle and its modern counterpart, the idea of respect for persons.

Firstly and most obviously, the modern concept of respect for persons is intended to be much more inclusive than Aristotle's doctrine of the free man. According to its recent proponents, the moral attitude of respect is due to all or most human beings qua persons. According to Aristotle's contemptuous doctrine of natural slavery – due to their lack of practical rationality – not all or even most human beings are by nature free and are, consequently, no proper objects of respect.[25] Hence Aristotle's conception of the morally required attitude towards free human beings is much more selective. Kant's ethics also exclude some human beings from the moral status of being a person, for example, heavily cognitively disabled individuals who are not able to independently enact the moral law (see Landesman 1982). But, unlike Aristotle, Kant does not hold the view that these human non-persons could and should be legitimately instrumentalized for the sake of someone else's well-being.

Secondly, since Aristotle develops his doctrine of the natural free man as one strain of his *theory of rulership*, the morally required attitude towards natural free human beings is *non-reciprocal*.[26] As a normative theory of rulership it only indicates the moral obligation s of a ruler towards his free subjects, and not the other way around. If, and to what extent free and ruled individuals must morally respond to the ruler's status as natural free beings is not discussed in *Pol*. 1.

Thirdly, the behavior that we morally owe to persons insofar as we respect them substantively differs from the behavior an Aristotelian ruler morally owes to his free subjects. The former is primarily of a negative or limitative character. To respect a person first and foremost means to approve her capacity to lead a self-governed and autonomous life and, therefore, the moral duty not to interfere in it unnecessarily. Respect for a person may sometimes also involve the moral demand on us for positive action, such as to remedy the disastrous material and physical shortcomings that endanger the bare subsistence of a per-

---

[24] For the latter case of application of Aristotle's doctrine of the natural free man see Weber 2015, pp. 204–208.
[25] In *Pol*. 1.2, 1252b5–7, Aristotle identifies barbarians with the "*to physei archomenon*", i.e. "what is ruled by nature". For the Greek elitism in Aristotle's doctrine of the natural free man, see also *Pol*. 7.7, 1327b20–34.
[26] I owe this and the following point to Christoph Horn.

son. But these positive obligations do not change the mainly negative or liberal direction of impact of the moral duties that we have towards persons insofar as we respect them. As opposed to this, the morally required behavior of an Aristotelian ruler towards his free subjects is primarily of a positive kind, since he has first and foremost the moral obligation to help them to flourish. Aristotle especially emphasizes the educational task that a ruler morally owes to his free subjects (see *NE* X.10; *Pol.* 1.13). In this regard the morally required attitude towards natural free human beings in Aristotle is much more 'paternalistic' than its modern counterpart. However, it should be noted that this conceptual difference should not necessarily be regarded as a defect in Aristotle's practical philosophy. In a famous article, Frankena argued that "respect for persons" is an empty moral principle, from which no concrete moral right, duty or virtue can be derived.[27] With regard to Franken's objection, Aristotle's eudaimonistic-paternalistic conception of the morally required behavior of a ruler towards his free subjects seems more attractive. This is so because the concept of the good human life has a substantive evaluative content. Thus, to "respect" someone as a potential subject of the good life tells us more precisely in what behavior the morally owed attitude of "respect" towards a being of such kind consists.

Finally, since – at least in the household – the realizable extent of *eudaimonia* seems to differ between different groups of free subjects, it is clear that the ruler's morally owed behavior towards the individual members of this different groups varies.[28] If so, the morally required attitude of a ruler towards natural free human beings in Aristotle, unlike moral recognition respect for persons, involves *grading*.

What should be made of these findings? Does Aristotle contribute to the history of the idea of respect for persons at least in the broad sense? As so often, the question is complicated. On the one hand, Aristotle's doctrine of the free man shares essential features of the idea of respect for persons: on the other, his doctrine significantly differs. Such an unsatisfactory area of tension is unfortunately symptomatic for the work of the historian of the ideas and his inquiries concerning the historical roots of philosophical concepts in general. Last but not least, how one answers this kind of question depends on the particular weight one

---

27 See Frankena 1986, p. 157f.: "The principle that we are to respect persons [...] says only that there are morally right and wrong, good and bad, ways of treating or relating to persons, as such or for their own sake. It does not tell us which ways of treating or relating to them are right or wrong, good or bad. In principle, one can acknowledge it and be no wiser about the rest of the moral law or the prophets."

28 For the different forms of virtue (and, therefore, happiness) open to household dependents, see especially *Pol.*1.13, 1260a14–24.

gives to each of the defining features of an idea. This, however, would require a much more detailed and extensive conceptual analysis of both the idea of respect for persons and of Aristotle's doctrine of the free man than is possible in a short article of this kind.

Bibliography

Annas, J. (1977): "Plato and Aristotle on Friendship and Altruism", *Mind* 86, pp. 532–554.
Birch, T.H. (1993): "Moral Considerability and Universal Consideration", *Environmental Ethics* 15, pp. 112–128.
Cooper, J.M. (1977): "Aristotle on the Forms of Friendship", *The Review of Metaphysics* 30, pp. 619–648.
Darwall, S.L. (1977): "Two Kinds of Respect", *Ethics* 88, pp. 36–49.
Deslauriers, M. (2006): "The Argument of Aristotle's 'Politics' 1", *Phoenix* 60, pp. 48–52.
Dillon, R.S. (2015): "Respect". In The Stanford Encyclopedia of Philosophy (Fall 2015 Edition), ed. by E.N. Zalta, http://plato.stanford.edu/archives/fall2015/entries/respect/. Date of last access: 05/20/2016.
Dobbs, D. (1994): "Natural Right and the Problem of Aristotle's Defense of Slavery", *Journal of Politics* 56, pp. 69–94.
Fortenbaugh, W.W. (1977): "Aristotle on Slaves and Women". In J. Barnes et al. (Eds.): *Ethics and Politics* (Articles on Aristotle, 2), London: Duckworth, pp. 135–139.
Frank, J. (2004): "Citizens, Slaves, and Foreigners: Aristotle on Human Nature", *American Political Science Review* 98, pp. 91–104.
Frankena, W.K. (1986): "The Ethics of Respect for Person", *Philosophical Topics* 14, pp. 149–167.
Garnsey, P. (1996): *Ideas of Slavery from Aristotle to Augustine*, Cambridge: Cambridge University Press.
Green, O.H. (1982): "Introduction". In O.H. Green (Ed.): *Respect for Persons* (Tulane Studies in Philosophy, 31), New Orleans: Tulane University Press, pp. 1–13.
Happ, H. (1971): *Hyle: Studien zum aristotelischen Materie-Begriff*, Berlin/New York: Hartmann.
Kahn, Ch. (1981): "Aristotle and Altruism", *Mind* 90, pp. 20–40.
Kahn, Ch. (1990): "Comments on M. Schofield". In G. Patzig (Ed.): *Aristoteles' 'Politik'. Akten des XI. Symposium Aristotelicum*, Göttingen: Vandenhoeck & Ruprecht, pp. 16–20.
Kant, I. (2002): *Groundwork for the Metaphysics of Morals*, ed. and trans. by A.W. Wood, New Haven/London: Yale University Press.
Kaser, M. (1992): *Römisches Privatrecht. Ein Studienbuch*, 16th ed., Munich: C.H. Beck.
Kraut, R. (1991): *Aristotle on the Human Good*, Princeton, NJ: Princeton University Press.
Kraut, R. (2002): *Aristotle. Political Philosophy* (Founders of Modern Political and Social Thought), Oxford/New York: Oxford University Press.
Landesman, Ch. (1982): "Against Respect for Persons". In O.H. Green (Ed.): *Respect for Persons* (Tulane Studies in Philosophy, 31), New Orleans: Tulane University Press, pp. 31–43.
Miller, F.D. (1995): *Nature, Justice, and Rights in Aristotle's 'Politics'*, Oxford: Clarendon Press.

Rabbås, Ø. (2015): "Virtue, Respect, and Morality in Aristotle", *The Journal of Value Inquiry* 49, pp. 619–643.

Rackham, H. (1934) (transl.): *Aristotle, 'Nicomachean Ethics'*. Cambridge, MA: Harvard University Press/London: William Heinemann Ltd (Aristotle in 23 Volumes, Vol. 19).

Rawls, J., (2000): *Lectures on the History of Moral Philosophy*, Cambridge, MA/London: Harvard University Press.

Schofield, M. (2005 [1990]): "Ideology and Philosophy in Aristotle's Theory of Slavery". In R. Kraut and S. Skultety (Eds.): *Aristotle's Politics: Critical Essays*, Lanham: Rowman & Littlefield, pp. 91–119.

Smith, N.D. (1991): "Aristotle's Theory of Natural Slavery". In D. Keyt and F.D. Miller (Eds.): *A Companion to Aristotle's Politics*, Oxford: Oxford University Press, pp. 142–155.

Tredennick, H. (1933) (transl.): *Aristotle, 'Metaphysics'*. Volume I: Books 1–9. Cambridge, MA: Harvard University Press/London: William Heinemann (Aristotle in 23 Volumes, Vol. 17).

Weber, S. (2015): *Herrschaft und Recht bei Aristoteles*, Berlin/Boston: De Gruyter.

Part II: **Respect in Modern Philosophy**

Elena Irrera
Human Interaction in the State of Nature: Hobbes on Respect for Persons and Self-Respect

> *Qui autem est fidens, is profecto non extimescit;*
> *discrepant enim a timendo confidere*
> (*But he who is full of faith is certainly under no fear;*
> *for there is an inconsistency between faith and fear*).
> Cicero, *Tusculan Disputations* III, VII.14

Abstract: In this chapter I shall attempt to identity different forms of respect in Hobbes' state of nature, by way of an identification and critical engagement with some of the key notions which, as I believe, inform his views of the mechanism of human interaction: power, recognition, honor, esteem and fear. My general contention is that the philosophical issues of respect for persons and self-respect offer a lens through which Hobbes can: (1) describe some features of the state of nature and the aspects which elicit a transition from such a state to the creation of a commonwealth; (b) some prescriptive indications on how human beings ought to behave towards each other with a view to a condition of peace and security. I will identify four kinds of respect: esteem, honor, an equal respect based on fear and one grounded in recognition of each other's legitimate needs and interests.

1 Introduction

Hobbes's reflection on human nature and the mechanisms of the constitution of political government exhibits a rich array of interrelated themes and philosophically problematic issues. Among them, the nature of the epistemic and the agential powers that human beings possess by nature or acquire over their lifetimes, the individual psychological motives inspiring their pursuits, and the strategies of reciprocal interaction that they usually enact to prevent conflict. Hobbes examines these issues and situates them in an elaborate philosophical edifice, set up with the following aim: a systematic discussion and a reconstruction of the conceptual mechanics that, in his view, enervate the transition from a supposedly pre-political condition of human coexistence (which Hobbes notoriously calls the "state of nature") to a civil society bereft of inner strife.

Within this framework of investigation, the philosophical issues of respect for persons and self-respect do not stand out (at least *prima facie*) as subjects which Hobbes is keen to discuss in a systematic way. On the one hand, this might explain a substantial absence of scholarly studies on the topic of respect in his philosophy; on the other, his concern for the ideal of respect is evident in his remarks on esteem, honor and the equal regard that persons owe to each other *qua* human beings. In this essay I will briefly review various expressions of respect for oneself and respect for others in the Hobbesian state of nature, stressing in particular the role that the idea of "recognition of power" plays in conceptually shaping each form of respect.

With a view to this, I shall focus on two of Hobbes's works:[1] the *Elements of Law Natural and Politic*, a philosophical tract written before the outbreak of the Civil War (1640) which represents a sort of "trial run for Hobbes's system" (Bobbio 1993, p. 26), and *Leviathan*, published in English in 1651,[2] where he provides a wide-ranging treatment of the theory of formation of civil society. As I believe, these works provide not only compatible, but also reciprocally enriching accounts of the ideal of respect.[3]

In the first section of this essay I give a short description of the main agential powers that guarantee human knowledge and agency, and show how these are at work in the state of nature. In the subsequent sections I address the following forms of respect in the state of nature: 1) respect as esteem and reputation; 2) respect as honor; 3) well-grounded and ill-grounded respect for oneself; 4) respect as reliance on oneself as an authoritative judge; 5) two kinds of equal respect for persons: (5a) one grounded on recognition of the human power to hurt other individuals; (5b) respect for one's agential powers (one prescribed by Hobbes's laws of nature).

---

[1] All the passages from Hobbes's works quoted in this essay are taken from *The Complete Works of Thomas Hobbes*, edited by Sir William Molesworth (1839–1845).

[2] As Bobbio (1993, p. 27) suggests, the Latin edition of *Leviathan* was probably written in part before the English version, but published only in 1670 with minor corrections.

[3] The *Elements*, by virtue of the systematic description of human powers provided by Hobbes, may contribute to a more accurate understanding of issues related to the ideal of respect. I follow Carlo Galli's view that *Leviathan* offers a less rigid and rigorous account of human nature than the *Elements of Law* and *De Cive* (Galli 2013, p. v).

2 The State of Nature: Its "Scientific" and Anthropological Premises

Both in the "Preface to the reader" of *De Cive* (EW II, xvii) and in the first chapter of *Leviathan* (I, XIV; EW 117), Hobbes notoriously declares that the state of nature is a condition of war of all against all (*bellum omnium contra omnes*). His urge to make such a forceful, apodictic statement in the opening sections of his work supposedly suggests that any attempt to understand the aims and strategies for the successful preservation of civil society must cope with the risk of returning to a pre-political state. On the one hand, as several scholars have pointed out, the state of nature represents a theoretical device by which Hobbes, in line with his method of exploration and presentation of reality to his readers, attempts to analyze the conceptual premises for the legitimacy of sovereign power (Kavka 1986, pp. 83–92).[4] On the other hand, the state of nature can also be viewed as one to which "politicized" human beings risk returning if the civil society in which they live suffers from inner strife and lack of regulation.[5] As Helen Thornton for instance maintains (Thornton 2005, p. 17), "the state of nature was also a constantly threatening possibility – a condition into which a weakened commonwealth had the potential to dissolve. In other words, it was a condition in which human beings living in civil society had the potential to fall, if they arrogated to themselves the judgment of good and evil, and in doing so disobeyed their rightful sovereign".[6] Whether conceived as the logical premise of the origins of society or as the nefarious outcome of civil disobedience, the state of nature represents a privileged space of observation from which Hobbes is able to draw consequences about human behavior (Thornton 2005, p. 17)[7] and, nonetheless, find reasons to justify the need for human beings to submit to the sovereign authority of civil society (Lloyd 2009, p. 212).

In order to understand how the state of nature generates (and is identified with) a condition of mutual conflict, it must be acknowledged that, in this

---

[4] For many of Hobbes's contemporaries, however, the state of nature represented a description of the pre-historic origin of society. For this interpretation see Ewin 1991, p. 94 and 96.
[5] See for instance Bobbio 1993, pp. 41–42, who claims that Hobbes, rather than considering the state of nature a pre-political condition, characterizes it as an *anti-political* situation, such as civil war in existing states.
[6] Thornton follows Sheldon Wolin (1960, p. 264) in regarding Hobbes' state of nature as a political version of the Biblical story of the Fall.
[7] On Hobbes's description of the state of nature as a theory of human behavior see Kavka 1986, p. 19; cf. Boonin-Vail pp. 21–50.

state, people appear to commit to the pursuit of what they believe makes up their personal good and the avoidance of whatever obstructs that pursuit. Hobbes does not seem to come to this conclusion from sheer experience.[8] On the contrary, he situates the human tendency to seek one's own good within the framework of natural necessity.[9] As he explains for instance in the *Elements of Law*, this necessity:

> [M]aketh men to will and desire *bonum sibi*, that which is good for themselves, and to avoid that which is hurtful; but most of all, the terrible enemy of nature, death, from whom we expect both the loss of all power, and also the greatest of bodily pains in the losing. (EL XIV, 6; EW IV, 83)

Here, the word "power" seems to evoke the generic idea of a man's "present means; to obtain some future apparent good", as Hobbes explains in *Leviathan* X, 41.1 (EW III, 74). In that chapter, Hobbes divides human powers into two classes: *natural* powers, which he describes as "eminence[s] of the faculties of body or mind: as extraordinary strength, form, prudence, arts, eloquence, liberality, nobility" and *instrumental* powers, that is, "means and instruments to acquire more [power]: as riches, reputation, friends" (EW III, 74).[10]

It should be noted, however, that in *The Elements of Law* Hobbes introduces a more "basic" sense of power, one on which the possibility of both natural and instrumental powers seems to rest. Here is the notion of "power" Hobbes employs while offering a definition of "human nature":

> [M]an's *nature* is the *sum* of *his natural faculties and powers*, as the faculties of *nutrition, motion, generation, sense, reason, etc.* These powers we do unanimously call *natural*, and are contained in the definition of man, under these words, *animal* and *rational*. (EL I, 4; EW IV, 2)

Unlike "eminent" or "instrumental" powers, the powers above are possessed by each and every human being, and so is the natural tendency to use them both in

---

[8] It is worth noting, however, that several scholars have stressed the relevance of empirical observation (and even of "self-inspection" in Hobbes' method of knowledge. See for instance Strauss 1936, p. 29; Oakeshott 1975, ix and Skinner 2002, p. 65; Kavka 1986, p. 7.

[9] Hobbes's insistence on the "causal" nature of scientific knowledge coexists with the belief that science in general (and, more specifically, the science of nature) is knowledge of mechanical causes (see Jesseph 1996, p. 86). In Hobbes's view, the notion of "motion" can be adopted as the unifying criterion for different branches of theoretical science, such as optics, physics, and geometry.

[10] A definition of "instrumental powers" is also given in EL VIII, 4; EW IV, 37–38.

cognitive and in practical endeavors with a view to the achievement of one's own good. In this light, people can not only recognize each other as equal, but also claim equal treatment by virtue of the act of recognition.

In the attempt to identify the sources of human interaction and its manifold expressions (conflictual or respectful), Hobbes sets aside the powers of the body and narrows the focus on the powers of the mind. As show in this essay, the various types of respect that human beings can display in the state of nature (as well as in the civil state) can be viewed as specific forms of rational recognition of these powers accompanied by the relevant passions (passion itself being a power that represents the outcome of recognition). Notably, Hobbes identifies two kinds of natural power of the mind: *cognitive* and *motive* (L I, VII; EW IV, 2). By putting his account of the connections between the human mind and external reality into a strictly deterministic framework, he maintains that both are to be understood as matter in motion.[11] Cognitive capacities as sense-perception, imagination, memory and rational understanding set off desires and processes like deliberation and choice. One cognitive power in particular, imagination,[12] is able to determine various kinds of "interior beginnings of voluntary motions": the so-called "endeavours" (L I, 6; EW III, 39). These are the motions that constitute the inherent mechanics of passions.[13] Hobbes employs the notion of "endeavour" to define two basic tendencies entrenched in each and every human being: appetite and aversion. Appetite is treated as interchangeable" with the notions of "desire", and "love" (L I, 6; EW III 39; cf. EL VII, 2; EW IV, 31–32),[14] and is defined as an endeavor toward something that delights (EL VII, 2; EW IV, 31). An expression of appetite is pleasure (or *contentment* or *delight*),[15] which in *The Elements* is described as a principle that helps the vital motion (EL VII, 1; EW IV, 3). By contrast, when the endeavor is fromward something, it is generally

---

[11] In this respect, Hobbes' view of the human mind is a stark departure from Descartes, who considers the mind incorporeal. For the Hobbesian view of the mind as a mode of organization of matter see Pettit 208, p. 12. See also Boonin-Vail 1994, pp. 34–38, who argues that both the minds and its inner workings can be viewed as natural bodies themselves.

[12] As Boonin-Vail (1994, p. 39) claims, the salient difference between vital and voluntary motion is that voluntary motions are caused by the imagination.

[13] From a mechanistic perspective, passions appear to derive from the action of external objects on the brain, going on to the heart (EL X, 1; EW IV, 54). They arise from that motion and agitation of the brain which Hobbes calls "conception" (EL VIII, 1; EW IV, 35).

[14] In L I, 6 (EW III, 40), however, Hobbes points out that by "desire" we always mean the absence of the desired object, whereas by "love" we most commonly signify the presence of the object.

[15] See L I, 6; EW III, 42: "But the appeareence, or sense of that motion [i.e. the motion in which appetite consists is that we either call *delight* or *trouble of mind*".

called *aversion* or *hate*. This tendency is accompanied by pain, i.e a principle that hinders and weakens the vital motion (EL VII, 1; EW IV, 3).

From the notions of "desire", "pleasure", "aversion"? and "pain" Hobbes derives his conception of good and evil in the state of nature. As he believes, good and evil do not exist as concrete realities in nature (L I, 6; EW III, 41; cf. Thornton 2005, p. 18). They are simply names, which individuals apply to their own and other people's actions on the basis of what they like or dislike (L I, XV; EW III, 146; cf. EL VII, 3; EW IV, 32; DC I, 2; EW II, 5). If considered in conjunction with the idea that every man differs from others in constitution and experiences, this implies the lack of an objective, absolute and unanimously accepted view of good and evil in the state of nature. Even one's own view is open to change over time, depending on what one desires and praises or opposes and disparages (L I, XV; EW III, 146). Hobbes concludes,

> from whence [i.e. this fact] arise disputes, controversies, and at last war. (L I, XV; EW III, 146)

Although Hobbes views appetites and aversions as the subjective measure of good and evil, that does not mean that he endorses a relativistic theory of morality (Kavka 1986, pp. 349–357; Boonin-Vail 1994, pp. 58–123[16]). On the contrary, there is some evidence that he held morality to be conventional (Gauthier 1979, p. 547[17]). In L I, 13 (EW III, 115), for instance, he claims that

> [T]o this war of every man, against every man, this also is consequent; that nothing can be unjust. The notions of right and wrong, justice and injustice have there no place. Where there is no common power, there is no law; where no law, no injustice.[18]

As I comment in the last section, there is an objective standard of conduct in the principles Hobbes calls "laws of nature", i.e., the laws a well-governed commonwealth ought to adopt.[19] It is primarily in the light of this moral standard that

---

[16] For a different view see Tuck (1989, p. 64), who claims that Hobbes's ethical vision is the "grimmest version of sceptical relativism". See also Reik (1977, p. 90), who claims that there are by no means objective, absolute ethical norms in Hobbes' system.

[17] Gauthier maintains that Hobbes establishes "a place for morality as a conventional constraint on our natural behavior".

[18] Cf. L I, 6, (EW III, 41), where Hobbes says that in the civil state there are common rules of good and evil as established by the person who represents it, or by an arbitrator (or judge) whom men agree to set up.

[19] See for instance L, II, 26 (EW III, 253), where Hobbes claims that civil and natural law "contain each other".

human beings may respect each other as equals. However, Hobbes also provides evidence that certain forms of respect for oneself and for persons (equal respect included) are at work even in a condition of war of all against all, where fellow humans refuse to abide by shared rational prescriptions. I will explore this by showing that some of the conceptual models of respect for oneself and for persons discussed by Hobbes (such as esteem, honor, glory and even embryonic forms of equal respect) not only prefigure practicable possibilities of human agency in the state of war, but also help Hobbes to conceptualize this state and to identify its causes.

3 From Potential to Actual Conflict. Forms of Respect for Oneself and Respect for Others in the State of Nature

Before identifying the kinds of respect that apply in the state of nature, it is interesting to note that Hobbes does not describe this state as a purely potential state of war, that is, characterized by the disposition to fight unless there are assurances to the contrary (Kavka 1986, p. 90). It is certainly true that, unlike the state of nature in John Locke,[20] Hobbes does not necessarily envisage active signs of hostility. Indeed, for Hobbes, the state of nature is primarily one in which people experience mutual distrust and, most crucially, fear (a passion of aversion generated from fear of receiving hurt, i.e. prompted by an anticipated displeasure; EL VII, 2; EW IV, 31–32; cf. L I, 6; EW III, 43). On the other hand, as in the Lockean state of war, Hobbes describes a state of paralysis hindering human cooperation based on common rules of conduct (Kavka 1986, p. 91). As Hobbes declares in L I, XIII (EW III, 113):

> [I]n such condition, there is no place for industry; because the fruit thereof is uncertain: and consequently no culture of the earth; no navigation [...] no arts; no letters; no society [...]; and which is worst of all, continual fear, and danger of violent death ...

What assumptions, then, does Hobbes make to identify the state of nature as a state of open conflict? Also, how does the issue of respect help to clarify the transition from the idea of potential conflict to an actual war? We might begin

---

20 See the second of the *Two Treatises of Government* (chap. 3, sec. 16, 319), where the state of war is described as one "declar[ed] by Word or Action, not a passionate and hasty, but a sedate settled Design, upon another Mans Life".

to answer these questions by stating that, as Hobbes himself declares in L I, XIII (EW III, 112):

> ... in the nature of man, we find three principal causes of quarrel. First, competition; secondly, diffidence; thirdly, glory. The first, maketh men invade for gain; the second, for safety; and the third, for reputation.

Here, competition is mentioned as a relational condition which Hobbes considers with reference to the human tendency to pursue gain. This tendency might be qualified as desire for either material goods, in which case Hobbes speaks of "covetousness", or office or precedence, which he calls "ambition" (L I, 6; EW III, 44). Both names are always used to indicate "blame"; what is blameworthy is not desire for certain goods in themselves, but the fact that the men contending for gain are displeased with one another.

In *The Elements of Law*, on the other hand, human beings are portrayed by Hobbes as naturally competitive even with regard to the passion for glory. In EL IX, 21 (EW IV, 52–53), for instance, Hobbes compares human life to a race which has "no other *goal*, nor other *garland*, but being foremost", and one's irreducible desire for superiority involves the search for glory, reputation and honor (Zagorin 2009, p. 32). These values, as we shall see, are viewed by Hobbes as goods that help people preserve and enhance a positive view of themselves. Moreover, like riches in a condition of limited resources, these are "inflationary" goods, i.e., if one person has them, another person is deprived of them. Competition over glory, reputation and honor can therefore be viewed as a "zero-sum game", in which one person's gain (or loss) of utility is exactly balanced by the losses (or gains) of the utility of others.[21]

For Hobbes the nature of the characteristic conflict between human beings in the state of nature is not determined by the lack of an absolute, objective good (a lack which, paradoxically, might compel people to look for different goods and therefore reduce competition), but by a desire to be and appear superior to others. This tendency is placed by Hobbes within the framework of a more basic inclination shared by human beings: the pursuit of one's own happiness, which he presents as "a perpetual and restless desire of power after power, that ceaseth only in death" (L I, 11; EW III, 85–86).

Hobbes's idea that each person always acts to satisfy her own desires has prompted scholars to argue that he endorses egoistic views of human nature.

---

[21] A well-established trend in contemporary Hobbesian scholarship analyzes Hobbes's theory of the state of nature in terms of "game-theory". For a discussion of the most important views on the matter see for instance Eggers 2011.

Understood in this light, however, egoism appears to be a sheer truism (Kavka 1986, p. 35),²² and it fails to account for the idea that people might have desires which, although aiming at their own happiness, go well with the pursuits and personal interest of others.²³ Non-tautological versions of human egoism are needed to support Hobbes's arguments against conflict and anarchy (Kavka 1986, p. 64). In other words, to explain Hobbes's state of nature as a condition of conflict, self-interested individual motives must be assumed to be "predominant" over other-regarding motives (see Kavka 1986, pp. 64–80, who speaks of a "predominant egoism").

Egoism can take the form not only of greediness for riches, knowledge and honors (that is, a desire to "have more"), but also of a desire to defend the powers and goods that are already possessed, i.e. a desire that can be fulfilled only by attempting to increase one's own powers (in which case, achieving more would not be an aim in itself, but simply a means to further ends) (cf. L I, 11; EW III, 86). In the following subsections I show that respect for oneself and respect for others help Hobbes to characterize this sort of egoism and, all the same, the conditions that prompt human conflict in the state of nature.

3.1 Reputation

In Hobbes' view, one's search for reputation (as good reputation) is a characteristic tendency of human beings, although he suggests that not every man is equally drawn to it.²⁴ Hobbes places reputation in the category of instrumental goods (L I, X; EW III, 74). People look for reputation not as a good in itself, but by virtue of the use they can make of it. A good reputation is achieved in relation to some kind of power and excellence, which consists in comparison and implies a form of superiority over others (cf. L I, VIII; EW III, 56). Unlike Aristotelian virtues, whose outstanding nature is rooted in an intermediacy between excess and defect in passions and actions (see especially Book II of Aristotle's *Nicomachean Ethics*), Hobbesian excellences are "relational" goods. Given

---

22 See also Gert 1972, p. 7, who has defined this form of egoism "tautological egoism".
23 See for instance those actions arising out of other-regarding passions like charity, benevolence and good will. These passions are defined by Hobbes as "desire of good to another" (L I, 6; EW III, 43). In EL IX, 17 (EW IV, 49–50) Hobbes explains that one's desire to assist other men in accomplishing their desires can ultimately be traced back to one's desire to advance one's own good and power.
24 See for instance L I, XI; EW III, 86, where Hobbes suggests that some desire fame from new conquest, others sensual pleasure, and others admiration for some excellence of their own.

people with similar or an equal degree of excellence, the power of each would lose value and its distinctive excellent nature would dissipate.

In this respect "reputation of power, is power" (L I, X; EW III, 74). For a good reputation draws with it the adherence of those that need protection (*Ibid.*), and it is plausible to suppose that the force of people's consent enables the person of high repute to achieve (at least some of) his plans. Moreover, a well-respected person represents for those who respect her a point of trust. This is for instance the case of people who excel in prudence:

> [R]eputation of prudence in the conduct of peace or war, is power; because to prudent men, we commit the government of ourselves, more willingly than to others (L I, X; EW III, 74).

To think highly of someone can be considered a form of "evaluative respect", and its basis may be any sort of identified excellence (whether other-regarding or not).[25]

One's striving for good reputation is successful only if desire is accompanied by a serious commitment to the achievement of natural powers including forms of excellence. The pursuit of a good reputation might represent a valuable motivational source for actions productive of power, and a sense of shame – a passion that Hobbes defines as the "apprehension of some thing dishonourable" (L I, 6; EW III, 47) – might be triggered by the prospect of failure to achieve the esteem of others. As he explains,

> in young men, [shame] is a sign of the love of good reputation, and commendable: in old men it is a sign of the same; but because it comes too late, not commendable. (L I, 6; EW III, 47)

By commending shame in young people, Hobbes probably means to say not only that the young are generally more inclined to act than the elderly, due to their energy and strength, but also that, by possibly having a longer life ahead, they can achieve a great deal through their individual powers.

Hence, being held in high esteem is not a good desirable in itself in Hobbes' view, but is instrumental in achieving one's aims. A good reputation is a starting point for the pursuit of greater power, and this pursuit (as well as the search for limited goods, riches and social position) exacerbates human competition. As Hobbes claims in L XI, 85 (EW III, 86),

---

25 This version of "evaluative respect" was conceptualized by Hudson (1980, pp. 71–73). A different version is provided by Stephen Darwall (1977, pp. 41–45), whose notion of "appraisal respect" applies not only to cases of respect for excellence of a moral nature, but also to respect for non-moral excellences employed in an other-regarding way.

> [C]ompetition of riches, honour, command, or other power, inclineth to contention, enmity, and war: because the way of one competitor, to the attaining of his desire, is to kill, subdue, supplant, or repel the other.

The following lines go on to show how the tendency to compete in the state of nature causes people to cultivate ill-grounded views of their own powers and those of others. A glaring example is the widespread inclination to show reverential respect for the ancients, rather than for one's competitors:

> [P]articularly, competition of praise, inclineth to a reverence of antiquity. For men contend with the living, not with the dead; to these ascribing more than due, that they may obscure the glory of the other. (L XI, 85; EW III, 86)

A reasonable implication is the idea that, when a person's view of herself (well-grounded or not) does not match the opinion of others, her expectations might be thwarted and her search for power be hindered by others. Mutual impediments, in their turn, generate conflict.

3.2 Honour

For Hobbes honour is a relational concept. One might recognize one's own powers by certain signs, that is, by the actions that proceed from those powers (EL VIII, 5; EW IV, 38); "honour", however, comes into play only when those signs are recognized by others. Honor is defined as "the acknowledgment of power" (or "opinion of power"; L I, X; EW III, 80) and, more to the point, of one's superiority regarding that power:

> to honour a man inwardly, is to conceive or acknowledge that man hath the odds or excess of that power above him with whom he contendeth or compareth himself. (L I, X; EW III, 80)

All the things that express the power from which they proceed are honorable, such as all actions and speeches that proceed or seem to proceed from experience, science, discretion or wit, because the sources from which they proceed are powers (L I, X; EW III, 79–80). By contrast, actions or speeches that proceed from error, ignorance or folly are dishonourable.

A power which, acknowledged, prompts a form of respect – honour – is not of absolute value; on the contrary, it is amenable to comparisons, as is the worth of a person.[26] As Hobbes points out in *Leviathan*,

> the *value*, or worth of a man, is as of all other things, his price; that is to say, so much as would be given for the use of his power: and therefore is not absolute; but a thing dependant on the need and judgment of another [...] to value a man at a high rate, is to *honour* him; at a low rate, is to *dishonour* him. But high, and low, in this case, is to be understood by comparison to the rate that each man setteth on himself. (L I, X; EW III, 76)

One's criteria of assessment of others, being based on the evaluation of one's own powers, appear unstable, especially if we consider that people tend to assess their own powers as superior to those actually possessed. Only in a commonwealth is value assigned according to public, shared criteria. Respect as honour, in this case, is recognition of the public worth of a man, his *dignity* (L I, X; EW III, 76). This can be expressed through the concession and establishment of professional and social positions, and is used by the sovereign to guarantee a stable, well-ordered political community.

In the civil state, each person is responsible and accountable for the lack of recognition of the worth of other persons (and the role assigned to each in the political community). The conceptual model of honour at work in this case seems to match Darwall's description of honour as a "second-personal" form of respect, one which, featuring a substantial asymmetry of power between those who respect and those who are respected, obliges the former to take the latter and to conduct themselves accordingly (Darwall 2008, pp. 5–7). By contrast, in the state of nature, the recognition of another's power is not normatively binding, nor does it contribute to preventing open conflict. Indeed, the addressees of honour in that state do not possess the authority to be treated with respect; hence the respecting subjects are not accountable for failing to honour them.

That the idea of respect for persons taking shape against the backdrop of a condition of mutual struggle and competition is all the more evident in Hobbes's definition of "reverence" in *The Elements of Law* (EL VIII, 7; EW IV, 40):

> *Reverence* is the conception we have concerning another, that he hath the *power* to do unto us both *good* and *hurt*, but not the *will* to do us *hurt*.

---

[26] In *De Cive*, however, Hobbes addresses the issue of value from a prescriptive point of view, suggesting that people should try to gain a "non-comparative" view of their own worth. In DC II, 2 (EW II, 5) he says that "every man must account himself, such as he can make himself without the help of others".

In Hobbes's account, a person is worthy of reverence not only through possession of a given power, but also the capacity and attitude which causes that person to refrain from using the power in ways that might damage others (for instance, by jeopardizing the pursuits undertaken by others). A pure conception, however, does not necessarily involve trust and confidence, and reverence for a person due to her attitude of restraint in specific situations does not dissipate distrust towards the person showing restraint.

3.3 Well-Grounded and Ill-Grounded Self-Respect

In Hobbes' view, acquiring a good reputation certainly helps a person to shape a positive view of herself and, as a consequence, develop the self-confidence needed to embark on certain pursuits. In this respect, Hobbes seems to foreshadow the idea of self-respect found in John Rawls's *A Theory of Justice*. Here, Rawls claims that

> [I]t is clearly rational for men to secure their self-respect. A sense of their own worth is necessary if they are to pursue their conception of the good with zest and to delight in its fulfillment. (Rawls 1971, p. 178)

In par. 67 he treats self-respect as a value endowed with two distinctive aspects: on the one hand,

> it includes a person's sense of his own value, his secure conviction that his conception of his good, his plan of life, is worth carrying out (Rawls 1971: p. 440);

on the other,

> self-respect implies a confidence in one's ability, so far as it is within one's power, to fulfill one's intentions. When we feel that our plans are of little value, we cannot pursue them with pleasure or take delight in their execution. (Rawls 1971: p. 440)

By endorsing a "proto-Rawlsian" view, Hobbes believes that self-respect does not rise simply from the opinions of external observers. Life-plans cannot be cultivated without recognition of one's own powers, that is, without an attempt to achieve a well-grounded self-knowledge.

As we have already seen, in the state of nature there are no public and agreed criteria for the assessment of one's powers. Nevertheless, Hobbes makes it clear that, even so, it is possible to develop a well-grounded opinion of oneself through experience of one's own actions, and consequently feel pleasure in relation to that opinion. The implicit premise of Hobbes' view is that the actions that enable some goals to be reached are proof of an authentically good power. In EL IX, 20 (EW IV, 52), for instance, Hobbes defines the virtue of "magnanimity" and claims that

> [M]agnanimity is no more than glory [...] but *glory well grounded* upon certain experience of a power sufficient to attain his end in open manner.

As Hobbes explains in *De Cive* (II, 2; EW II, 5), glory is a good opinion of oneself, and all the pleasures of the mind are either glory or refer to glory in the end. In the same passage, he states that

> [A]ll society therefore is either for gain, or for glory; that is, not so much for love of our fellows, as for the love of ourselves.

By "glory" Hobbes also means an "internal gloriation or triumph of the mind", that is,

> the passion which proceedeth from the imagination or conception of our own power above the power of him that contendeth with us. (EL IX, 1; EW IV, 40; cf. L I, 6; EW IV, 46)

This concept retains an aristocratic flavour (Slomp 2000, p. 48; cf. Pacchi 1987, p. 115), incorporating a sense of superiority over others; as proof of this, as already mentioned in L I, XIII (EW III, 112), Hobbes includes it among the causes of competition. On the other hand, he also seems to understand glory as self-respect, a passion that accompanies a specific kind of rational recognition: the acknowledgment of one's own powers.

As Hobbes explains in *The Elements*, (EL IX, 1; EW IV, 40–41), the acknowledgment of one's worth can be well-grounded:

> this passion, of them whom it displeaseth, is called *pride;* by them whom it pleaseth, it is termed a *just valuation* of himself. This imagination of our power or worth, may be from an assured a certain *experience* of our own actions; and then is that glory *just*, and well grounded, and begetteth an opinion of *increasing* the same by other actions to follows.

Ill-grounded self-respect, in contrast, is of two possible kinds. Firstly, it may be false glory, a passion stemming from an improper opinion of oneself, nourished by fame and the trust of others (EL IX, 1; EW IV, 41). False glory is described as a passion prompting those who feel it to act on the basis of their conceptions of themselves, causing them to fall short of their ambitions (*Ibid.*)

The second kind of "fallacious" self-respect is represented by the so-called "vain glory", a passion consisting in the mere presumption of power, without action. This passion consists "in the feigning or supposing of abilities in ourselves, which we know are not" (L I, VI; EW III, 45–46). As Hobbes clarifies in L I, XI (EW III, 88),

> [V]ain-glorious men, such as without being conscious to themselves of great sufficiency, delight in supposing themselves gallant men, are inclined only to ostentation; but not to attempt: because when danger or difficulty appears, they look for nothing but to have their insufficiency discovered.

Understood in general terms, the search for glory is unstable in the state of nature. Human beings feel the seductive allure of power (Cooper 2010, pp. 245–246), which causes them to see themselves as superior to others (EL XIV, 4; EW IV, 82), so even a well-grounded confidence can easily become fallacious self-respect.

We might expect Hobbes to see false-glory as a source of conflict, given its capacity to produce real agency. Nevertheless, as some scholars have suggested, (Cooper 2010; Slomp 2000) Hobbes appears to present vain-glory (more than false-glory) as the primary cause of conflictual interactions. Why should vain-glory, perhaps more than false-glory, exacerbate conflict? The answer may lie in the idea that

> vainly glorious men hope for precedency and superiority above their fellows, not only when they are equal in power, but also when they are inferior (EL XIV, 4; EW IV, 82).

The ill-grounded expectations cultivated by vainly glorious men, as Hobbes concludes in this passage of *The Elements*, produce an attempt to subdue even those who are equal or superior in power. Although vain-glory in relation to one's powers does not lead to the realization of those specific powers, it is a passion that, in the long run, can fuel anger, which, as Hobbes states in *Leviathan*, is an excess of pride prompting the overwhelming desire for revenge (L I, VIII; EW III, 62; DC II, 4; EW II, 7).

4 From the Right of Nature to the Law of Nature

In the Hobbesian state of nature, every man has a right to all things, that is to say, to do whatever he wishes and to possess and use whatever he wants (EL XIV, 10; EW IV, 84). Hobbes calls this (*Jus*) "right of nature", characterizing it as "*blameless liberty* of using our own natural power and ability" (EL XIV, 6; EW IV, 83). The right of nature (which we could think of a "permission right"; cf. Kavka 1986, p. 296) is not opposed to reason, given that it is natural and legitimate for everyone to preserve their own body and limbs from death and pain (EL XIV, 6; EW IV, 83). On the other hand, the phrase "right of nature" does not indicate a series of entitlements enabling people to call for equal respect (such as those enshrined for instance in liberally-oriented contemporary Charters of rights). In the state of nature, everyone is the judge of their pursuits, of the necessity of the means to their established goals, and also of the degree of the danger involved in pursuing them (EL XIV, 8; EW IV, 83). It could be said that we are ourselves the yardsticks of our own agency. We might say, then, that one holds oneself as a yardstick for one's own agency; we are a sort of "epistemic authority" to be respected.[27]

Hobbes explains this concept by means of a *reductio ad absurdum:*

> [F]or if it be against reason, that I be judge of mine own danger myself, then it is reason, that another man be judge thereof. But the same reason that maketh another man judge of those things that concern me, maketh me also judge of that that concerneth him. And therefore I have reason to judge of his sentence, whether it be for my benefit, or not. (EL XIV, 8; EW IV, 83)

As we have already seen, however, the lack of shared criteria for assessing pursuits and dangers generates ill-grounded expectations, claims and conflicts. In the state of nature, the idea of respect for oneself as "judge" legitimatizes not only one's right to action, but also to resist action, and this is what sparks off open conflict:

> [S]eeing then to the offensiveness of man's nature one to another, there is added a right of every man to every thing, whereby one man invadeth with right, and another man with right resisteth, and men live thereby in perpetual diffidence, and study how to preoccupate each other; the estate of men in this natural liberty, is the estate of war. (EL XIV, 11; EW IV, 84)

Having said this, the human capacity to actively experience (or simply mentally represent) a condition of conflict gradually leads to the universal acknowledgment that what seemed, in itself, to be rational, i.e., the arbitrary pursuit of the good, becomes incompatible with the actualization of peace. This is the only condition under which life-plans can be pursued without the danger of mutual hindrance. Rationality, ultimately, recommends cooperation rather than conflict (Hampton 1986, p. 76). The need to achieve peace calls for an urgent re-definition of the standard criteria of rationality in the state of nature, and

---

[27] See Darwall 2008, pp. 8–9, who outlines the conceptual model of respect as "recognition of an epistemic authority".

also, as I argue in the last section of this essay, of the criteria for the respect of persons.

The transition from a life ruled according to subjective criteria of agency to one requiring the employment of a shared rationality (directed towards the promotion of a stable condition of peace and respectful interaction) takes shape through the universal recognition of the substantial equality of all human beings. What makes human beings equal to one another, in Hobbes' view, is not a presumed dignity possessed by all, but the equal power to hurt others. The capacity to inflict damage on others (including the stronger and more virtuous ones) neutralizes the undeniable differences between people in their natural and instrumental powers (i.e. differences which might cause superior people to demand higher amounts of goods than those they would be willing to assign to others). In *The Elements of Law*, Hobbes suggests that

> if we consider how little odds there is of strength or knowledge, between men of mature age, and with how great facility he that is the weaker in strength or in wit, or in both, may utterly destroy the power of the stronger; since there needeth but little force to the taking away of a man's life, we may conclude, that men considered in mere nature ought to admit amongst themselves equality. (EL XIV, 2; EW IV; 81–82)

I maintain that the need to imagine ourselves equal to others can be understood as an embryonic form of equal respect, based on recognition of the equal power of human beings to hurt one another. This form of respect combines a rational aspect, the acknowledgment of this power, and the passions of fear and distrust, aroused by imagining the effects of this power. A similar form of respect was conceptualized by Hudson, who spoke of "respect as obstacle" with reference to objects worthy of consideration by virtue of their power to block the plans of others (among whom the same person who respects) (Hudson 1980).

In my view, in addition to representing a sort of "prudential recognition" and caution, this opens up the possibility of respect for oneself and others as equally dangerous subjects. Of course, the concept of respect as an obstacle is far from expressing the recognition of equal worth (or "dignity") of human beings *qua* human. Nevertheless, this kind of equal respect might be the basis for the idea that each and every human being needs to be recognized as a subject whose existence should be taken seriously and perhaps even adopted as a constraint against the agency of others (see Darwall 1977). I would also suggest that, by virtue of the recognition of the power of subjects to inflict damage on one another, rationality, initially employed to promote strategies implementing individual life plans, gradually transcends the sphere of the right of nature and comes to be a reflection on the most promising strategies for successful arbitration and the production of agreement between incompatible points of view.

A rationally-informed treatment of conflicts in the direction of peace does not represent a way out of the state of nature. Indeed, as Hobbes claims, reason is no less "nature" than passion (EL XV, 1; EW IV, 87), and even in the state of nature can be used for strategies of respectful interaction between people. In my view, it is primarily by means of the concept of the "law of nature" that Hobbes establishes a basis for equal respect as mutual recognition of an equal entitlement to survival and happiness. Departing from a tradition of thought that assimilates the law and right of nature,[28] Hobbes draws a stark distinction between the two. More pointedly, the law of nature and its various expressions, if understood and accepted universally as a legitimate source of human conduct, reduces the risk of conflict (the very conflict the right of nature itself, if freely pursued, ends up producing).

The nature of the laws of nature has been the object of intense debate among scholars, especially with regard to its supposed foundations. Some hold that these laws ought to be primarily understood as theorems of reason (see for instance Gauthier 2001), whereas others regard them as prescriptions ultimately issued by divine command (see for instance Martinich 1992). A detailed treatment of the laws of nature is beyond the scope of this paper. Suffice it to say that these are precepts or general rules found by rational argument (L I, XIV; EW III, 116–117) of a normative nature. By abstracting from subjective plans, opinion and sensitivities, they provide the seeds for well-regulated human coexistence. The prescriptions do not oblige *in foro externo*, but only *in foro interno*, i.e. in one's conscience (L I, XV; EW III, 145), implying that the failure to comply with the laws of nature would not be punishable under the laws established by a certain commonwealth.

The laws of nature can be thought of as "hypothetical imperatives" (Pacchi 1965, p. 118, note 1), rules that ought to be observed as an indispensable step towards the achievement of a condition of peace. From the founding law of nature, which prescribes that human beings act to preserve peace (L I, XIV; EW III, 117–118), Hobbes derives a second law, according to which every man who desires peace and the defense of himself thinks that it is necessary

---

28 For a detailed discussion of this issue, see Zagorin 2009, pp. 20–29. Zagorin mentions in particular Suárez (16th century), who points out that the word *lex* can be used interchangeably with *ius* (p. 24).

to lay down this right to all things; and be contented with so much liberty against other men, as he would allow other men against himself. (L I, XIV; EW III, 117–118; cf. DC II, 3; EW II, 17; EL XV, 2; EW IV, 87)

The readiness to relinquish the right can be seen as a form of regard for other persons and their existence. This is all the more evident since depriving oneself of absolute liberty may be not only general in nature, but a transfer of rights. Unlike the act of *renouncing*, in which it does not matter to whom the benefit adheres, the act of *transferring* involves concern for the benefit to certain persons (L I, XIV; EW III, 118–119). This idea emerges for instance in EL XV, 3 (EW IV, 88):

> [T]o *transfer* right to another, is by sufficient signs to declare to that other accepting thereof, that it is his will not to resist, or hinder him, according to that right he had thereto before he transferred it.

In order to achieve peace, no one should do to others what they would not want done to themselves (Cf. L I, XIV; EW III, 118), a notion, as Hobbes states, that can be found in Gospels:

> whatsoever you require that others should do to you, that do ye to them. And that law of all men, *quod tibi fieri non vis, alteri ne feceris*. (L I, XIV; EW III, 118)

Respecting persons, in this sense, would amount to calibrating one's expectations to fit in with the equal expectations that other subjects, in their turn, ought to hold in order to attain peace. The idea of equal respect suggested here appears to be premised on a form of reciprocity which is not simply built against the backdrop of mutual fear, but on the capacity to open oneself up to the needs and expectations of others (Lloyd 2009). It is a reciprocity of respectful attitudes making of respect a genuinely "moral" value in Hobbes's theory. This emerges in particular in the following excerpt from *The Elements of Law* (XVII, 2; EW IV, 104), where Hobbes states that

> ... reason and the law of nature dictateth, *Whatsoever right any man requireth to retain, he allow every other man to retain the same* [...] for there is no acknowledgment of worth, without attribution of the equality of benefit and respect.

Hobbes points out in the following lines that the law of nature presupposes a principle of distributive justice which consists in allowing "*proportionalia proportionalibus*", a principle that, in his view, demonstrates that equal respect is an attribution of *aequalia aequalibus* (XVII, 2; EW IV, 104). The distributive principle at stake is premised on a human inclination mentioned by Hobbes in

DC II, 4 (EW II, 7): the inclination to permit as much to others as one assumes for oneself, according to natural equality. This, he says

> is an argument of a temperate man, and one that rightly values his power.

The above law of nature, accepted and followed *in foro interno*, is not in itself a guarantee of safety in a state and does not make human beings accountable for their own conduct. Only the transition from the state of nature to a civil state can reduce (possibly even eliminate) distrust and mutual fear. It is primarily in the state of nature, however, that Hobbes seems to identify the anthropological premises underlying the transition. A founding act of mutual recognition between human beings as equal is the outcome of people with a firm view of themselves, their powers and limits.

Bibliography

Bobbio, N. (1993): *Thomas Hobbes and the Natural Law Tradition*, Chicago: University of Chicago Press.
Boonin-Vail, D. (1994): *Thomas Hobbes and the Science of Moral Virtue*, Cambridge: Cambridge University Press.
Cooper, J.E. (2010): "Vainglory, Modesty, and Political Agency in the Political Theory of Thomas Hobbes", *The Review of Politics* 72, pp. 241–269.
Darwall, S.L. (1977): "Two Kinds of Respect", *Ethics* 88 (1): 36–49.
Darwall, S.L. (2008): "Due tipi di rispetto come riconoscimento per le persone". In I. Carter, A.E. Galeotti and V. Ottonelli (Eds.): *Eguale Rispetto*, Milan: Mondadori, pp. 1–23.
Eggers, D. (2011): "Hobbes and Game Theory Revisited. Zero-Sum Games in the State of Nature", *Southern Journal of Philosophy* 49 (3), pp. 193–226.
Ewin, R.E. (1991): *Virtues and Rights: The Moral Philosophy of Thomas Hobbes*, Boulder: Westview Press.
Galli, C. (2013): *Introductory essay to Hobbes*, *Leviatano*, Milan: Bur.
Gauthier, D. (2001): "Hobbes: The Law of Nature", *Pacific Philosophical Quarterly* 82 (2), pp. 258–284.
Gert, B. (1972): *Introduction to Thomas Hobbes, Man and Citizen*, Garden City, NY: Doubleday.
Hampton, J. (1986): *Hobbes and the Social Contract Tradition*, Cambridge: Cambridge University Press.
Hobbes, Th. (1839–1845): *The English Works of Thomas Hobbes of Malmesbury*, ed. by W. Molesworth, London: Bohn.
Hudson, S.D. (1980): "The Nature of Respect", *Social Theory and Practice* 6 (1), pp. 69–90.
Jesseph, D. (1996): "Hobbes and the Method of Natural Science". In T. Sorell (Ed.): *The Cambridge Companion to Hobbes*, Cambridge: Cambridge University Press, pp. 86–107.
Kavka, G. (1986): *Hobbesian Moral and Political Theory*, Princeton: Princeton University Press.

Laslett, P. (Ed.) (1965): *John Locke, Two Treatises of Government*, New York: New American Library.
Lloyd, S.A. (2009): *Morality in the Philosophy of Thomas Hobbes. Thomas Hobbes. Cases in the Law of Nature*, Cambridge: Cambridge University Press.
Martinich, A.P. (1992): *The Two Gods of Leviathan*, Cambridge: Cambridge University Press.
Oakeshott, M. (1975): *Hobbes on Civil Association*, Oxford: Oxford University Press.
Pacchi, A. (Ed.) (1968): *Thomas Hobbes. Elementi di legge naturale e politica*, Florence: La Nuova Italia.
Pacchi, A. (1987): "Hobbes and the Passions", *Topoi* 6, pp. 111–119.
Rawls, J. (1971): *A Theory of Justice*, Cambridge, MA/ London: Harvard University Press.
Reik, M. (1977): *The Golden Lands of Thomas Hobbes*, Detroit: Wayne State University Press.
Skinner, Q. (1996): *Reason and Rhetoric in the Philosophy of Hobbes*, Cambridge: Cambridge University Press.
Slomp, G. (2000): *Thomas Hobbes and the Politics of Glory*, New York: St. Martin's Press.
Strauss, L. (1952): *The Political Philosophy of Hobbes: Its Basis and Genesis*, Oxford: Oxford University Press.
Thornton, H.C. (2005): *State of Nature or Eden? Thomas Hobbes and His Contemporaries on the Natural Condition of Human Beings*, Rochester, NY: University of Rochester Press.
Tuck, R. (1989): *Hobbes*, Oxford: Oxford University Press.
Wolin, S. (1960): *Politics and Vision – Continuity and Innovation in Western Political Thought*, Boston: Little, Brown & Co.
Zagorin, P. (2009): *Hobbes and the Law of Nature*, Princeton: Princeton University Press.

Christine Bratu
The Source of Moral Motivation and Actions We Owe to Others: Kant's Theory of Respect

Abstract: In the contemporary debate about respect, the writings of Immanuel Kant constitute an important point of reference. I argue that Kant distinguishes between *two different kinds of respect: reverentia* is a feeling that a person experiences towards whatever is morally warranted and that will lead her to do what is morally warranted, provided that she has cultivated a calm state of mind. In contrast, *observantia* consists in a set of actions she has to perform in response to certain morally relevant features of persons, for instance their dignity. So both kinds of respect are different stances and directed towards different objects. What they have in common is that they both consist in the *acknowledgment of some morally relevant feature*. But while in the case of *reverentia* this acknowledgment takes place on the level of feelings and motivations, in the case of *observantia* it takes place on the level of actions.

1 Introduction

For many contemporary authors who work on the concept of respect, the writings of Immanuel Kant constitute an important point of reference. Thomas Hill for instance takes up Kant's idea that we have a moral duty to respect each other and ourselves (cf. Hill 1995, p. 85). Stephen Darwall contends that the notion of respect can be spelled out by drawing on Kant's demand always to treat persons as ends in themselves and never only as means (cf. Darwall 1995, p. 181), and Robin Dillon makes use of Kant's famous idea of the dignity of persons to establish her concept of recognition self-respect (cf. Dillon 2001, p. 65). But what exactly does Kant mean when he talks about respect ("Achtung")? In this chapter, I argue that Kant uses the notion of respect to discuss two distinct phenomena and therefore distinguishes between *two different kinds of respect:*[1] One kind of respect is the feeling that constitutes the source of moral motivation, the other consists in a specific set of actions we have the duty to perform in response to

---

[1] Other authors remarking that Kant distinguishes between different kinds of respect are Darwall 2008, Singleton 2007 and Sensen 2014.

certain morally relevant features of persons. The latter kind of respect is presented by Kant only in the *Metaphysics of Morals* (MM), while the former is first introduced in the *Groundwork of the Metaphysics of Morals* (G) and then extensively discussed in the *Critique of Practical Reason* (CPrR).[2] To distinguish between these two kinds of respect, Kant uses in MM the Latin notions of *reverentia* (cf. MM 6:402) for respect understood as the source of moral motivation and of *observantia* (cf. MM 6:449) for respect understood as the performance of specific actions.

In what follows, I will explain what we are to understand by respect as *reverentia* (from now on: respect$_r$) and respect as *observantia* (from now on: respect$_o$). In doing so, I will touch upon the following two questions every account of respect should address: Firstly, what kind of stance is respect, i.e. *what does a person A have to do to respect another person B?* Does A have to experience a particular feeling towards B, does A have to entertain a specific belief about B (for instance, about B's achievements or her merits) or does A have to behave in a certain way towards B? And secondly, what is it that warrants respect, i.e. *what should the object of A's respect be?* I will argue that respect$_r$ is a feeling that a person A experiences towards whatever is morally warranted and that will lead her to do what is morally warranted, provided that A has cultivated a calm state of mind. In contrast, respect$_o$ consists in a set of actions A has to perform in response to certain morally relevant features of persons, for instance their dignity. So both kinds of respect Kant discusses are different stances and directed towards different objects. What they have in common is that they both consist in the *acknowledgment of some morally relevant feature*. But while in the case of *reverentia* this acknowledgment takes place at the level of feelings and motivations, in the case of *observantia* it takes place at the level of actions. In my reconstruction, I will focus mainly on MM, since it is there that the concept of respect$_o$ first surfaces, so that Kant has to distinguish between the two kinds of respect. But whenever necessary, I will draw on his earlier practical works to illuminate Kant's position.

2 Respect Understood as *reverentia*: The Source of Moral Motivation

In MM, Kant first mentions respect$_r$ in section XII of the introduction, where he talks about what concepts "on the Part of Feeling" (MM 6:399), i.e. what psycho-

---

[2] All citations from Kant are taken from Kant 1996.

logical concepts we have to presuppose, if we want to assume that beings like us can act from duty alone. One such concept is respect understood as *reverentia*. Of this, Kant says the following:

> Respect (*reverentia*) is [...] something merely subjective, a feeling of a special kind, not a judgment about an object that it would be a duty to bring about or promote. For such a duty, regarded as a duty, could be present to us only through the respect we have for it. A duty to have respect would thus amount to being put under obligation to [have] duties. (MM 6:402)

According to what Kant says in MM, $respect_r$ is *a special kind of feeling* (1). This feeling *plays some part in moral action*, because it is through this feeling that duties are present to us (2). And precisely because of the part $respect_r$ plays in moral action, having a duty to feel $respect_r$ would be tantamount to having a duty to have duties, which to Kant is nonsensical. Therefore, *there can be no duty to feel respect* (3). Going by these scarce remarks alone, it is hard to understand what Kant means by $respect_r$. But Kant can afford to keep his treatment of $respect_r$ short in MM, as he has already explained the concept at length in CPrR (albeit without using the term "reverential"). To learn more about $respect_r$, we therefore have to turn to CPrR. From here it transpires that $respect_r$ is *the source of moral motivation*, i.e. the feeling that gives rise to the incentive a person acts upon when she acts from duty alone.[3] In arguing for this claim, I will take the three remarks Kant makes about $respect_r$ in MM as guidelines.

How does Kant justify claim (1)? In book I of CPrR, where he discusses the "incentives of pure practical reason" (CPrR 5:71), Kant specifies that the feeling of $respect_r$ "is inseparably connected with the representation of the moral law in every finite rational being" (CPrR 5:80). So for finite beings like us – who are capable of acting reasonably, but who do not do so necessarily – understanding what the moral law demands is inseparably connected with the feeling of $respect_r$. Put differently, realizing what we are morally required to do does not take place purely on an intellectual level but has a certain feel to it, namely the feeling of $respect_r$.

Why should the insight into what is morally required lead to or imply any particular feeling?[4] Kant offers the following explanation: When we realize what we ought to do, we also realize that there is a rational constraint on what we desire,

---

[3] *Reverentia* as the source of moral motivation is also discussed by Stratton-Lake 2000, pp. 29 – 44, Ameriks 2006, Klemme 2006, Timmons 2007 and Singleton 2007, pp. 43 – 50.
[4] I will presently discuss what kind of connection holds precisely between a moral insight and $respect_r$. For now, I only want to assume that there is such a connection.

i.e. on our will. Imagine, for instance, that a person A comes to realize that all things considered she should give back a sum of money she has kept safe for a friend to its rightful heirs.[5] From this it follows that it would be morally wrong of A to want to keep the money and spend it all herself. According to Kant, this realization results in a feeling of "pain" (CPrR 5:73) or humiliation (cf. CPrR 5:73), as A comes to understand that some of her desires are wrong and that she should stop having them. But A will also come to feel elevated (cf. CPrR 5:81), since the rational constraint she finds herself under is set by no one but herself, since she came to understand what she should or should not want through the exercise of her own practical reason. So for Kant, realizing what we are morally required to do results in a mixture of feelings – a negative feeling (cf. CPrR 5:74) of humiliation or frustration as we are not allowed to want whatever comes to our minds and, at the same time, a positive feeling (cf. CPrR 5:75) of elevation as we realize that the authority issuing these prohibitions is our own (cf. Singleton 2007, pp. 45–46). And it is this mixture of feelings – which he also describes as a feeling of necessitation ("Nötigung", cf. G 8:413 and CPrR 5:80) – that Kant calls respect$_r$.

So far I have explained why Kant believes that realizing what we are morally required to do has a phenomenal aspect. Put differently, I have explained why Kant believes that respect$_r$ is a feeling. But in the passage quoted above from MM, Kant states that respect$_r$ is a *special* feeling – so in what regard does the feeling of respect differ from other feelings? Before I spell this out, I will first point out a similarity between respect$_r$ and other feelings: For Kant, "all inclination [...] is based on feeling" (CPrR 5:72–73) and respect$_r$, like all feelings, can give rise to specific inclinations. By inclination Kant means something akin to a desire, i.e. a psychological state with a world-to-mind direction of fit and a propositional content similar to "I wish that it were the case that x". Having a world-to-mind direction of fit, inclinations are mental states that motivate their bearers to become active in such a way as to effect the state of affairs they are about. Kant does not spell out the exact relationship between the feeling of respect$_r$ and the inclinations it results in, but the following model comes to mind: After some deliberation, a person A realizes that all things considered she ought to do x. This realization frustrates A because she now understands that she is under a rational constraint to want to do x; but at the same time A feels elevated as she is aware that it is by her own reasoning and thereby by her own authority that this constraint has been placed upon her. This feeling of elevation in turn gives rise to an inclination, namely the inclination to do x.

---

[5] This is, of course, an example Kant himself discusses in CPrR 5:50.

But even though the feeling of respect_r resembles other feelings insofar it can give rise to inclinations, in other regards respect_r is special. Firstly, we come to experience respect_r in a different way than other feeling. According to Kant, apart from respect_r, all our feelings are pathological (cf. CPrR 5:75) in the sense that we are assailed by them. For instance, whether we feel pain or pleasure is usually not up to us. Respect_r, on the other hand, is up to us insofar as experiencing respect_r depends on the exercise of our own practical reason. Only by thinking about and understanding what we are morally required to do, do we come to feel both the frustration and elevation this insight entails. As "the cause determining it [i.e. the feeling of respect_r, C.B.] lies in pure practical reason", Kant concludes that "this feeling, on account of its origin, cannot be called pathologically effected but must be called *practically effected*" (CPrR 5:74). In the words Kant uses in G, respect_r is "a feeling self-wrought" (G 8:401, footnote).

Secondly and relatedly, Kant claims that as a feeling, respect_r "is the only one that we can cognize completely a priori and the necessity of which we can have insight into" (CPrR 5:73). So according to Kant, we can have a priori knowledge about when we are going to feel respect_r. Regarding all other feelings, there is no way to know a priori which feeling we are likely to experience under which circumstances. For instance, whether a person A will feel anxious or confident when presented with a task depends on A's abilities to cope with the problem and the experiences A has made in similar situations. Therefore, the only way to anticipate how A will feel regarding a new task is to get to know her, i.e. to get experiential knowledge of her. But given that Kant assumes that the insight into what the moral law demands and the feeling of respect_r are inseparably connected, the same does not hold for respect_r. For if there is such an inseparable connection, we know in advance that a person A who gains moral insight will experience the corresponding feeling of respect_r. Admittedly, A can hide the fact that she experiences respect_r and it is an open question (to which I will return presently) whether it will influence A's actions. Nevertheless, if we accept Kant's claim that the feeling of respect_r is inseparably tied to having a moral insight, we do not need to be intimately acquainted with A to know that she will experience respect_r whenever she has understood what the moral law calls for.

Kant's claim about the a priori status of respect_r hinges on his assumption that the insight into what the moral law s requires and the feeling of respect_r are inseparably connected. But how should we conceive of this connection? Either the connection between a moral insight and respect_r is a *causal* one, so that realizing what we are morally required to do causes us to feel respect_r; or it is a *constitutive* connection, so that realizing what we are morally required to do consists (at least) in part in experiencing the feeling of respect_r. There is textual evidence to support both interpretations. On the one hand, when Kant characterizes respect_r as "self-wrought" (G 8:401, footnote.) or "practically effected" (CPrR 5:74), this suggests a causal connection. And as something that has a feel to it, i.e. as part of the phenomenal world, we should expect respect_r to abide by the laws of the phenomenal world and thus have a cause. On the other hand, we have already seen that, according to Kant, respect_r is a special feeling insofar as it is brought about in a radically different way from any other feeling. Also, if respect_r were only the causal effect of an insight into the moral law, Kant could not claim that we can know a priori about when a person is going to experience respect_r, as a causal connection only ever establishes a contingent connection of whose existence we cannot have a priori knowledge (cf. Stratton-Lake 2000, p. 35). Therefore, I conclude that we should settle for the constitutive interpretation. According to this interpretation, respect_r is best understood as a constitutive part of a complex mental state comprising both cognitive and affective components. Thus, realizing that an action x is morally warranted does not only consist in having an appropriate belief (such as "I ought to do x/I must not do x"), but also in feeling a kind of necessitation to do x. Or as Kant himself says: "Respect for the law, which in its subjective aspect is called moral feeling, *is identical with* consciousness of one's duty." (MM 6:464, emphasis added)[6]

Having established that experiencing respect_r is a constitutive part of realizing what we ought to do, we are in a position to understand remark (2) concerning respect_r in MM. Here, Kant says that our duties can only be present to us through respect_r, i.e. that we can only come to understand that we are under a particular moral duty by experiencing respect_r. If we take experiencing respect_r to be a constitutive part of understanding what we ought to do, this statement turns out to be a necessary truth.

This necessary truth helps to bridge a gap between two parts of Kant's practical philosophy, namely his theory of action and his moral theory. What does this gap consist in? In his theory of action, Kant accepts what some have called the Aristotelian model of human action (cf. Timmons 1985, p. 384 and 386). According to this model, every action consists of a cognitive and a conative (or affective) element, where both these elements are distinct from one another. For Kant, the conative states that propel us into activity are – at the most general level – inclinations. In contrast, the cognitive element behind an action is a

---

[6] This interpretation was first put forward by Stratton-Lake (2000, p. 36) and then picked up by Singleton (2007, pp. 49–50).

so-called maxim, i.e. a rule a person A sets herself which states how A is going to react when faced with a particular type of situation. In the case of non-moral action, the conative takes precedence over the cognitive element in the sense that the inclination A finds herself in the grip of is not the result of A's practical deliberation. Rather, A's inclination results from a pathological feeling (for instance, pleasure or displeasure). A's practical reason only comes into play to find out which means are most suited to satisfying the inclination she experiences – a discovery which is then is reflected in A's maxim. But in the case of moral action, something else has to go on. For in his moral writings, Kant famously claims that moral action is autonomous action, i.e. action the course of which the agent has charted herself, independently of any pathological influences.[7] So in the case of moral action, practical deliberation needs to take precedence over any pre-existing pathological inclinations. If all inclinations were the result of pathological feelings and thus pathologically effected themselves, Kant's theory of action and his moral theory would be irreconcilable. For according to his theory of action, an inclination is a constitutive part of every action, but according to his moral theory, in order to be moral an action (and thereby each of its constitutive parts) has to be the result of practical reason alone. It is here that respect$_r$ comes into play. For as a practically effected feeling, respect$_r$ is strictly connected to practical deliberation, as respect$_r$ is nothing but the phenomenal aspect of our understanding of what we ought to do. Nevertheless, respect$_r$ is still a feeling and can as such give rise to corresponding inclinations, which in turn can form a constitutive part of moral action. Therefore, as a constitutive part of the understanding of what is morally warranted, respect$_r$ reconciles Kant's theory of action with his moral theory.

Kant himself admits that his attempt to reconcile his theory of action with his moral theory "is for human reason an insoluble problem" (CPrR 5:72). Usually, this insoluble problem is presented as the problem of free will (cf. CPrR 5:72): How can reason alone become practical and cause us to feel respect$_r$ and, consequently, be inclined to act in a particular way? Given that I have argued that we should understand respect$_r$ not as an effect of rational insight but as a constitutive part thereof, I have to restate the problem in the following terms: With respect$_r$ Kant posits a mental state that has both cognitive and conative aspects, but according to the Aristotelian model of human action there are no mental states with both a world-to-mind and a mind-to-world direction of fit. So how

---

[7] Indeed, this is where Kant thinks that all moral theorists before him went astray, as "it never occured to them that he (i.e. a person while acting morally, C.B.) is subject only to law given by himself" (G 8:432).

can there be such a feeling as respect$_f$? In his treatment of respect$_f$ in MM, Kant says nothing in answer to this question. Instead, he relies on what he claims to have shown in CPrR, namely that it is simply a fact of reason that reason alone can become practical (and that, consequently, there are mental states with both cognitive and conative aspects, cf. CPrR 5:56). Given this assumption, Kant argues that there is no need to show "how a law can be of itself and immediately a determining ground of the will" but only "what it effects […] in the mind insofar as it is an incentive" (CPrR 5:72). Put differently, in explaining respect$_f$, Kant limits himself to showing *how* respect$_f$ works, because he takes it for granted *that* it works.[8]

And how exactly does respect$_f$ work? In MM Kant states that "feelings arising from sensible impressions lose their influence on moral feeling only because respect for the law is *more powerful* than all such feelings together". (MM 6:409, emphasis added) So according to Kant, a person A acts from respect$_f$ only if her respect$_f$ for what is morally warranted is stronger than all the pathological feelings she is also experiencing. This implies that there might be cases in which A realizes what she ought to do and therefore experiences respect$_f$, but will nevertheless not do what is morally required of her, simply because her other feelings outweigh her feeling of respect$_f$. So while there is an inseparable connection between moral insight and the feeling of respect$_f$, the connection between experiencing respect$_f$ and acting upon this feeling is more tenuous. Thus, Kant drives a wedge between realizing what is morally required to do and acting because of this insight. Only a person who has cultivated a calm state of mind and is not chased around by her pathological feelings and inclinations will regularly act because of respect$_f$. Two important points follow from this: Firstly, Kant is not committed to the claim that understanding what is morally required will inevitably lead to acting on this insight. Since weakness of the will seems to be a common phenomenon, such a commitment would be implausible.[9] And secondly, because our wills can be weak, we have "the duty of apathy" (MM 6:408), i.e. the duty to cultivate "a tranquil mind with a considered and firm resolution to put the law into practice" (MM 6:409).

---

[8] Russell remarks skeptically on Kant's reticence when it comes to explaining how respect$_f$ is even possible (cf. Russell 2006, p. 296).

[9] Kant himself wants to make room for the possibility of weakness of will, when he writes about a person facing the gallows. For this person knows what is morally required to do, but nevertheless he will "not venture to assert whether he would do it or not" (CRP 5:54). By making room for weakness of will, Kant avoids an implausibly tight connection between moral insight and moral motivation while still holding what in contemporary metaethical debates has been called an internalist position (cf. Wallace 2004, p. 183, and Klemme 2006, p. 133).

But while we have a duty to cultivate a tranquil mind so that the feeling of respect$_r$ can outweigh all our pathological feelings, we cannot have an outright duty to experience respect$_r$ as Kant states in remark (3) from MM. Kant does not make his reasoning for this claim explicit, but the following argument comes to mind: like most practical philosophers, Kant accepts the principle that *ought implies can*. Therefore, A's having the duty to experience respect$_r$ presupposes that A can come to know that she has the duty to experience respect$_r$. Otherwise how could A fulfill a duty she does not know she has? In order to come to know that she has the duty to experience respect$_r$, A has to have the moral insight that she ought to experience respect$_r$. But as I have argued above, Kant maintains that A's having the moral insight that she ought to do x is tantamount to A's experiencing respect$_r$ for x. Therefore, to come to know that she has the duty to experience respect$_r$, A has to experience respect$_r$ for experiencing respect$_r$. So in placing the duty of experiencing respect$_r$ on A, Kant would presuppose that A was already experiencing the stance he was in the process of demanding from her. Thus, a duty to experience respect$_r$ is nonsensical.

To sum up: According to Kant, respect in the sense of reverentia is the feeling we experience towards what we have understood to be morally required, as respect$_r$ is a constitutive part of our moral insight. Phenomenologically, respect$_r$ presents itself as a mixture of frustration and elevation. Like all feelings, respect$_r$ can give rise to inclinations. More specifically, respect$_r$ gives rise to the inclination to do what we have understood to be morally required. Therefore, respect$_r$ serves as the source of moral motivation and thus bridges the gap between Kant's theory of action and his moral philosophy. Unlike other feelings, respect$_r$ is not a feeling we are assailed by; rather, we can induce ourselves to experience respect$_r$ by thinking about what we are morally required to do. Since respect$_r$ is part and parcel of our insight into morality, we cannot be morally required to experience respect$_r$, because in order to be assigned a moral duty we already have to experience respect$_r$ for what we are supposedly morally required to do.

3 Respect Understood as observantia: Actions That We Owe to Others

I concluded the second part of this chapter by pointing out that according to Kant there can be no moral duty to experience respect$_r$. Therefore, Kant has to speak about a different kind of respect when he introduces respect$_o$ as "observatia aliis praestanda" (MM 6:449) which translates as "respect that we have to grant to others", discussed in the section where he treats the duties of virtue to others merely as human beings (cf. MM 6:462). Another indication that we are dealing with a second kind of respect is that Kant states that $respect_o$ is not "to be understood as the mere feeling" (which is how we are to understand $respect_r$) but "as respect in the practical sense" (MM 6:449). In what follows, I will argue that *$respect_o$ consists in a set of specific actions we have the duty to perform in response to certain morally relevant features of other persons*. Different morally relevant features call for $respect_o$ in different ways; the feature that Kant discusses most extensively in MM is the dignity of persons, but he also touches upon the $respect_o$ due to other persons because they have helped us. Since Kant focuses on $respect_o$ for the dignity of persons, so will I; I will return to the $respect_o$ due to others because they have helped us only briefly at the end of this section. I will distinguish between these two versions of $respect_o$ by calling them $respect_{o,d}$ ($respect_o$ for the dignity of persons) and $respect_{o,b}$ (respect for our benefactors).

What are we to understand by $respect_{o,d}$ that we owe to other persons in virtue of their dignity? According to Kant, $respect_{o,d}$ consists in the "recognition of a dignity (*dignitas*) in other human beings, that is, of a worth that has no price, no equivalent for which the object evaluated (*aestimii*) could be exchanged" (MM 6:462). The meaning of this remark has to be spelled out, since it is far from obvious what exactly it means to recognize the dignity of others. Do we recognize the dignity of another person A by believing that A has inherent moral worth instead of a price? Or do we also have to profess this belief publicly? Or do we even have to perform further, more demanding actions such as, for instance, treating A's requests and commands as authoritative?[10] In what follows, I will argue for a *narrow understanding of $respect_{o,d}$*, according to which a

> person A $respects_o$ another person B in virtue of B's dignity if and only if A refrains from explicitly denying that B has dignity because A believes that B in fact has dignity.

I will contrast this narrow understanding of $respect_{o,d}$ with a *wide interpretation* according to which

> a person A $respects_o$ another person B in virtue of B's dignity if and only if A treats B in accordance with her dignity because A believes that B in fact has dignity.

Both interpretations assume that to $respect_{o,d}$ B's dignity, A must perform certain actions (discussed below), but also that she has to do so for a specific reason: A has to refrain from explicitly denying B's dignity or treat B in accordance

---

[10] This is what Darwall takes $respect_o$ to consist in. See Darwall 2008, pp. 190–192.

with her dignity because she believes that B has dignity. By assuming this, both interpretations try to make good on Kant's claim that the duty to respect$_{o,d}$ is a duty of virtue. For duties of virtue are duties "for which only internal lawgiving is possible" (MM 6:394), i.e. where the duty cannot be discharged by simply performing a specific action, but where the action has to be performed because of a specific reason (which is reflected in the agent's maxim).

Where the narrow and the wide interpretation differ is in the actions they hold the duty of respect$_{o,d}$ to call for. According to the narrow interpretation, A has to perform a specific type of action or rather, A has to refrain from performing a specific type of action, since A has to refrain from explicitly denying that B has dignity. In contrast, it is impossible to state in advance what specific actions respect$_{o,d}$ requires under the wide interpretation. For Kant, we treat another person in accordance with her dignity by treating her as the Categorical Imperative (CI) requires;[11] but what actions CI calls for cannot be ascertained *in abstracto* since this depends on the actors involved and the circumstances they find themselves in. Therefore, all that can be said about the wide interpretation in general is that A has to treat B as CI requires, where this can involve any specific kind of action. Another way of putting the difference between the narrow and the wide interpretation would be the following: according to the narrow interpretation, recognizing B's dignity is an *explicit matter*, a matter of explicitly stating that B has dignity or rather of not explicitly denying B's status as a dignified being; whereas, according to the wide interpretation, recognizing B's dignity is an *implicit matter*, which transpires only from A's acting as CI requires whenever B is involved.

Of course, there are affinities between the interpretations. For instance, if A were to treat B disrespectfully$_{o,d}$ according to the narrow interpretation, i.e. if A were to explicitly deny that B had dignity, this might eventually lead to her treating B disrespectfully$_{o,d}$ according to the wide interpretation, i.e. to her not observing CI whenever B is involved. For why should A bother to treat B as morality requires if she explicitly denies that B has the feature needed to be an equal member of the kingdom of ends (cf. G 8:433)? Likewise, if A were to constantly and openly violate CI in her interactions with B, B might have the impression that with her actions A implicitly expresses her belief that B has no dignity

---

[11] The following reasoning serves to establish the connection between treating a person A in accordance with her dignity and observing CI: That A has dignity means that A has "a worth that has no price" (MM 6:462) and thus is a being "the existence of which is in itself an end" (G 8:428). To treat A in accordance with her dignity, we therefore have to treat her "always at the same time as an end, never merely as a means" (G 8:433). But to treat A in such a way is to treat her as CI requires.

and is therefore not worthy of moral consideration. Thus, A disrespecting$_{o,d}$ B in terms of the narrow interpretation can lead to A disrespecting$_{o,d}$ B in terms of the wide interpretation, while A disrespecting$_{o,d}$ B in terms of the wide interpretation can be taken to imply an act of disrespect$_{o,d}$ by A towards B in terms of the narrow interpretation. Notwithstanding these affinities, the interpretations are not equivalent. For while any case of disrespect$_{o,d}$ in terms of the narrow interpretation is also a case of disrespect$_{o,d}$ in terms of the wide interpretation (at least if we assume that CI calls for us to truthfully report on other people's dignity), the reverse is not true. To see this, think of a case of physical abuse. If A physically abuses B, A clearly violates CI in her interaction with B and is therefore disrespectful$_{o,d}$ towards B given the wide interpretation. But physically abusing someone is not necessarily identical with (nor does it necessarily imply) explicitly denying their dignity. Therefore A's action does not constitute an instance of disrespect$_o$ according to the narrow interpretation.

Which of these two interpretations of respect$_{o,d}$ should we adopt? Several commentators settle on the wide interpretation. For instance, Darwall remarks that according to Kant "[w]*hatever* we owe others mobilizes the duty of respect" (Darwall 2008, p. 196). Whenever we fail to treat a person as CI requires or – as Darwall says paraphrasing Rawls – as a self-originating source of valid claims, we "also violate the duty of respect" (Darwall 2008, p. 196). So according to Darwall, Kant claims that treating others as their dignity requires and treating others with respect$_{o,d}$ are coextensive – which is only the case in the wide interpretation of respect$_{o,d}$. Oliver Sensen has a similar opinion when he argues that for Kant, to be respectful$_{o,d}$ towards other people is to "not have an attitude of exalting oneself above others" (Sensen 2014, p. 117), where this is then spelled out in terms observing CI (cf. Sensen 2014, p. 118). Sensen can conclude that "it might be a sign of respect to speak very slowly, and use simple grammar if one meets a small child or a foreigner who hardly understands any English" (Sensen 2014, p. 121), since this is what CI calls for in these interactions. But these two types of action cannot count as respect$_{o,d}$ in the narrow interpretation since they are not about refraining from explicitly denying anybody's dignity.[12]

In contrast, I contend that we should settle for the narrow interpretation. There are four reasons for this reading. Firstly, if we accept the wide interpretation, "to be respectful$_{o,d}$" does not designate any particular virtue just as "to be disrespectful$_{o,d}$" does not distinguish any particular vice. Instead, in the wide in-

---

[12] Singleton also distinguishes between respect$_r$ and respect$_o$, but she does not spell out any further what she takes respect$_o$ to be. All she says is that to respect$_o$ another person we have "to recognize the rationality and free agency (humanity) of others as well as ourselves" (Singleton 2007, p. 56), but she does not go on to say what concrete actions this implies.

terpretation, calling a person A disrespectful$_{o,d}$ is just another way of saying that A violates CI and therefore behaves in a morally objectionable way, but it does not state in which specific way A's behavior is morally objectionable. To put it differently, in the wide interpretation "acting respectfully$_{o,d}$" and "acting disrespectfully$_{o,d}$" are simply synonyms of the thin ethical concepts "acting morally right" and "acting morally wrong". Since Kant already has terms for designating such behavior, there is no need for him to introduce the notion of respect$_{o,d}$.

Also, MM strongly suggests that Kant did not intend simply to introduce a synonym. For after presenting respect$_{o,d}$ as the "recognition of a dignity (*dignitas*) in other human beings" (MM 6:462), Kant goes on to explain the particular "vices that violate duties of respect for other human beings" (MM 6:465). If Kant had had the wide interpretation of respect$_{o,d}$ in mind, he could have listed any number of morally objectionable actions, since very diverse types of action can amount to a violation of CI, such as for instance stealing from or lying to another person. But instead of drawing on different cases in which CI is violated, Kant cites three very particular vices, namely arrogance, defamation and ridicule. These three vices share a common element in that they all consist in the explicit and deliberate belittling of other people. For according to Kant, to be arrogant is to "demand that others think little of themselves in comparison with us" (MM 6:465), while to defame other persons consists in the "immediate inclination […] to bring into the open something prejudicial to respect to others" (MM 6:466) and to ridicule is to hold up "a person's real faults, or supposed faults as if they were real, in order to deprive him of the respect he deserves" (MM 6:467). So people prone to arrogance, defamation and ridicule rejoice in vilifying others, i.e. in calling others less worthy than they are. But then, what is common in these three vices is simply what the narrow interpretation holds disrespect$_{o,d}$ to be, namely the explicit denial of somebody else's dignity. That Kant holds these three vices to violate the duties of respect for other human beings therefore suggests that we should accept the narrow interpretation of respect$_{o,d}$.

The narrow interpretation of respect$_{o,d}$ also fits nicely with what Kant has to say about self-respect. According to Kant, we have a duty to respect ourselves, since not only other persons have dignity, but we ourselves do too. We violate this duty if we display "false servility", i.e. by "[w]aiving any claim to moral worth in oneself" (MM 6:435). So to discharge our duty of self-respect we have to refrain from explicitly denying our dignity. Let's assume that the duty of self-respect is analogous to the duty of respect insofar as it calls for the same type of actions only that, in the case of self-respect, these actions are directed towards ourselves rather than towards others. If we accept this assumption, then the way Kant describes the duty of self-respect speaks in favor of adopting the narrow interpretation of respect$_{o,d}$. To be self-respecting we only have to refrain from denying our own dignity and not – as the wide interpretation would have it – to treat ourselves as CI requires.

Finally, Kant repeatedly stresses that the "respect we are bound to show other human beings [...] is only a *negative* duty" (MM 6:467; cf. also MM 6:464). So according to Kant, respecting$_{o,d}$ another person always consists in refraining from doing something, since negative duties are duties that "*forbid* a human being to act" (MM 6:419), in contrast to positive duties "which *command* him to make a certain object of choice his end" (MM 6:419). This characterization of the duty of respect$_{o,d}$ as a negative duty is better suited to the narrow interpretation. For given the wide interpretation, the duty to respect$_{o,d}$ another person can also amount to a positive duty, since treating another person as CI requires may call for both refraining from certain actions (such as slandering her reputation) and for performing certain actions (such as helping a person in need). To put it differently, given that in the wide interpretation respect$_{o,d}$ for another person can mean performing any action CI authorizes, it is far from clear that the duty to respect$_{o,d}$ another person will always amount to a negative duty. In contrast, if we settle on the narrow interpretation, this is necessarily the case since in this interpretation to respect$_{o,d}$ another person is specifically to refrain from explicitly denying her status as a dignified being.

So far I have argued that the evidence from MM supports the narrow interpretation of respect$_{o,d}$. This gives rise to the question why Kant should have considered refraining from explicitly denying the dignity of another person of such eminent importance as to coin a specific term for it. Of course, the fact that he assumes persons to have dignity justifies why Kant holds respectful$_{o,d}$ behavior to be morally warranted and disrespectful$_{o,d}$ behavior to be morally forbidden. But not every type of morally right or wrong action gets its own account in MM. So what is so important about respect$_{o,d}$ and disrespect$_{o,d}$ that they call for a separate discussion?

In MM Kant worries that if people disrespect$_o$ each other, this will lead to the degradation or even the collapse of our shared moral community. For instance, Kant states that "an example of disregarding respectability [...] might lead others to follow it" (MM 6:464). Likewise, the

> intentional spreading (*propalatio*) of something that detracts from another's honor – even if it is not a matter of public justice, and even if what is said is true – diminishes respect for humanity as such, so as finally to cast a shadow of worthlessness over our race itself, making misanthropy (shying away from human beings) or contempt the prevalent cast of mind (MM 6:466).

So according to Kant, it is important that we respect$_{o,d}$ each other not only because it is warranted by that fact that we have dignity, but also because it serves to stabilize our moral community. For if we hear too often how other people are denied their rightful moral standing or if we too often yield to this denial, we might start to consider human beings as such to be worthless. In this, Kant foreshadows the arguments made today by advocates of hate speech regulation. For instance, Jeremy Waldron explains the harm that is caused by explicitly denying the dignity of others thus:

> [T]here is a sort of public good of inclusiveness that our society sponsors and that it is committed to. [...] This sense of security in the space we all inhabit is a public good, and in a good society it is something that we all contribute to and help sustain in an instinctive and almost unnoticeable way. Hate speech undermines this public good, or it makes the task of sustaining it much more difficult than it would otherwise be. [...] In doing so, it creates something like an environmental threat to social peace, a sort of slow-acting poison, accumulating here and there, word by word, so that eventually it becomes harder and less natural for even the good-hearted members of the society to play their part in maintaining this public good. (Waldron 2012, p. 4)

In fact, Kant is so worried about the slow-acting poison of systematic disrespect$_{o,d}$ that he also urges us to be careful in our pronouncements of negative judgments concerning other features of persons apart from their dignity. For instance, according to Kant it is "a duty of virtue not to take malicious pleasure in exposing the faults of others [...], but rather to throw the veil of philanthropy over their faults" (MM 6:466).

So far, I have discussed respect$_o$ as it is called for by a particular feature of persons, namely by their dignity. But dignity is not the only feature persons possess that calls for respect$_o$; according to Kant, so can their "age, sex, birth, strength or weakness, or even rank" (MM 6:468). So at least in theory, respect$_o$ is a manifold phenomenon. But in MM, Kant cannot elaborate on possible other versions of respect$_o$. The reason for this is that, as a work of metaphysics, MM only deals in necessary and therefore a priori truths. And while it is a defining and therefore necessary feature of persons to have dignity,[13] it depends "in part on arbitrary arrangements" (MM 6:468) which of the other features mentioned above of persons are accorded moral relevance by a society. Therefore, Kant concludes that

> [t]he different forms of respect to be shown to others in accordance with differences in their qualities or contingent relations [...] cannot be set forth in detail and classified in the met-

---

[13] While it is clear that Kant holds all persons to have dignity, it is doubtful whether he takes all human beings to be persons. This problem is discussed extensively in Hay 2013, pp. 158–179.

aphysical first principles of a doctrine of virtue, since this has to do only with its pure rational principles. (MM 6:468)

The only exception Kant makes to this can be found in his short treatment of the respect we owe to our benefactors (cf. MM 6:454). As this respect towards our benefactors (respect$_{o,b}$) is another instance of respect$_o$, we have to perform certain actions (rather than just experience certain feelings) to display it. But which actions we have to perform to show respect$_{o,b}$ varies in accordance with "how useful the favor was to the one put under obligation and how unselfishly it was bestowed on him" (MM 6:456). Kant limits himself to stating the minimum we have to do to be respectful$_{o,b}$, which is "to render equal services to the benefactor if he can receive them" (MM 6:456) and to not consider "the kindness received as a burden" (MM 6:456).

To sum up, according to Kant, respect in the sense of *observantia* is shown by performing a certain set of actions. Which actions in particular depends on the object of respect$_o$. For instance, to show the proper respect$_o$ for the dignity of another person B, a person A has to refrain from explicitly denying that B has dignity. In contrast, to show proper respect$_o$ for the fact that B has helped her, A must at least return the favor. Since Kant believes that we have the duty to react to certain features of persons – for instance their dignity or the fact that they have been of assistance to us – with respect$_o$, the concept of respect$_o$ is part of Kant's moral philosophy.

4 Conclusion

In this chapter, I have argued for the claim that Kant knows of and distinguishes between two different kinds of respect, namely respect as *reverentia* and respect as *observantia*. Between these two kinds of respect there are a number of important differences. While respect$_r$ is the feeling a person experiences when she has understood what she is morally required to do, to show respect$_o$ consists in performing certain actions. The object of respect$_r$ is what the moral law requires, while respect$_o$ can be directed towards different morally relevant features of persons, most importantly towards their dignity. While we have a moral duty to show respect$_o$ for the dignity of persons, there cannot be any moral duty to experience respect$_r$ since experiencing respect$_r$ is a condition of possibility for being placed under a duty in the first place. What unites the two concepts of respect is that they both consist in the acknowledgment of some morally relevant feature. But while this acknowledgment takes place at the level of feelings and motivations when it comes to respect$_r$, it plays out at the level of actions in the case of respect$_o$.

Another way to distinguish the two kinds of respect Kant identifies is to stress that they belong to different parts of his practical philosophy. Kant uses the concept of respect$_r$ to explain how acting from duty alone is possible, as he introduces this feeling as the source of moral motivation; therefore, the concept of respect$_r$ belongs to Kant's theory of action. In contrast, in arguing for our duty to respect$_o$ the dignity of others by refraining from calling it into question, Kant engages in moral philosophy. Therefore, if we want to take Kant as our inspiration when we think about respect, we first have to clarify what intellectual endeavor we are engaged in. The authors I have cited at the beginning of this paper, who draw on Kant's work to spell out their own theories of respect, are all interested in practical matters. Therefore, the concept of respect they can take from Kant is that of respect$_o$, in particular respect$_o$ for the dignity of other persons. For this concept to have any content of its own – instead of simply being a synonym for "acting morally right" – we must see it along the lines of the narrow interpretation I have presented. Put differently, when Kant claims that we owe it to other persons to respect$_o$ their dignity, we have to understand him to be saying that we have to refrain from explicitly denying their status as dignified beings. Thus, analyzing the concept of respect$_o$ shows that Kant was one of the first authors to acknowledge the harm that lies in what nowadays is called hate speech.

Bibliography

Ameriks Karl (2006): "Kant and Motivational Externalism". In Heiner Klemme, Manfred Kühn and Dieter Schönecker (Eds.): *Moralische Motivation. Kant und die Alternativen*, Hamburg: Meiner, pp. 3–22.

Darwall, Stephen (1995): "Two Kinds of Respect". In Robin Dillon (Ed.): *Dignity, Character, and Self-Respect*, London/New York: Routledge, pp. 181–197.

Darwall, Stephen (2008): "Kant on Respect, Dignity, and the Duty of Respect". In Monika Betzler (Ed.): *Kant's Ethics of Virtue*, Berlin/New York: De Gruyter, pp. 175–199.

Dillon, Robin (2001): "Self-Forgiveness and Self-Respect", *Ethics* 112, pp. 53–83.

Hay, Carol (2012): *Kantianism, Liberalism, and Feminism. Resisting Oppression*, London: Palgrave Macmillan.

Hill, Thomas (1995): "Servility and Self-Respect". In Robin Dillon (Ed.): *Dignity, Character, and Self-Respect*, London/New York: Routledge, pp. 76–92.

Kant, Immanuel (1996): *Practical Philosophy*, trans. and ed. by Mary J. Gregor, General Introduction by Allen Wood, Cambridge: Cambridge University Press.

Klemme, Heiner (2006): "Praktische Gründe und moralische Motivation. Eine deontologische Perspektive". In: Heiner Klemme, Manfred Kühn and Dieter Schönecker (Eds.): *Moralische Motivation. Kant und die Alternativen*, Hamburg: Meiner, pp. 113–154.

Russell, Paul (2006): "Practical Reason and Motivational Scepticism". In Heiner Klemme, Manfred Kühn and Dieter Schönecker (Eds.): *Moralische Motivation. Kant und die Alternativen*, Hamburg: Meiner, pp. 287–298.

Sensen, Oliver (2014): "Respect Towards Elderly Demented Patients", *Diametros* 39, pp. 109–124.

Singleton, Jane (2007): "Kant's Account of Respect: A Bridge between Rationality and Anthropology", *Kantian Review* 12, pp. 40–60.

Stratton-Lake, Philip (2000): *Kant, Duty and Moral Worth*, London/New York: Routledge.

Timmons, Mark (1985): "Kant and the Possibility of Moral Motivation", *The Southern Journal of Philosophy* 3, pp. 377–398.

Wallace, Jay (2006): "Moral Motivation". In: James Dreier (Ed.): *Contemporary Debates in Moral Theory*, Malden et al.: Blackwell, pp. 182–196.

Waldron Jeremy (2012): *The Harm in Hate Speech*, Cambridge MA/London: Harvard University Press.

Marie Göbel
Respect as the Foundation of Human Rights: To What Extent Can This View Be Attributed to Kant?

Abstract: In this essay I consider to what extent the view that respect for persons is the foundation of human rights might be an adequate characterization of Kant's philosophical position on this subject. I distinguish the claim that Kant was a defender of human rights (which I reject) from the possibility of a Kantian theory of human rights (which I affirm). I then address the question how Kant's concept of respect might fit into the latter as a foundation. The answer is developed via a systematic (re)construction of two concepts of respect in Kant, and two different "foundational claims" accordingly. This makes it possible to evaluate whether the relevant view can properly be attributed to Kant.

In the last decades the systematic efforts in the field of the philosophy of human rights have been accompanied by an increased interest in the historic-philosophical sources of current human rights-thought, both as a matter of historical curiosity and theoretical inspiration. This search for historical predecessors concerns in particular the – by now somewhat notorious – question about the foundation(s) of human rights (cf. Cruft, Liao and Renzo 2015). Unsurprisingly this development has also led to a fresh engagement in certain aspects of Kant's practical philosophy: Was Kant a defender of human rights, and if so, how did he justify them?

In current systematic debates arguably the two most prominent candidates for a foundation of human rights are human dignity and respect for persons.[1] The quintessence of the resulting view(s) is that the (moral) reason why all human beings have certain fundamental rights is their dignity or the respect they owe to one another.[2] These views are regularly attributed to Kant. Accordingly, Kant's practical philosophy is frequently treated as *the* historical reference point for our modern understanding of human rights. However, the question if

---

[1] In this essay I take no account of the difference between human beings and rational beings or persons and the well-known problems that come along with it.
[2] Depending on how one understands both concepts and their relationship one might not regard these views as alternatives but hold that they eventually amount to one and the same view (as I do). I will briefly consider this point in section 4.

this attribution is warranted is of course highly controversial. This applies to the question of whether one finds a concept of human rights in Kant at all as well as to their alleged foundation(s).

In this essay I consider to what extent the view that respect for persons is the foundation of human rights might be an adequate characterization of Kant's philosophical position on this subject.[3] Two levels of analysis need to be kept apart here. On the exegetical level the question is whether Kant developed a concept or conception of human rights in his writings, and if so, how he related it to the concept of respect.[4] As distinguished from this, the systematic question is whether a conception of human rights and of respect as their foundation can be developed from certain constitutive elements of Kant's philosophy. Depending on which one of these levels or questions is concerned I will refer to "*Kant's*" or a "*Kantian*" conception, theory etc. respectively.[5]

The argument essentially comes in two parts, one that focuses on human rights (1–2) and one that focuses on respect for persons (3–4). I begin by considering whether Kant has a concept of human rights at all (1). My answer will be negative. Accordingly, as an exegetical matter the possibility that respect might serve as the foundation of *human rights in Kant* is ruled out. Instead, the argumentative place of the latter is taken by a *Kantian conception of human rights* in the systematic sense. I argue for the possibility and for what I take to be the core elements of such a conception in section 2. The question is then whether

---

[3] Although throughout this essay I mention Kant's concept of "respect for the moral law", from time to time I limit my analysis to his concept of "respect for persons". (In case I only speak of "respect" this is always what I mean.) The latter has the advantage that it is much closer to our moral language today. Furthermore, the two concepts are so intimately connected in Kant's philosophy that I do not expect that adding an analysis of the former concept would considerably change my results: According to Kant, the feeling of respect is directed exclusively toward the moral law. Yet the only beings who can impose the law upon themselves, i.e. who can be law-giving, are rational beings or beings capable of pure practical reason – in other words, "persons". Respect for persons then ultimately *is* respect for the moral law: "Any respect for a person is properly only respect for the law […] of which he gives us an example." (G 8:401)

[4] I do not strictly distinguish here between the questions of whether Kant has a "concept" or "conception" of human rights. In the present context they come down to the same question, namely whether Kant had anything close to our current understanding of human rights. In the same breath I sometimes refer to Kant as a "defender" of human rights. Of course it would in principle be possible that Kant developed a concept or conception of human rights yet rejected the human rights-idea. However, I do not see that this option is currently on the agenda.

[5] A third question one might ask is whether Kant's philosophy rates among the historical factors that prompted and shaped our modern human rights-thought (it helped to "pave the way" for human rights). This is a question that to my knowledge nobody seriously negates.

and, if so, in what sense precisely Kant's concept of respect (which he unquestionably has) might be the foundation of Kantian human rights. To this end, in section 3 I distinguish two concepts of respect in Kant and accordingly two *prima facie* different foundational claims. I work out the precise meaning of each claim and specify how they relate to each other. Finally, in section 4 I draw conclusions regarding the leading question of this paper and add some further-reaching thoughts on the relationship between respect and dignity. Section 5 summarizes the argument.

Two conceptual and terminological remarks are appropriate at this point. First, in contemporary debates the term "foundation" is notoriously ambiguous. In my understanding the concept of a foundation is as simple as indispensable: A foundation is that which morally justifies something else.[6] So if the assumption in question is that there are human rights then whatever morally justifies this assumption is its foundation. In my terminology, the claim that "X is the foundation of Y" is then a "foundational claim", where the qualifier "about respect" etc. specifies the foundation proposed.[7]

Secondly, what do I understand by human rights? In current human rights-debates it is frequently not clear if scholars refer to human rights as (a particular kind of) moral rights or as (a particular kind of) legal rights, by which they typically mean those legal rights that are included in the UN-based system of human rights law (cf. Buchanan 2013, pp. 3–23). Here I use the term in the former sense, for obvious reasons. According to the dominant and rather minimalist understanding of the concept, human rights are then those moral rights that belong to all human beings simply by virtue of being human (e.g. Griffin 2008, p. 13). As such, they are universal in scope, valid independently of space and time, and they belong to human beings unconditionally and inalienably. Furthermore, they are or express categorical or overriding demands: Human rights ought to be respected by everyone and under all circumstances (feasibility presupposed), and they may only be weighed against one another (if at all; cf. Gewirth

---

[6] In particular, by employing the term "foundation" I am not committed to the epistemological theory of "foundationalism". I should also add that in my view the very concept of a foundation does not yet imply anything specific with regard to the features of this justification – for instance: that the relevant moral reasons need to be "ultimate" in some sense; whether or not there can be more than one such justification; how exactly the foundation and that which it justifies relate and so forth. These are substantive claims that are not conceptually implied but require argument. Accordingly, when I refer to a foundation throughout this paper I am not assuming any of them.

[7] For clarity it might be added that whereas a foundational claim is in itself a substantive claim it is usually an interpretative claim (about Kant's or Kantian philosophy) in the context of this paper.

1982) but not against other moral or prudential considerations. I will turn to the political and legal implications of this concept in the next section.

1 Human Rights in Kant?

Regardless of the countless references to Kant in the human rights-literature the question whether one finds a concept of human rights in Kant's work divides scholars up to the present day. Those who argue that he does possess such a concept often point to his thoughts on the law of peoples in *On Perpetual Peace*,[8] to the innate right to freedom from the *Doctrine of Right* (MM 6:237–238) and to the way he justifies the *exeundum* in the same work (MM 6:306). In addition to these elements of Kant's political thought they emphasize his ethical notions of the rational being as an "end in itself" (G 8:428–431), of the "dignity" of rational beings (G 8:434–440) and of "respect for persons" (G 8:401, CPrR 5:71–89) – all of which figure in contemporary justifications of human rights. Beside this, there is of course the general expectation that a moral universalist like Kant should be a political or rights-universalist as well (cf. Horn 2014, p. 68) and that under the terms of his ethical standpoint he should at least defend a moral conception of law, if not a human rights-based conception.

I agree with the opponents of this view that Kant does *not* have a concept of human rights (cf. Flikschuh 2015; Horn 2014; Sangiovanni 2015). To be sure, the picture that emerges from his writings is not unambiguous, and I have not come across an interpretation so far that I would consider conclusive without reservations (partly because the question cannot be addressed without touching larger issues about Kant's political and moral philosophy as a whole, which again allow for different interpretative options). Still, all in all the better arguments to me seem to lie on the side of the opponents. In what follows, I will briefly sketch some of them. The aim of this is not to provide a thorough discussion of the matter (which would require a paper of its own) nor do my remarks add up to an argument in any way. They will remain rather selective and one-sided, which however will do for present purposes, namely to clear the ground for turning to a Kantian conception of human rights.

Assuming that Kant had a human rights-conception: What would one expect to find in his work, and where would one expect to find it? Let us first recall what one does clearly *not* find in his writings: Kant did not work out a human rights-

---

[8] All references to Kant follow the pagination of the Akademie-Ausgabe. All translations are taken from Kant 1996a.

theory, nor did he explicitly and systematically introduce a concept of human rights. He uses expressions like *"Menschenrecht"* (e.g. MM 6:321), yet not in the sense of a subjective right of individuals. He does not develop a list of human rights as did for instance John Locke and political declarations at the time. Finally, he does not express his unequivocal commitment to (the major implications of) the human rights-idea (cf. Horn 2014, pp. 68–84).

The concept of a (moral) human right has direct implications with regard to states and their legislation, especially in light of its feature of categoricity or overridingness.[9] Clearly, it would be contradictory to assume that all human beings have moral human rights if there did not exist a corresponding moral obligation whatsoever to ensure that they can actually enjoy (the objects of) their rights, i.e. to realize their enforcement.[10] For this reason, laws and legal systems ought to be *compatible* with human rights, i.e. they may not violate them, and they ought to *protect* them. From a human rights-perspective a state and its laws are not morally legitimate unless they meet these two requirements. Crucially, the concept of a moral human right hence implies a moral concept of legal legitimacy: It is an immediate consequence of the human rights-idea that legitimate law must be founded on (the recognition of) moral human rights (although it can of course be disputed in what way precisely they might function as such a foundation).[11]

The human rights-concept is then, among others, a concept of political morality that carries a particular view on the relationship between morality and law. The question whether Kant possesses (and endorses) such a concept can be taken up from two angles: by looking at the foundation(s) of the legal system or at features of the resulting state. For both clues Kant's *Doctrine of Right* is the obvious place to start out, and I will focus on this work exclusively in what follows.

The *Doctrine of Right* has the declared aim to establish the a priori principles of right upon which a possible positive legislation ought to be built (MM 6:230). Here Kant mentions in one single passage what a number of interpreters hold to

---

9 For pragmatic reasons I do not distinguish here between states on the one hand and their legislation, laws and legal systems on the other; it is clear that this largely simplifies the matter.
10 Needless to say, this raises difficult questions about who the relevant duty-bearers are, what their duties amount to, and so on. I cannot discuss these issues here.
11 I distinguish a moral concept of legal legitimacy from a moral concept of law: The claim is not that only morally legitimate law counts as law (for this is not necessarily implied in a concept of moral human rights). Rather, the claim is that what counts as *legally* legitimate can at least partly be reduced to what is *morally* legitimate and what is morally legitimate is again at least partly understood in terms of moral human rights.

be the most promising or even the only true candidate for a human right in Kant, namely the right to freedom (MM 6:237–238). Kant writes:

> *There is only one innate right.*
> *Freedom* (independence from being constrained by another's choice), insofar as it can coexist with the freedom of every other in accordance with a universal law, is the only original right belonging to every man by virtue of his humanity. (MM 6:237)

He goes on to list several "authorizations" which "[t]his principle of innate freedom already involves" and "which are not really distinct from it (as if they were members of the division of some higher concept of a right)" (MM 6:238) – among them: "innate *equality*, that is, independence from being bound by others to more than one can in turn bind them", and "being a human being *beyond reproach* [...], since before he performs any act affecting rights he has done no wrong to anyone" (MM 6:237–238). In short, according to some interpreters the natural right ("innate") to freedom is a moral human right ("belonging to every man by virtue of his humanity") or a principle of human rights from which Kant derives a number of lower-level rights ("authorizations") that constitute the foundation (in the dual sense of justification and basis) of the state to be erected.

If the right to freedom were a human right and as such the foundation of Kant's state we should expect him to spell out (1) at least some of the concrete substantive rights that follow from it, and (2) how it affects the positive legal order. Yet this is not what he does. Regarding (1), the "authorizations" just mentioned are purely formal principles, and they are highly indeterminate content-wise. For instance, the "innate equality" of human beings does not point to any material standard of non-discrimination (of human beings as human beings) or equal wellbeing. Rather, Kant refers here to a formal principle of reciprocity as part of his concept of law (cf. Horn 2014, p. 115; Flikschuh 2015, p. 663). Accordingly, "these 'authorizations' essentially set out aspects of persons' equality in formal juridical status", e.g. "formal equality before the law" (Flikschuh 2015, p. 662). This suggests that the right to freedom cannot be properly interpreted as a human right. Instead, this right and its implications specify the abstract, procedural and formal principles which a legal order that regulates the external actions of free individuals presupposes.[12] In this sense they constitute something

---

[12] In this essay I use the terms "external" and "internal" exclusively with regard to actions, and always in the following sense: The external aspect of actions regards bodily movements in space (e.g. the movement of an arm), including the interpretation of this movement as a specific action. The internal aspect of actions regards the reasons and motives that underlie them.

like the "core" of Kant's state but not in the sense of a human rights-idea. This interpretation is also supported by the fact that (2) the right to freedom does not play *any* role in the main text of the *Doctrine of Right* and hence *in* Kant's state. (See on this Flikschuh 2015, pp. 662–663.)

Let me briefly mention two other objections that support this argument before moving on. First, there is Kant's notorious rejection of a right to resistance. There can be no doubt that Kant does radically reject such a right, and it should be noted that he rejects it both as a moral and as a legal right (cf. MM 6:318–323). No matter how one attempts to make sense of Kant's position, it remains strictly incompatible with our contemporary understanding of human rights. Secondly, Kant ties the possession of (legal) fundamental rights on a domestic level in a peculiar way to the possession of (active) citizenship. It is crucial here who counts as a citizen: In order to be a citizen one has to be "fit to vote"; this presupposes "civil independence" [*bürgerliche Selbständigkeit*], which means nothing but *economic* independence; for only then does one have a "civil personality" (MM 6:314–315). In short, fundamental rights are not grounded in the human but in the civil personality, and consequently they are legally guaranteed only to economically independent members of the community. The fact that all human beings are free and equal (MM 6:315) does hence not lead to their legal recognition as free and equal citizens. Again, this is incompatible with the way "our" human rights are commonly supposed to work on the domestic level.[13] All of this suggests that the assumption that Kant advocated a human rights-idea does not sustain critical scrutiny.

2 A Kantian Theory of Human Rights?

A much more promising line of arguing is to defend the view that a human rights-theory follows from certain core elements of Kant's philosophical thinking. Again, here I can only hint at what such a theory might look like. Whether we *need* a Kantian theory of human rights is clearly a question of its own. However, if we intend to make Kant's philosophy fertile for current thought about human rights then we should go with the widespread intuition that there is something about his philosophy that makes one think he *should* have been a de-

---

[13] The interesting point here is that Kant does not exclude members of a state who lack civil personality, i.e. "passive citizens" from the group of human or rational beings, but he does not grant them fundamental rights. This makes this case different from e.g. his view on women who are not regarded as rational in the first place.

fender of human rights – we should just not mix that up with the assumption that he *was*.

Whether one deems a Kantian theory of human rights to be possible largely depends on what one understands as the core elements of his philosophy. For instance, Andrea Sangiovanni has recently defended the position that "there cannot be a truly Kantian theory of human rights" (Sangiovanni 2015), because in his view it would only then be "truly Kantian" if it

> remains faithful to three constituent planks of Kant's practical philosophy, namely, (1) Kant's division between the domain of morality and the domain of right, (2) Kant's arguments for our moral obligation to exit the state of nature, and (3) Kant's arguments for unitary sovereignty. (Sangiovanni 2015, p. 671)

Apart from reservations about the first point I largely agree with Sangiovanni that these aspects of Kant's philosophy are indeed hardly compatible with a human rights-theory. The difference is that I do not regard them as "constituent planks of Kant's practical philosophy". They *might* be constitutive of his *political* philosophy (the first feature clearly is, though I hesitate to agree with how Sangiovanni reconstructs it). However, this just pushes the question one level up: How far can and should Kant's political philosophy be considered a "constituent plank" of his practical philosophy at all? In my view, in order to keep the distinction between "Kant's" and "Kantian" philosophy productive we should (re)construct the relevant Kantian premises as cautiously and sparingly as possible. Briefly, in light of the well-known interpretative and substantive problems with the *Doctrine of Right* this speaks for a certain priority of his (early) ethical writings when it comes to formulating these premises.

I want to suggest then that there are three such premises that arise from Kant's practical philosophy as a whole. The first is his method of transcendental arguing or the way he ties his ethical considerations to what it means for every one of us to be a being with practical reason. The second premise is the categoricity of moral norms, as instantiated first and foremost by the Categorical Imperative. The third feature – which I am somewhat uncertain about – is the priority of duties to rights. Generally speaking, a moral theory of human rights that is in line with these three requirements might well be referred to as Kantian.[14]

---

[14] Needless to say, the question which features ought to be included and which not is disputable and ultimately a matter of degree. Yet I clearly plead for concentrating on the bigger picture of Kant's practical philosophy when selecting them. Otherwise we run the risk of carrying over a whole range of interpretative problems regarding Kant's philosophy to a Kantian philosophy, which might ultimately undermine the very point of the latter.

Why am I uncertain about the third feature? In order to be a theory *of human rights* (in the sense explained above) the relevant moral theory needs to meet two major challenges: to justify the step from duties to rights and from (a specific conception of) morality to (a specific conception of) law. The second challenge concerns the debate about the relationship between morality and law in Kant. Very briefly and in simplified terms, the opposing positions in this debate can be summarized like this: According to the proponents of the "Inseparability Thesis" or "Derivation View" Kant derives the a priori principles of right from the Categorical Imperative. Consequently, the latter serves as the sole moral standard both for moral and legal norms. In contrast to this, proponents of the "Separability Thesis" or "Independency Thesis" defend the view that Kant justifies both kinds of norms by reference to different standards, at least to some extent. Consequently, the Categorical Imperative forfeits its absolute status as the highest and uncircumventable moral guideline. For present purposes it should be noted that this debate also (and crucially) concerns the question to what extent in the *Doctrine of Right* Kant departed from his earlier ethical position as exemplified in particular in the *Groundwork*. In light of the latter work it would be impossible to assert that a (legal) norm might be morally legitimate even though it does not conform to the Categorical Imperative. Briefly, what follows from this is that to some extent it simply does not matter for a Kantian theory of human rights what Kant's actual view on these matters was. Rather, suffice it to say that only the Derivation View is compatible with his earlier ethical position, in particular with the categoricity of moral norms. Consequently, some version of the Derivation View must constitute one pillar of a Kantian theory of human rights and will be presupposed in what follows.

Quite the opposite applies concerning the question how (human) rights can be derived from (categorical) duties. It is undisputed that Kant champions the priority of duties to rights as regards their justification (hence the talk of the notorious "duty-centeredness" of his practical philosophy) (cf. MM 6:239, MMV 27:521). Whereas this interpretative claim is thus clearly correct, the systematic question if rights can be derived from duties is highly controversial: How do you get from the assumption that you have a categorical moral duty to the assumption that you have a corresponding moral right? This is why I wonder if Kant's principle of the priority of duties to rights should also be considered a Kantian principle (or whether it might be dropped): On the one hand, it is important for his practical philosophy as a whole, also if one considers its "spirit". On the other hand, I doubt that it is important enough to justify the impossibility of a Kantian theory of human rights in case the derivation of moral rights from moral duties turns out to be impossible.[15] As I cannot further discuss this point here for the rest of this paper I will assume that such a derivation is indeed possible. Of the three premises mentioned above I will leave the first, methodological premise out of consideration. The second and third premise can be summarized in one thesis that I conveniently refer to as the "Foundational Claim of Kant's Ethics": *"The Categorical Imperative is the ultimate foundation of moral duties."* The term "ultimate" indicates that there is no higher moral principle than the Categorical Imperative. I use the term "duties" instead of "norms" to indicate that they are prior to rights. We can then say that there is at least one necessary condition that the claim that *respect* is the foundation of Kantian human rights has to meet in order to be plausible: It needs to be compatible with the Foundational Claim of Kant's Ethics. I will come back to this condition in section 4.

Against this background, in a highly condensed fashion the large contours of a Kantian theory of human rights might look like this. The theory starts with the assumption that we cannot coherently deny the truth of certain moral claims unless we also want to deny that we are beings with practical reason (which we cannot coherently deny in the first place). The moral claims in question assert that all human beings categorically ought to be treated in a particular way. The reason for this is that anything else would be incompatible with their self-understanding as beings with practical reason. The latter hence confers a particular moral status to them. Starting from the fundamental moral obligation just mentioned this status can be interpreted as that of a right-holder, which means that all human beings have certain moral human rights. Let us now consider how respect in Kant's terms might fit into that framework as a foundation.

3 Two Ways to Understand the Foundational Claim about Respect

To begin with, one might wonder why of all notions in Kant respect should be taken into account as a moral foundation of (Kantian) human rights. The concept of respect for persons is commonly associated with Kant's ethics in two different yet related senses. First, it serves as a non-literal circumscription of the moral requirement that Kant expresses in the so called "Humanity Formula", i.e. one of the "formulas" of the Categorical Imperative that he develops in the *Ground-*

---

[15] Furthermore, one might wonder if replacing moral duties with rights at the top of the chain of moral norms would really be so "un-Kantian" after all. Would we for example not regard Gewirth's moral theory as Kantian? That would seem like a counterintuitive result.

work. The Humanity Formula famously states: "So act that you use humanity, whether in your own person or in the person of any other, always at the same time as an end, never merely as a means." (G 8:429, emphasis deleted) Although it does not contain the term "respect", the content of this formula is usually (and rightly) understood as the moral obligation to *respect* human beings in a particular way, namely as "ends in themselves" or persons (cf. G 8:428–431). What this might mean and imply specifically is a question that, though doubtlessly crucial, is negligible for present purposes. All that matters here is that the idea of human beings as ends in themselves occupies a central place in Kant's ethics and that from here it seems just a small step to the assumption that the respect we owe to one another as persons is the reason why we ought to attribute to every human being certain fundamental moral rights.

The second sense is literal: "Respect" [*Achtung*] figures prominently in Kant's ethics as the only possible motive or "drive" [*Triebfeder*] to morally good action, or (which amounts to the same in Kant's terms) the only morally good motive for action (G 8:400–403, CPrR 5:71–89). Consequently, this concept of respect that corresponds to "respect" as a technical term of Kant's ethics must be understood in the specific context of his theory of moral motivation.[16]

In both senses respect for persons plays a central role in Kant's ethics and hence clearly qualifies as a possible candidate for a moral foundation of Kantian human rights. However, it is important to note that there are at least prima facie two different concepts of respect at stake here, and accordingly two different foundational claims. In what follows I will first address them separately and then consider how they relate.

How does respect for persons, understood in the context of the Humanity Formula, translate into a foundational claim? What does it mean to regard respect in *this* sense as the foundation of human rights? Essentially the answer is quite straightforward. In the *Groundwork* Kant contrasts beings with reason or a (partly) rational nature, i.e. "persons", with beings and entities that lack reason, i.e. "things" (G 8:428). He argues that only the former are "objective ends" or "ends in themselves" (as opposed to "subjective" and "relative ends") and that only they have "absolute worth" (as opposed to a worth that is relative to someone's ends). (G 8:427–428) Leaving all details of Kant's argument (and a myriad of interpretative issues) aside, this is so because by virtue of their capacity to reason [*Vernunftvermögen*] human and all other rational beings are capable of acting in accordance with the moral law (for the moral law de-

---

[16] Kant neither developed a theory of action in general nor a theory of motivation in particular. For a systematic reconstruction of both from Kant's works cf. Willaschek 1992.

mands just what pure practical reason demands).[17] Consequently, only they have the power to realize that which alone is unconditionally good in the world, namely a "good will" or what Kant later calls "pure practical reason". According to the dominant interpretation and contrary to our language use today, Kant uses the term "humanity" to signify precisely this capacity of pure practical reason (Hill 1992, pp. 38–41; Mohr 2007, pp. 18–19). The Humanity Formula then expresses the categorical moral obligation to always also treat any person as an end, never merely as a means, due to him or her *being* a person, i.e. a being with the capacity to act morally. Persons, in other words, should be *respected as* persons. Consequently, the foundational claim in terms of this concept of respect ("Foundational Claim I") states that it is implied in or follows from this moral obligation that every person is a bearer of human rights. Put somewhat more schematically, this variant of the claim then takes the following form: *"The categorical moral obligation to respect persons is the moral foundation for the ascription of moral human rights."* Let us now turn to the second version of this claim and then consider how the two of them relate.

As mentioned above, the concept of respect (for persons or the moral law) figures centrally in Kant's ethics as the unique motive or drive to morally good action. Famously, according to Kant for an action to have moral worth it is not sufficient that it externally conforms to what the moral law demands. Rather, a morally good action is performed precisely because the moral law demands that it be performed – it is not only "in conformity with duty" [*pflichtgemäß*] but "from duty" [*aus Pflicht*]. Hence, decisive for the moral worth of an action is the *motive* or the property of the *will* that underlies it.

In order to determine more precisely the systematic place of the concept of respect in Kant's ethics we need to have a closer look at how this moral requirement relates to Kant's theory of action, and in particular his theory of motivation. Central in this regard is Kant's concept of a "determination of the will" [*Willensbestimmung*] (cf. Horn 2002). The expression reads as a *genitivus objectivus* (the will *is determined* – though in an action from duty "by itself") and roughly means "choice" (for a particular action). According to Kant, one can generally distinguish two different levels or aspects of the will of a sensual-rational being (like a human being) (Allison 1990, pp. 120–128). The first is a cognitive aspect: Human beings act on the basis of rational practical principles, i.e. "imperatives" in Kant's terminology. These principles are either prudential ("hypothetical imperatives") or moral ("categorical imperatives") in kind. They regard

---

[17] I am using the terms "willing" and "acting" interchangeably here; it should be clear in each case if I refer to an internal or external action.

the *reasons* for a particular course of action, as provided e.g. by moral considerations, reflections on ends-means-relationships, and so on. In as much as this aspect of volition is concerned Kant speaks of an "objective determination of the will".

As distinguished from this, the will also has a conative or motivational aspect. According to Kant, rational principles alone cannot "move" sensual-rational beings to action. For this it takes a *sensual* drive, i.e. some kind of *feeling*. In so far as this level of volition is concerned Kant refers to a "subjective determination of the will".

It is important to see that both aspects must always be present in any determination of the will to action, be it moral or prudential. In the case of actions against or in conformity with duty the conative aspect of volition is provided by an "inclination" [*Neigung*]. However, inclinations or "empirical feelings" are precisely what must not determine the will in the case of a morally good action, for then it would not be from duty. Therefore, taken together this moral requirement and the motivational requirement just sketched seem to pose a dilemma.

Kant solves this dilemma by introducing the motive of respect (for the moral law or persons). Respect is the only feeling that is produced by reason, more precisely: by the insight into the superiority of the moral law. Kant also calls it a "self-produced feeling" (G 8:400), and as such it is a priori. Furthermore, as a motive respect is intentionally directed exclusively towards the realization of the demands of the moral law. Finally, respect is the only feeling of this kind and hence the only genuine "moral feeling" or "moral drive" (CPrR 5:78, 85): As a *feeling* it fulfills the motivational condition that a conative or sensual aspect of volition is part of any determination to action. As a feeling that is *produced by reason* it fulfills the moral condition that no (empirical) inclinations may be part of the determination of the will to a morally good action.

This short sketch shows that within Kant's theory of motivation the emergence of respect as a moral incentive is inseparably connected with the recognition of the superiority of the moral law, and thus with the Categorical Imperative: Actions that are performed for the sake of the moral law are actions out of respect (for the moral law or persons) and vice versa. Put differently, an action that is (objectively) determined by the Categorical Imperative is always at the same time an action that is (subjectively) determined by respect. To act "from duty" means to act "from respect".

What does a foundational claim in terms of this notion of respect amount to? To begin with, the preceding considerations make it clear that the foundational claim as formulated with regard to the Humanity Formula (Foundational Claim I) cannot simply be transferred to the concept of respect as a moral drive: If "foundation" signifies "morally justifying ground" then respect in the latter sense cannot serve as a foundation of human rights. In contrast to a practical principle a (sensual) motive in itself is nothing normative and hence cannot play a central role in moral justification.[18] This applies regardless of respect being a *moral* incentive: The qualifier "moral" tells us something about its origin and function yet it does not affect the kind of entity that respect is. Consequently, we need to formulate the second claim ("Foundational Claim II") as follows in order to bring it in line with Kant's understanding of respect: *"The categorical moral obligation to act out of respect for persons is the moral foundation for the ascription of moral human rights."*

On the face of it the two claims now look almost equivalent. But do they really mean the same? The gap between "to respect" (Foundational Claim I) and "to *act out of* respect" (Foundational Claim II) invites the following objection: Both claims entail a moral duty (to respect persons). However, only the second claim additionally entails the duty to respect persons *out of* respect for them, i.e. to act as the moral duty demands because it demands it. In other words, the first claim relates to a morally *legitimate*, the second to a morally good or *worthy* action. Therefore – so the objection goes – the two foundational claims are not equivalent.

However, this anticipated objection does not hold for the following reason. On the level of the description of an action we can distinguish between actions that only externally comply with a categorical obligation (actions in conformity with duty) and actions that also internally comply with it (actions from duty). However, this distinction does not apply once we consider an action on the level of obligation, i.e. we ask what practical principle or imperative underlies the action. What the Categorical Imperative demands is to adopt only such maxims that are universalizable. To act under a maxim only under the condition that it is universalizable means nothing else than to act "from duty": The maxim is adopted because of its moral rightness, which is precisely what the Categorical Imperative requires. In contrast to this, acting on a maxim that is not universalizable does certainly not exclude that one ends up acting in conformity with duty. However, it does exclude that the action follows the Categorical Imperative. From this it is clear that only morally worthy actions that internally conform to the moral law follow a Categorical Imperative, whereas all others ultimately stem from a prudential practical principle. As has been shown above, actions "from the Categorical Imperative" are always at the same time actions "from respect", and the Humanity Formula is just one variant of this very imperative. Conse-

---

[18] I assume here without argument that nothing that is non-propositional like a feeling can serve as a justification in this sense.

quently, from Kant's perspective there simply is no other option than to respect persons *out of* respect for them, as long as the level of obligation is concerned.

The difference between the two foundational claims then comes down to a matter of emphasis: One claim stresses the (rational) reason, the other the (sensual) motive for action. But in obligational terms their contents amount to precisely the same. The two claims might then be summarized to one more comprehensive claim ("Foundational Claim"): *"The categorical moral obligation to respect persons out of respect for them is the moral foundation for the ascription of moral human rights."*

This formulation invites a second objection. In its current form (and in line with the preceding considerations) the Foundational Claim contains a reference to respect as a motive of action. Put differently, if the Foundational Claim pertains then the justifiability of the assumption that there are moral human rights depends not only on a moral obligation to act in a specific way but also to do so out of a specific motive. This might entail a certain tension with regard to the assumption that moral human rights point, in one way or another, to positive legislation – which implies that the Foundational Claim explicates to some extent the foundation of a morally qualified legal system as well. Why might there be a tension?

In the *Metaphysics of Morals* Kant famously distinguishes between "duties of virtue" and "duties of right" (MM 6:218–221, 239–240). The juridical realm is made up of norms or rules that are (legally) enforceable. Yet enforceable are only external actions and not the motives out of which they are performed. It is therefore the role of motives that distinguishes ethical from juridical duties: From an ethical standpoint the moral worth of an action depends entirely on the underlying motive. In contrast to this, from a legal standpoint the motive is completely irrelevant as long as one acts in accordance with the legal norm. Consequently, the *motive* of respect does not seem to play any role for a legal system and the duties of right that it contains. How could it then be part of its foundation?

The resolution of this alleged tension leads at the same time to a clearer idea in what ways respect might serve as the foundation of a human rights-based legal system, and in what ways not. From a juridical perspective there cannot be a legal obligation to follow legal duties out of the moral motive of respect. However, this does not mean that we might not be morally required to do so (cf. Höffe 2006, pp. 87–91).[19] In short, there is no tension or even contradiction

---

19 In fact, at least part of the troubles with Kant's rejection of a right to resistance arise on the basis of precisely this assumption: We are morally obliged to follow laws that are morally appropriate, hence we are equally morally obliged to resist laws that are not.

in holding that from an ethical perspective there is a moral obligation to act in accordance with each other's legal rights out of respect whereas from a juridical perspective there is only a more limited legal obligation to act in accordance with each other's legal rights.

What does this tell us about the relationship between respect for persons and the legal realm, broadly defined? We need to distinguish between three aspects of the legal realm that this question might concern: its establishment (1), its moral property (2) and the legal duties that it contains (3). To the extent that it is true that everyone's moral human rights can only or much more effectively be protected under legal conditions (as opposed to some state of nature) the Foundational Claim applies to the establishment of a legal system as well (1). If moral human rights are justified by respect (as specified in the Foundational Claim) and the concept of a moral human right implies the concept of a correlative moral obligation to its protection, then indirectly the categorical moral obligation to respect persons (out of respect for them) justifies the establishment of a legal system. (Directly it is justified by moral human rights.) However, it goes without saying that respect does not justify just any legal system but only one that protects moral human rights (therefore, again, the troubles with Kant's rejection of a right to resistance). Hence the Foundational Claim only applies to (1) in combination with (2) (it justifies a *human rights-based* system of law). Finally, regarding (3) the answer is multi-layered: Respect justifies the *existence* of legal duties inasmuch as they serve the purpose of (1) and (2). Under this condition, it also justifies a *moral* obligation to act in accordance with those legal duties *out of respect*. However, it does *not* justify a *legal* obligation to act in accordance with them out of respect, because this is precisely what a juridical perspective cannot provide.

4 Respect and Human Dignity

On this basis it is now possible to evaluate the plausibility of the Foundational Claim. In light of the limited scope my considerations will have to be brief.

One simple fact that speaks in favor of respect as a foundation of Kantian human rights is that in both of its meanings it figures so centrally in Kant's ethical work. This matters because whatever the details of the relevant human rights-theory might be one should expect the human rights-idea around which it revolves to be (morally) justified by considerations that are central to Kant's ethical thought. There are only a couple of other candidates that fulfill this criterion, such as the concept of a Categorical Imperative, of an end in itself, of human dignity and of autonomy. It is an important feature of both concepts of respect that *at least* with the first two alternative candidates they are conceptually so intimately intertwined that the Foundational Claim encompasses foundational claims in their terms as well (which does not make them real alternatives after all). This is particularly important with regard to the Categorical Imperative: In as much as it describes the content of the Humanity Formula, respect or the moral obligation to respect persons is *nothing but* one version of the Categorical Imperative. Similarly, respect as a moral incentive is *inseparably bound* to the Categorical Imperative insofar as an action from duty *is* an action from respect. Consequently, the Foundational Claim is fully compatible with the Foundational Claim of Kant's Ethics: It does not undermine the absolute priority of the Categorical Imperative regarding the justification of moral norms, and with that neither does it touch the priority of duties to rights.

It might be argued that this compatibility gives the Foundational Claim a certain advantage against its most prominent competitor, namely the claim that *human dignity* is the foundation of – here: Kantian – human rights. Let me finally consider the plausibility of this assumption.

The last years have seen an intensified scholarly discussion about whether the "contemporary paradigm of dignity" (Sensen 2009, p. 312) is properly attributed to Kant. According to this paradigm, human dignity is a particularly high or absolute value of all human beings that justifies that they have human rights. In other words, "human dignity is a non-relational value property human beings possess that generates normative requirements to respect them" (Sensen 2009, p. 312). Apart from criticisms based on how Kant actually uses the term "dignity", the ascription of this view to Kant has provoked two substantive objections, among others: First, it conflicts with Kant's view on the priority of duties to rights; and secondly, it replaces the absolute normative priority of the Categorical Imperative (i.e. a principle of right) with a value (i.e. a principle of the good) (cf. Sensen 2009). The foundational claim about human dignity is hence incompatible with what I called the Foundational Claim of Kant's Ethics.

I believe that this critique is apt. Consequently, in the version just presented the foundational claim about human dignity should be rejected, both as a Kantian and as Kant's position. However, this does not mean that there cannot be a different, more plausible version of this claim; nor does this presuppose that the concept of human dignity that it implies is in line with Kant's usage of the term "human dignity". Instead, as indicated in the end of section 2, human dignity might be understood as a particular *status* (cf. Waldron 2013, pp. 24–27), for instance the status of being a *right-holder* (i.e. a holder of moral human rights), which again might follow from or be implied in the status of being a *person* that ought to be *respected*. Far from being implausible, *this* foundational claim about human dignity might then itself be either implied in or equivalent to the foundational claim about respect.

5 Conclusion

I started from the assumption that it is highly unlikely that Kant was a defender of human rights, understood as an exegetical thesis: There is insufficient textual evidence for this view, and it substantively contradicts important theorems of his political philosophy. Nevertheless, there are good reasons to assume that there can be a Kantian theory of human rights, based on a further systematic development of certain constitutive elements of Kant's practical philosophy. I have argued that there are three such elements: A methodological requirement which I have here left out of consideration, the categoricity of moral duties, and the priority of duties to rights. I have summarized the second and third element in the "Foundational Claim of Kant's Ethics": "The Categorical Imperative is the ultimate foundation of moral duties." I have also argued that apart from this any Kantian theory of human rights needs to assume some version of the Derivation View.

In a second step I have asked what the claim might mean that respect, (re-)constructed in Kant's terms, is the foundation of moral human rights, constructed in Kantian terms, and if it might be plausible. Section 3 was mainly devoted to the first part of this question. The leading assumption here was that the claim that according to Kant respect is the foundation of human rights is easily made in passing, but that it acquires a very specific meaning once it is systematically reconstructed in Kant's terms. I have explained the meaning of the claim by distinguishing two concepts of respect in Kant and two foundational claims accordingly, which turned out to be reducible to the one I coined the Foundational Claim. I have defended the Foundational Claim against two objections and hinted at what it might imply with regard to the legal realm.

In section 4 I came to the conclusion that it is indeed plausible to assume that respect is the foundation of Kantian human rights. Finally, I suggested that this claim might be equivalent to the – allegedly competing – claim that human dignity is the foundation of Kantian human rights, as long as the latter would be based on a Kantian rather than on Kant's concept of human dignity.

Bibliography

Allison, H. E. (1990): *Kant's Theory of Freedom*, Cambridge: Cambridge University Press.
Buchanan, A. (2013): *The Heart of Human Rights*, Oxford-New York: Oxford University Press.
Cruft, R., Liao, S. M. and Renzo, M. (Eds.) (2015): *Philosophical Foundations of Human Rights*, Oxford-New York: Oxford University Press.
Flikschuh, K. (2015): "Human Rights in Kantian Mode. A Sketch". In R. Cruft, S. M. Liao and M. Renzo (Eds.) (2015): *Philosophical Foundations of Human Rights*, Oxford/New York: Oxford University Press, pp. 653–670.
Gewirth, A. (1982): "Are There Any Absolute Rights?". In A. Gewirth: *Human Rights. Essays on Justification and Applications*, Chicago-London: The University of Chicago Press, pp. 218–233.
Griffin, J. (2008): *On Human Rights*, Oxford-New York: Oxford University Press.
Hill, T. E. (1992): *Dignity and Practical Reason in Kant's Moral Theory*, Ithaca-London: Cornell University Press.
Höffe, O. (2006): *Kant's Cosmopolitan Theory of Law and Peace*, Cambridge et al.: Cambridge University Press.
Horn, C. (2002): "Wille, Willensbestimmung, Begehrungsvermögen (§§ 1–3, 19–26)". In O. Höffe (Ed.) (2002): *Immanuel Kant. Kritik der praktischen Vernunft*, Berlin: Akademie, pp. 43–61.
Horn, C. (2014): *Nichtideale Normativität. Ein neuer Blick auf Kants politische Philosophie*, Berlin: Suhrkamp.
Kant, I. (1996a): *Practical Philosophy*, trans. and ed. by M. J. Gregor, Cambridge: Cambridge University Press.
Kant, I. (1996b): "Critique of Practical Reason (1788)". In Immanuel Kant: *Practical Philosophy*, trans. and ed. by M. J. Gregor, Cambridge: Cambridge University Press, pp. 133–272.
Kant, I. (1996c): "Groundwork of the Metaphysics of Morals (1785)". In I. Kant: *Practical Philosophy*, trans. and ed. by M. J. Gregor, Cambridge: Cambridge University Press, pp. 37–108.
Kant, I. (1996d): "The Metaphysics of Morals (1797)". In I. Kant: *Practical Philosophy*, trans. and ed. by M. J. Gregor, Cambridge: Cambridge University Press, pp. 353–604.
Kant, I. (1996e): "Toward Perpetual Peace (1795)". In I. Kant: *Practical Philosophy*, trans. and ed. by M. J. Gregor, Cambridge: Cambridge University Press, pp. 311–351.
Kant, I.. (1997): "Kant on the Metaphysics of Morals: Vigilantius's Lecture Notes (1793–94)". In I. Kant: *Lectures on Ethics*, trans. by P. Heath, Cambridge: Cambridge University Press, pp. 249–452.
Mohr, G. (2007): "Ein 'Wert, der keinen Preis hat' – Philosophiegeschichtliche Grundlagen der Menschenwürde bei Kant und Fichte". In H. J. Sandkühler (Ed.): *Menschenwürde. Philosophische, theologische und juristische Analysen*, Frankfurt a.M.: Peter Lang, pp. 13–39.
Sangiovanni, A. (2015): "Why there Cannot be a Truly Kantian Theory of Human Rights". In R. Cruft, S. M. Liao and M. Renzo (Eds.): *Philosophical Foundations of Human Rights*, Oxford: Oxford University Press, pp. 671–689.
Sensen, O. (2009): "Kant's Conception of Human Dignity", *Kant-Studien* 100, pp. 309–331.

Waldron, J. (2013): "Is Dignity the Foundation of Human Rights?", *Public Law and Legal Theory Research Paper Series*. Working Paper No. 12–73. Available at: http://ssrn.com/abstract=2196074, accessed 04/03/2016.

Willaschek, M. (1992): *Praktische Vernunft. Handlungstheorie und Moralbegründung bei Kant*, Stuttgart-Weimar: Metzler.

Part III: From Modern to Contemporary Perspectives on Respect

Arto Laitinen
Hegel and Respect for Persons

Abstract: This essay discusses Hegel's theory of "abstract" respect for "abstract" personhood and its relation to the fuller, concrete account of human personhood. Hegel defines (abstract) personhood as an abstract, formal category with the help of his account of free will. For Hegel, personhood is defined in terms of powers, relations to self and to others. After analyzing what according to the first part of *Philosophy of Right* it is to (abstractly) respect someone as a person, the essay discusses the implications for private property and market. Then the paper turns to discuss pathologies of ideologies that stress these aspects only. Finally, the essay discusses the way in which Hegel's full social theory aims to overcome such pathological tendencies; most notably in his theory of Family and the State.

Hegel, following Fichte's initiative, developed an intersubjectivist account of human personhood, where relations of recognition are constitutive of personhood. Personhood is not merely a social status: it is also constituted by capacities and relations to self (see Ikäheimo and Laitinen 2007).

Hegel's *Philosophy of Right* puts forward a *multidimensional* account of relations of recognition, which concern different aspects of human personhood or selfhood and human freedom. Mutual respect, alongside social esteem and love, is for Hegel to be analyzed as one form that mutual recognition can take (see Honneth 1992, 2014; Siep 2014). And further, respect comes in different forms; some forms of recognition are clearly forms of respect (abstract respect for personhood, moral respect for autonomous subjectivity) whereas some others are forms of respect more contestable (possible forms of respect that are constitutive of aspects of ethical life such as civil society and state).

Philosophy of Right has three main parts. First, what Hegel calls *abstract right* concerns external legal personhood and negative liberty, and secondly *morality, Moralität*, concerns more or less Kantian self-determining moral subjectivity and inner "reflective freedom".[1] Both these spheres are constituted as forms of mutual recognition that can be approached as forms of respect: respect for abstract personhood and respect for autonomous moral subjectivity (nowadays also called moral personhood). Legal personhood is best understood as a protec-

---
1 See Honneth 2014.

tive mask, and moral subjectivity as a set of inner capacities – they both fall short of the concreteness and detail of actual ethical life, which is analyzed in the third part of *Philosophy of Right*.

Thirdly, *Sittlichkeit* or *ethical life* concerns humans in particular concrete roles, as members of family, civil society and the state. In contrast to mere negative liberty or the reflective freedom, they constitute forms of "social freedom" (Honneth 2014, Neuhouser 2000). Each of these aspects of ethical life is constituted by relations of recognition: love is constitutive of family, arguably a kind of respect is constitutive of market relations, bonds of solidarity and social esteem are constitutive of division of social labor, and further universal concern – and for contemporary Hegelians, respect for democratic participation – is constitutive of the state (see Honneth 1992, Knowles 2002).

It is therefore important to distinguish the *abstract* personal respect – presented in the section of Abstract Right – not only from other "thicker" forms of recognition such as esteem, love, or solidarity, but also from other forms of recognition that can appropriately be called "respect": respect for moral subjectivity, and respect for each other as democratic members in collective self-determination (which is not part of Hegel's story, but is stressed e.g. by Honneth 2014 and Habermas 1996). Further, the pre-institutionalized form of respect in Abstract Right, taken in abstraction from institutional structures, resembles forms of respect in concrete market relations as realized by economic institutions.

It is well understood that the main specificity of Hegel's ethical and political philosophy is the way that *Sittlichkeit* supersedes *Moralität*, echoed in the communitarian criticism of atomistic tendencies in liberalism. Another much discussed topic in the debates on mutual recognition is Hegel's defense of the sociality of self-consciousness in *Phenomenology of Spirit*, in terms of a struggle for recognition. Hegel's account of abstract personhood in *abstract right* has been less discussed but is worth serious attention, together with Hegel's analysis of morality and recognition of moral responsibility.

This essay will focus on Hegel's "abstract" respect for "abstract" personhood, and its relation to the fuller, concrete account of human personhood. Hegel defines (abstract) personhood as an abstract, formal category with the help of his account of free will. Like Rawls (1972, 1993), for whom persons have two powers, for Hegel personhood is defined in terms of powers, but Hegel differs in also holding relations to self and to others as constitutive: mere capacities do not suffice (presented in sections 1–2 in this essay).[2] After

---

[2] Further, for Hegel "personhood" has metaphysical significance: it is one layer in the realiza-

that this essay will analyze what according to the first part of *Philosophy of Right* it is to (abstractly) respect someone as a person (section 3), and what the implications of this for private property and market are (section 4). Then it turns to discuss the pathologies of an ideology of a roughly Neo-Liberal kind that stresses these aspects only (section 5) and also the way that Hegel's full social theory of *Sittlichkeit* and *Social Freedom* aims to overcome such pathological tendencies; most notably in his theory of Family and the State (section 6).

It is in the context of this fuller theory that we can understand why Hegel in *The Philosophy of Right* (§ 35 A) claims that being a person is "the highest achievement of a human being" and yet in his *Phenomenology of Spirit* writes that "to describe an individual as a 'person' is an expression of contempt".[3] We have other identities than (abstract) personhood that capture our being more fully, but nonetheless respect for (abstract) personhood constitutes a significant protective mask or shell for our existence.

1 The Structure of Free Will

As for Rawls (1972, 1993), for whom persons have two powers, for Hegel the capacity for personhood can be said to be defined first of all in terms of certain powers.

As outlined in § 5–7 of *Philosophy of Right*, free will has three moments. The first moment resembles 20th-century existentialism in its uncompromising emphasis on the capacity to negate any inclination or traditional injunction. Unlike any other natural beings, we are radically free, not necessitated by our natural inclinations. As argued e.g. by Yeomans (2012), Hegel's view on freedom and determinism preserves the libertarian insight that alternate possibilities and genuine control are needed for freedom. It is not enough that one is recognized as a free agent, or has a self-relation as a free agent; there are also metaphysical aspects of freedom that need to be taken into account. Free agents are able to say "no" to any alternative. Even when being coerced, being held at gunpoint, an agent with free will can in principle refuse the offer. And indeed, coercion by threats is only possible in the case of persons.

---

tion of the concept – but I will here ignore the metaphysical setting. For Hegel, it is not merely a historical construction, there is a speculative justification for it.

3 Hegel 1977, § 480; quoted in Poole 1996. Poole (1996, p. 48) also notes "that a derogatory sense of the French 'personne' is alive and well is indicated by Simone Weil's discussion in 'Human Personality' in Weil 1986.

That on its own does not yet suffice. The second aspect of free will is the capacity to set a positive end to oneself. The capacity to say "yes" to a goal, set it as one's aim, is equally important – otherwise one would not be able to act at all. It would be a misguided conception of freedom that would see any positive content, even commitments to self-determined ends, as a threat to freedom. The capacity or power to set oneself an end is thus a necessary second aspect of free will.

Thirdly, what completes the analysis of the structure of the will is the capacity to still see the end as "mine" once it is realized in the external world: the capacity to find oneself in externalized deeds. Hegel has a developmental account about "finding oneself": as explained e.g. by Charles Taylor (1975), for Hegel one gains self-understanding in acting – one grasps more fully what one is once one sees the results. The paradigm for such gains in self-understanding via self-expression is that of an artist who proceeds via different drafts and versions. In the process of acting, and pursuing means, the agent's ends are specified and reformulated, so that she can retrospectively take external deeds to express her will.

This analysis of the capacity of free will forms one aspect of the background of Hegel's theory. *That* one can freely set ends to oneself will be relevant to moral and legal respect, whereas *what* ends to set rather is at stake in concrete ethical life.

2 Conditions of Responsible Agency: Capacities, Self-Relations, Recognition

Mark Alznauer's (2015) recent study discusses responsible agency from the illuminating viewpoint of "innocence" in the sense of not being fit to be held responsible.[4] A responsible, non-innocent, agent must meet three conditions: first, he or she must have the required psychological capacities; second, he or she must have the self-conception of himself or herself as being free; third, he or she must be a recognized member of the state (2015, p. 21).

Accordingly, there are three ways in which beings can be "innocent". They can, first of all, lack the psychological capacities needed for responsibility. There are three of these capacities, and Alznauer illustrates them with Hegel's views about animals, children and "the mentally deranged" (who suffer from local irrationalities due to obsessions and fixed ideas):

---

[4] I have discussed Alznauer's views in Laitinen 2016a, this section draws on that text.

> An individual must be capable of thought (unlike an animal), she must be capable of having personal insight into right and wrong (unlike a child), and [...] her thoughts and desires must be fully responsive to her judgments about the world and about what she has grounds to do (unlike the mentally deranged). [...] A normal human adult is one that has all three of these capacities and so fully satisfies the psychological conditions for responsible agency. (Alznauer 2015, p. 75)

There are also sociological conditions of "innocence" that Alznauer (2015, p. 62) highlights with Hegel's views about "savagery, tribal patriarchy, and slavery". They are related to the second and third ways of being "innocent": these sociological conditions prevent the individual from developing the required *self-conception* and getting the right kind of *recognition*. Savagery and tribal patriarchy "do not allow individuals to achieve a certain self-conception, one in which they take themselves to be bound only to those standards whose justification they have insight into" (Alznauer 2015, p. 81). They lack exposure to norms that are understood to be valid only if rationally justified. Slaves typically do not lack such exposure, but they lack the required relation to self. Alznauer writes:

> [Hegel] characterizes the slave as someone who is not conscious of his freedom and so has not yet become "his own property as distinct from that of others" (PR § 57), and he goes on to say that it is precisely in "the act whereby I take possession of my personality and substantial essence" that "I make myself [mache mich] a being capable of rights and accountability [Rechts- und Zurechnungsfähigkeit], morality and religiosity" (PR § 66, [Alznauer's] translation) (Alznauer 2015, p. 81).

Such "taking possession of one's personality" may be part of the reason why non-human animals are often regarded as not bearing rights, but one may wonder whether it is plausible concerning children: arguably children have actual rights – it is wrong to harm them in ways which hinder the actualization of their potentials – despite them not yet having taken possession of their personality.

Without the requisite self-relation, the agents remain rational and responsible only implicitly and potentially, or "in themselves", but not actually or "for themselves". Unlike for example Robert Brandom's (2006) more existentialist Hegel, according to whom the content of our essence or concept depends on our self-conception as well, Alznauer's Hegel thinks that the essence or Hegelian "concept" is the same for all of us independently of our different self-interpretations. The self-interpretations make a difference in the degree to which the essence or "concept" is actualized. It is only when we regard ourselves as free, rational beings, and as having objective reasons and necessary ends, that the concept of free will is fully actualized. In this limited respect "humans can change what they are merely by arriving at a different self-conception. When a slave, for example, becomes conscious of his own freedom and refuses to accept his position of dependency, Hegel says he 'makes himself' a 'responsible being' (PR § 66R)" (Alznauer 2015, p. 42).

Thus, when non-human animals fight for food or attack each other, they do not violate each others' rights, as they have not constituted themselves as rights-bearing agents:

> a true right to our bodies is only generated insofar as that possession is posited as rightful by the agent. In order for any possession to be rightful ownership, the agent needs to be conscious of her freedom, of her status as a person who can rightfully express her will in external existence. (Alznauer 2015, p. 103)

An analogue to Alznauer's position could be a political system where one must register to vote: although voting rights are the same for everyone, one needs to register to vote to get the rights "activated" for oneself. There is no voting in the state of nature, and unless one is socialized in the system one would not have any idea of what is going on. But in addition, one must register oneself, and this registering partly consists in being recognized as a rights-bearer by the registrar.

The relevant kind of self-conception is, according to Alznauer's Hegel, possible only when one is recognized by others as free. Further,

> the kind of recognition responsible agency requires in order to exist fully and completely is political recognition: the sort of recognition that states give their citizens, not the sort that individuals could bilaterally give each other outside of the specific political context of a legitimate state. (Alznauer 2015, p. 63)

Alznauer (2015, p. 84) quotes Hegel, PR § 258 A: "it is only through being a member of a state that the individual himself has objectivity, truth, and ethical life", and that someone who rejects citizenship is "devoid of rights, wholly lacking in dignity". The necessity of recognition from the state is a highly interesting thesis, but ultimately it seems that recognition is not directly constitutive of responsible agency for Alznauer: it is merely a precondition of the required self-conception, and a precondition of responsibility.

Alznauer sees Hegel as radicalizing the view of Kant, who thought that ownership of external property is indeterminate in a state of nature (while possession of one's body, or being subject to duties, is not). First of all, outside a shared normative structure or a general will, unilaterally taking something into possession does not obligate others to regard it as property. Secondly, there is no assurance that others will respect my property. Thirdly, it is indeterminate who owns what in the absence of a shared mechanism of settling disputes. The rights to external property in a state of nature are provisional or tentative, not yet conclusive or valid (Alznauer 2015, p. 89). Those who violate these tentative claims, Kant writes, "do one another no wrong at all" (MM 6:307).[5]

Thus, all and all, persons must have certain capacities, certain relations to self, and they have to stand in certain relations of recognition to others. In different sections, different capacities, self-relations and relations of recognition are relevant. The relations of recognition within Abstract Right are the most formal ones – to be superseded by relations of recognition in the sections of Morality and Ethical Life.

3 Respect for Persons in *Abstract Right*

Baynes (2002, p. 6) aptly summarizes the kind of recognition at play in Abstract Right:

> "Abstract Right", the first section of the *Philosophy of Right*, introduces the most formal and minimal mode of recognition. The social status mutually attributed to members is that of legal persons with basic rights, including the right to own property and form contracts. It is a relatively uncomplicated form of recognition in that it abstracts from all motives and intentions of persons and considers them solely in terms of their "external" relations to one another.

The crucial thing in (abstractly) *respecting* a person is taking into account only *that* the person has a free will. Respect need not be sensitive to *what* they

---

[5] Alznauer's Hegel argues the same is true of all rights and obligations – there are none in the state of nature (Alznauer 2015, p. 92–93). Alznauer argues then that the state of nature is a normative vacuum. There can be no rights or any "way to wrong [each other] at all" (p. 95), good or evil (p. 87), no independent reasons (p. 97), nor responsible agency – all there is to being right is taking oneself to be right (p. 96). Evaluability or responsibility depend on "the establishment of some normative framework within which we can be evaluated for what we do. If that framework has social preconditions, then so will action itself." (p. 12). Now the assumption of a total normative vacuum seems to go too far, and in any case Alznauer might not need it. He could try to defend the interesting claims concerning personhood (that actualization of the capacities requires a certain self-conception, which in turn requires recognition) without making such an assumption of a normative vacuum, which is not that plausible (are there not objective reasons, say, to avoid poisonous food outside a political state? Are not the tyrants outside a developed state at all responsible for their deeds? Are there no reasons at all not to torture animals outside a political state?).

will. The particularities will be important in concrete relations, but respecting someone as a person abstracts from that.

> Personality [or better: personhood, AL] contains in general the capacity for right and constitutes the concept and the (itself abstract) basis of abstract and hence formal right. The commandment of right is therefore: be a person and respect others as persons. (Hegel 1991, § 36)
>
> The universality of this will which is free for itself is formal universality, i.e. the will's self-conscious (but otherwise contentless) and simple reference of itself in its individuality [*Einzelheit*]; to this extent, the subject is a person. It is inherent in personality [or better: personhood] that, as this person, I am completely determined in all respect s (in my inner arbitrary will, drive, and desire, as well as in relation to my immediate external existence [*Dasein*]), and that I am finite, yet totally pure self-reference, and thus know myself in my finitude as infinite, universal, and free. (Hegel 1991, § 35)
>
> Personality [or better: personhood, AL] begins only at that point where the subject has not merely a consciousness of itself in general as concrete and in some way determined, but a consciousness of itself as a completely abstract "I" in which all concrete limitation and validity are negated and invalidated. (Hegel 1991, § 35, Rem.)

Schmidt am Busch (2008, p. 578) explains that

> As a person, the human individual ("subject") stands in relation to himself, and this type of relationship has two crucial aspects. First, such an individual is, in Hegel's words, "completely determined in all respects" and "finite." As a biological and social being, this individual is "determined" in a number of ways: he has specific convictions, needs, desires, and interests, and in most cases, he also knows which convictions, needs, desires, and interests he has. With this knowledge, the individual refers to himself as a "concrete" being; he is, as Hegel puts it, a "finite self-reference." Second, the individual in question is said to be, at the same time, a "totally pure self-reference," that is, "a completely abstract 'I' in which all concrete limitation and validity are negated and invalidated." This is supposed to mean that the individual who refers to himself as a concrete being also believes that he is able to distance himself from every one of his convictions, needs, desires, and objectives. For him, there is indeed no belief he could not call into question, no need and no desire he could not decline to act on, and no objective he could not stop willing and pursuing. It is in this sense that such an individual has "a consciousness of [him]self as a completely abstract 'I.'"

Schmidt am Busch argues that an individual "not only believes that he has the capacity to distance himself from his desires, objectives, etc., but that he also takes this capacity to be of value and importance to him. This in turn means that he wants to be somebody who actually exercises the capacity in question and decides on his own which goals to pursue. In this sense, such an individual wants to be a person." (Schmidt am Busch 2008, p. 578) This has two aspects: first, particular features, but also universal capacities or powers of persons.

If personal respect is to be analyzed as an intersubjective relation, we should ask: what do individuals respect each other as when they respect one another as persons? Schmidt am Busch continues, that Hegel answers this question on the basis of his distinction between the aforementioned moments of the will: personhood and particularity. Respect as a person concerns only personhood, and abstracts from particularities.

> Hegel argues that human beings who respect each other as persons respect one another as individuals who can distance themselves from their particular needs, desires, and objectives, and who can decide on their own which goals they will pursue. As persons, human beings take each other to be independent actors in this sense. To be sure, they may also appreciate the particular objectives other people pursue and hold these people in esteem on the basis of the particularity of their goals – it is important to note, however, that this type of esteem is not part of what Hegel calls personal respect. As far as personal respect is concerned, there is, as Hegel (1991, § 37) says, "not a question of particular interests, of my advantage or welfare, and just as little of the particular ground by which my will is determined, i.e. of my insight and intention". (Schmidt am Busch 2008, p. 579)

4 Personal Respect and Private Property

Perhaps surprisingly, Hegel ties the notion of personal respect to private property. To be a person is to be an owner, to have external property rights. It is perhaps quite readily understandable why being a person is to have rights – and in an imagined "Nowheresville" where individuals would not have rights they would lack something central: not only would they lack the normative protection, but also the self-understanding as a locus of claims, which is central to self-respect (see Feinberg & Narveson 1970, Honneth 1992). But it is perhaps less clear why among these rights, there should be a right to privately owned property.

In Schmidt am Busch's (2008, p. 579) analysis, Hegel 'derives' the institution of private property from his concept of the person with the help of four theses:
(1) "The person must give himself an external sphere of freedom." (Hegel 1991, § 41)
(2) This sphere of freedom must consist of entities that are "immediately different and separable" from the person.
(3) The human body, human capacities, and external things can be said to meet Hegel's criterion of difference and separability; however, they do so in different ways.[6]

---

[6] Schmidt am Busch (2008) also notes that with respect to the human body, Hegel emphasizes the person's possibility of committing suicide: "[A]s a person, I [...] possess my life and body, like

(4) The person can only give himself a "sphere of its freedom" in private property.[7]

The need for such an external sphere can be highlighted developmentally: what would a child lack without any chance to have his or her own say and own control over external things such as toys? If one could never be in charge of what happens in a play? Presumably one's will and sense of responsibility could not develop. Similarly, Virginia Woolf famously argued for the need of a room of one's own (see also Honneth 2014 for arguments for the need for such an external sphere). The external sphere is that of negative liberty – and Hegel's argument is that although it cannot be the full story, it is a necessary aspect of the full story.

In evaluating this thesis one may ask whether less individualistic forms could not do as well: why not common property governed by a deliberative democracy in light of general interests? Why not common property of the family? Indeed, one could argue that as long as one has an equal say as others, why could not all of one's life, including the choice of one's marriage partner and career, be a matter of common choice – and yet one would be treated in terms of "respect" as long as one has an equal say. This would however be to reduce personal respect to democratic respect, and thus to lose one dimension of self-relations and relations to others: the very dimension that Hegel's abstract right tries to articulate. Since Roman Law this idea has been part of Western Civilization, and in modernity it has been gradually institutionalized with the aim to cover all adults with the relevant capacities.

Here, a comparative evaluative argument would state that individualistic forms of private property have their pros and cons, as does common property. Hegel's approach is not merely comparative (although it makes a claim about historical progress in this respect) but argues that individualistic property is necessary for personhood: abstract right forms a necessary aspect of full personhood.

---

other things, only in so far as I so will it." (Hegel 1991, § 47) And he explains: "[T]he animal cannot mutilate or destroy itself, but the human being can." (Hegel 1991, § 47, Rem.)

7 Schmidt am Busch (2008) further continues: "Why is it that the person's external sphere of freedom must be made up of private property? In this connection, Hegel puts forth the following thesis: "Since my will, as the will of a person, and so as a single will, becomes objective to me in property, property acquires the character of private property [...]." (Hegel 1991, § 46) To this, Hegel adds by way of a hand-written remark: "Private property, because person [is] single [and because] I shall be, shall be there as such." (Hegel 1991, § 46, Marginal Remark)

Other economic implications of "personal respect" include the ban of slavery or bondage as incompatible with personal respect. Yet, *markets* are not a necessary condition of personal respect.

Schmidt am Busch argues that, however,

> Personal respect gives individuals who wish to cooperate economically a prima facie reason to favor market-like exchanges over state-regulated distributions of goods. Two points are responsible for this. (a) Market-like exchanges can be understood as possible institutionalizations of personal respect. (b) The sphere of activities that realize the structure of personal freedom seems to be larger in market economies than in state-regulated economies. (Schmidt am Busch 2008, p. 584)

5 The Pathology of Mistaking Abstract Personhood for the Concrete Individual

What is wrong with a one-sided view according to which we all would conceive of each other and of ourselves as just persons, characterized by such respect? It would, according to e.g. Honneth 2014 and Poole 1996, be a pathological development.[8] The reason personal respect cannot be the whole story is by now pretty evident: it abstracts from all the concrete features that provide our distinctiveness and provide meaning for our lives; as persons we are all alike, share the same relevant capabilities. As Poole (1996, p. 48) puts it:

> For Hegel, the concept of a person is an artefact of those systems of law which recognize the equal rights of all those subject to it. The identity which the law imposes abstracts from all those characteristics which differentiate one subject from another.[9]

---

[8] One may also stress its social-ontological impossibility in a state of nature (see Alznauer 2015).

[9] Poole continues by describing the Hegelian understanding of Modernity and modern personhood: "When it is divorced from actual life, as it was in the Roman Empire, the concept of a person is a mere empty formalism. The modern world provides, on Hegel's view, a far richer form of ethical life than the Roman imperium. The family, life in civil society and the institutions of the state provide the social purpose necessary to sustain the legal structure of abstract right (property, contract, and the like). Insofar as an individual enters this sphere of abstract right, that is, he makes contracts, owns property and so on, he counts as a person, i.e., as a bearer of rights. But this abstraction is not a self-sufficient form of existence: it arises on the basis of an individual's substantive ethical life in the family, civil society, and the state."(1996, p. 49)

In Poole's words:

> The concept of personhood invites us to abstract our identity from those very narrative resources – birth, growth and development, sexuality, procreation, friendship, decay, death – which we require to make sense of our lives. It is through these resources that we are able to form conceptions of ourselves which do justice to our existence as individuals and which at the same time provide us with a location within a larger framework. Personhood does not provide a story at all, let alone a story which is mine. (Poole 1996, p. 50)[10]

In Honneth's (2014) view, there are real pathologies, which consist in people relating to each other and to themselves in these formal and abstract terms as "persons" when they should regard each other as suffering beings and cooperators in concrete roles. Overlegalization of other social spheres brings with it such pathological relations to others as "mere" persons with claims to privacy, and a related empty relation to self. Regarding others as "black boxes" whose intentions and motives do not matter for their rightful claims is an appropriate relationship in abstract and contractual relations, but it would be a very pathological relation to take to oneself: that my motives and intentions do not matter to me, because I can always set myself different ones.[11] It is good to value the capacity to set oneself ends, but it is also good to see that the ends that one has set to oneself indeed matter.

The main point then is that respect for personhood is a necessary but not a sufficient form of recognition of personhood. Thicker notions of recognition are at play in the contexts of family, civil society and the state. They provide concrete roles, which are (in the good cases) not obstacles to self-realization, but something *through* which self-realization can take place. In those ways, they add to the layers of recognition of individuals. But additionally, they seem to break the bounds of the so far individualistic analysis: in some sense a family and a state are themselves collective agents, collective persons even.

6 Family and State

In his article, David Ciavatta (2006) notes how collective ownership and personhood of the family break the bounds of the individualistic notion of personhood:

---

[10] Cf. Raz 1986, who argues that morality does not provide meaning; here abstract personhood, as being a rights-bearer, provides no meaning.

[11] I have discussed Honneth's view in more detail in Laitinen 2016c.

As Hegel writes, one is in one's family "not as an independent person but as a member," and the ethical core of the family involves the "identification of personalities [*Persönlichkeiten*, Ciavatta writes "personhoods", AL], whereby the family becomes one person and its members become its accidents (though substance is in essence the relation of accidents to itself)." Rather than being separate, self-standing persons, each with her own individual will, and each thus affirming her familial involvements through the mediation of her own independent reasons and motivations, the individual family member *finds* her own will, and, more generally, her affirmation of her own individual self-identity, to be already concretely implicated in an inherently intersubjective will – in a collectively affirmed, familial "we" – that serves as a fundamental background context that gives ethical legitimacy and determinate meaning to her own agency (Ciavatta 2006, p. 156).

And later Ciavatta notes that this is in tension with the argument that abstract personhood involves private property:

> For, in Hegel's account of Abstract Right – and we can infer that this point would apply generally to the civil sphere – collective ownership is claimed to be counter to the very notion of personhood, for ownership *necessarily* involves an *individual* person's unilateral control over a thing, and thus involves the recognized freedom to exclude all others from being able to lay claim to that thing. In the family, in contrast, I own things only insofar as my family members own them too, for what I own here is not merely the expression of my unconditioned freedom as an individual, but rather the concrete expression of the unconditioned bonds of mutual recognition that allow us to be the particular selves we are (Ciavatta 2006, p. 164).

Thus, one must say that there are two rival forms of recognition – as an abstract person and as a concrete family member – which come with rival understandings of property being either private or shared. Presumably then, while these may be in tension, they are both necessary aspects of full human personhood.

In family, the ethical nature of the relationship, despite involving owning, is a more intimate one, and provides what is missing in mere abstract respect:

> The collective ownership of such priceless familial resources is thus not defined primarily in terms of natural need, or in terms of the sheer assertion of the individual self's independence from the world (as is the case in the realm of Abstract Right), but is an essentially ethical matter, defined essentially in terms of the project of maintaining a concrete, living field of intersubjective recognition that allows the family members to be who they are in relation to one another. (Ciavatta 2006, p. 165)

Further, the dialectics of Family and Civil Society show how Family is not an ethically self-sustaining whole, but contains its own seeds of destruction:

> Although the family's property has a unique and self-sufficient ethical significance within the context of its family life, family members must implicitly rely on the fact that their prop-

erty attains its full, objective status as property only through the actual recognition of a civil order that preserves formal property relations in general. Each family as a whole, qua a collective property owner, thus implicitly claims to be a recognized legal person externally related to other recognized families. In tension with its incomparable, ethical significance as embodying familial self-identity, then, this family property implicitly takes on for family members a generic – but very real and objective – market value that is determined in the light of its external significance for any legal person who might seek to possess it. For Hegel, it is precisely in having to deal with inheritance which is essentially "the transfer to private ownership of property which is in principle common," in that the family's common property now appears as something that has to be divided into separable shares. The fact that these shares are, in principle, something that can be given to anyone, and thus no longer possess the concrete, ethical significance of uniting these specific family members together into a common project, signals that the principle of personhood has emerged from within the family itself. (Ciavatta 2006, p. 167)[12]

As Hegel writes, civil society "tears the individual from his family ties, estranges the members of the family from one another, and recognizes them as self-subsistent persons" (PR, § 238).

No discussion of Hegel's notion of respect for persons can be complete without a reference to how Hegel seems to suggest that states, and not only individual humans, can actualize the conceptual structure of personhood. Let me therefore end with a quotation, which serves to remind us that it is not only within family that there is a tension between individuality and membership in a bigger unity:

> Personality, like subjectivity in general, as infinitely self-related, has its truth (to be precise, its most elementary, immediate, truth) only in a person, in a subject existing "for" himself, and what exists "for" itself is just simply a unit. It is only as a person, the monarch, that the personality of the state is actual. Personality expresses the concept as such; but the person enshrines the actuality of the concept, and only when the concept is determined as person is it the Idea or truth. A so-called "artificial person", be it a society, a community, or a family, however inherently concrete it may be, contains personality only abstractly, as one moment of itself. In an "artificial person", personality has not achieved its true mode of existence. The state, however, is precisely this totality in which the moments of the concept have attained the actuality correspondent to their degree of truth. (Hegel, PR § 279)

---

[12] Ciavatta adds: "The family is, then, an inherently unstable institution in Hegel's view: It is an institution that must recognize the unconditional legitimacy of the individual person and of the civil sphere, and yet it cannot do so without at the same time giving up its status as an original and independent source of normativity and self-identity – without, in short, risking becoming just another civil institution among many. This inherent tension is not simply done away with once we move on to a consideration of the civil sphere. Rather, Hegel seems to be suggesting that the ethical order is founded on this tension, and can never fully rid itself of it." (Ciavatta 2006, p. 167)

Bibliography

Alznauer, M. (2015): Hegel's Theory of Responsibility, Cambridge: Cambridge University Press.
Baynes, K. (2002): "Freedom and Recognition in Hegel and Habermas", *Philosophy and Social Criticism* 28 (1), pp. 1–17.
Brandom, R. (2007): "Hegel on the Structure of Desire and Self-Consciousness", *Philosophy and Social Criticism* 33 (1), pp. 127–150.
Ciavatta, D. (2006): "The Unreflective Bonds of Intimacy: Hegel on Familial Ties and the Modern Person", *The Philosophical Forum* 37 (2), pp. 153–181.
Feinberg, J. and Narveson, J. (1970): "The Nature and Value of Rights", *Journal of Value Inquiry* 4 (4), pp. 243–260.
Habermas, J. (1988): *Theorie des kommunikativen Handelns*, vol. 2., Frankfurt a.M.: Suhrkamp.
Habermas, J. (1996): *Between Facts and Norms*, Cambridge, MA: MIT Press.
Hartmann, M. and Honneth, A. (2006): "Paradoxes of Capitalism", *Constellations* 13 (1), pp. 41–58.
Hegel, G.W.F. (1977): *The Phenomenology of Spirit*, trans. by A.V. Miller, Oxford: Oxford University Press.
Hegel, G.W.F. (1991): *Elements of the Philosophy of Right*, ed. by A.W. Wood, trans. by H.B. Nisbett, Cambridge: Cambridge University Press.
Hegel, G.W.F. (2015): *Encyclopedia of the Philosophical Sciences in Basic Outline*, Cambridge: Cambridge University Press.
Honneth, A. (1992): *Kampf um Anerkennung. Zur moralischen Grammatik sozialer Kämpfe*, Frankfurt a.M.: Suhrkamp.
Honneth, A. (2003): "Umverteilung als Anerkennung. Eine Erwiderung auf Nancy Fraser". In N. Fraser and A. Honneth (Eds.): *Umverteilung oder Anerkennung? Eine politisch-philosophische Kontroverse*, Frankfurt a.M.: Suhrkamp, pp. 129–224.
Honneth, A. (2012): *The I in We*, Cambridge: Polity Press.
Honneth, A. (2014): *Freedom's Right*, New York: Columbia University Press.
Ikäheimo, H. (2014): *Anerkennung*, Berlin: De Gruyter.
Ikäheimo, H. and Laitinen, A. (Eds.) (2007): *Dimensions of Personhood*, Exeter: Imprint Academic.
Kant, I. (1996): *Metaphysics of Morals*, Cambridge: Cambridge University Press.
Knowles, D. (2002): *Hegel and the Philosophy of Right*, London: Routledge.
Laitinen, A. (2016a): Review of "Hegel's Theory of Responsibility" by Mark Alznauer, *Notre Dame Philosophical Reviews*, http://ndpr.nd.edu/news/65311-hegels-theory-of-responsibility. Last accessed 31st October 2016.
Laitinen, A. (2016b): Review of "Freedom and Reflection: Hegel and the Logic of Agency" by Yeomans Christopher, Oxford: Oxford University Press, 2012. ISBN 978–0-199–79452–2 (hbk). Pp. 275. $74.00.', *Hegel Bulletin*, pp. 1–5. doi: 10.1017/hgl.2016.39. Published online 17 October 2016.
Laitinen, A. (2016c): "Freedom's Left? Market's Right? Morality's Wrong?". In J.D. Rendtorff, A. Sørensen and G. Baruchello (Eds.): Ethics, Democracy, and Markets: Nordic Perspectives on World Problems, Copenhagen: NSU Press, pp. 258–281.
Neuhouser, F. (2000): *Foundations of Hegel's Social Theory. Actualizing Freedom*, Cambridge, MA: Harvard University Press.

Quante, M. (1997): "'Die Persönlichkeit des Willens' als Prinzip des abstrakten Rechts. Eine Analyse der begriffslogischen Struktur der §§ 34–40 von Hegels Grundlinien der Philosophie des Rechts". In L. Siep (Ed.): *Hegel: Grundlinien der Philosophie des Rechts*, Berlin: Akademie, pp. 73–94.

Quante, M. (2004): *Hegel's Concept of Action*, Cambridge: Cambridge University Press.

Quante, M. (2007): *Person*, Berlin: De Gruyter.

Patten, A. (1999): *Hegel's Idea of Freedom*, Oxford: Oxford University Press.

Poole, R. (1996): "On Being a Person", *Australasian Journal of Philosophy* 74 (1), pp. 38–56.

Rawls, J. (1972): *Theory of Justice*, Oxford: Clarendon Press.

Rawls, J. (1993): *Political Liberalism*, New York: Columbia University Press.

Raz, J. (1986): *Morality of Freedom*, Oxford: Clarendon Press.

Schmidt am Busch, H.-C. (2008): "Personal Respect, Private Property, and Market Economy: What Critical Theory Can Learn From Hegel", *Ethical Theory & Moral Practice* 11, pp. 573–586.

Siep, L. (2014): *Anerkennung als Prinzip der praktischen Philosophie. Untersuchungen zu Hegels Jenaer Philosophie des Geistes*, 2nd ed., Hamburg: Meiner.

Taylor, C. (1975): *Hegel*, Cambridge: Cambridge University Press.

Taylor, C. (1989): *Sources of the Self*, Cambridge, MA: Harvard University Press.

Weil, S. (1986): *An Anthology* ed. by S. Miles, London: Virago,

Williams, R. (1992): *Hegel's Ethics of Recognition*, Berkeley-Los Angeles/London: University of California Press.

Yeomans, C. (2012): *Freedom and Reflection: Hegel and the Logic of Agency*, Oxford: Oxford University Press.

Antis Loizides
John Stuart Mill: Individuality, Dignity, and Respect for Persons[1]

Abstract: This chapter explores the idea of respect for persons in John Stuart Mill's thought, focusing on individuality and the sense of dignity. Following a brief discussion of the grounds for the protection of individuality and self-development in Mill's *On Liberty* (1859), the chapter attempts to bring to the surface the implications of individuality and self-development for social relationships, particularly those of gender, class and race. But can Mill's utilitarian theory really incorporate the idea that human dignity ought never to be violated, whatever the social gains? The chapter turns for answers to Mill's theory of an "Art of Life", his argument on kinds of pleasure, and consequently his views on the relationship between justice and utility. At this point the sense of dignity – a feeling of self-respect – and its relation to self-development and the life of justice comes to the fore. As the chapter argues, the sense of dignity is the foundation upon which the respect of the rights, liberty and individuality of others is to be built.

In April 1854, just before abandoning the experiment of registering at least one "worthy" thought per day, John Stuart Mill scribbled down an interesting idea in his "little book" ("Diary" (1854), 8 Jan. 1854. In: Mill 1963–1991, vol. XXVII, p. 641)[2]:

> All systems of morals agree in prescribing to do that, and only that, which accords with self-respect. The difference between one person and another is mainly in that with which their self-respect is associated. In some it is with worldly or selfish success. In others, with the supposed favour of the supernal powers. In others, with the indulgence of mere self-will. In others, with self-conceit. In the best, with the sympathy of those they respect and a just regard for the good of all. (Diary, 9 Apr. 1854, CW:XXVII.667)

Mill made the note at a time when he was working on essays soon to turn into *On Liberty* (1859), *Utilitarianism* (1861), and *The Subjection of Women* (1869) and

---

[1] I would like to thank Elena Irrera, Georgios Varouxakis, Gregoris Molivas, Giovanni Giorgini, and Sophia Kanaouti for extremely helpful comments on earlier drafts of this chapter.
[2] All subsequent references to John Stuart Mill's works are by title, followed by volume and page number of the *Collected Works* (CW).

while he and Harriet Taylor Mill were advocating women's rights (*Autobiography* (1873), CW:I.249; letter to H. Taylor Mill, 7 Feb. and 14 Jun. 1854, CW:XIV.152, 212). With a view to fully sketching out the idea in the near future, Mill pointed to two kinds of respect: first, respect associated with a feeling of approbation; second, respect associated with an acknowledgment of what is good for all members of a society, irrespective of approbation. This short note suggests that Mill linked these two kinds of respect to each other, and that he considered the link important. However, it is not clear how or why; neither is it clear that such concepts or the link itself made sense in terms of Mill's utilitarian theory. In this chapter, I attempt to clarify these issues.

In short, I explore the idea of respect for persons in Mill's thought as a concern with individuality and the sense of dignity. In Section 1, I offer some contemporary definitions of key terms in the discussion of respect for persons, that is, recognition respect and appraisal respect as well as dignity. These definitions serve as conceptual tools when turning to Mill's thought. In Section 2, I discuss the grounds for the protection of individuality and self-development in Mill's *On Liberty*. In Section 3, I attempt to bring to the surface the implications of individuality and self-development for social relationships, particularly those of gender, class and race, as worked out in *Subjection* and *Principles of Political Economy* (1848), among other works. Section 4 deals with a potential problem for Mill: can his utilitarian theory incorporate the idea that human dignity ought never to be violated, whatever the social gains? I turn for answers to Mill's theory of an "Art of Life", his argument on kinds of pleasure, and consequently his views on the relationship between justice and utility. Section 5 focuses on the sense of dignity – a feeling of self-respect – and its relation to self-development and the life of justice. I take the discussion to an aspect of respect for persons which is not as readily apparent as Mill's thesis on individuality: although our character is formed during our childhood and early experiences, it is possible through appraisal respect to initiate self-culture in maturity. As I try to show, in Mill's thought the two kinds of respect are inextricably bound: the sense of dignity is the foundation upon which the respect of the rights and liberty of others is to be built.

1

In Section 1, first, drawing from Stephen Darwall,[3] I distinguish between "recognition respect" and "appraisal respect". Second, drawing from John Rawls and Bernard Williams, I state the deontological challenge to utilitarian theories: can a utilitarian really accommodate the idea of respect for persons, irrespective of losses in social utility? Identifying the essential elements of the idea of respect for persons delineates and, concurrently, tests Mill's arguments.

On one hand, appraisal or evaluative respect, as Darwall puts it, is a kind of esteem: a positive or favorable attitude towards a person as a (moral) agent. That is, appraisal respect for a person has to do with some form of evaluation of a person's character or conduct. To appraise, to evaluate, or to assess a person means that her/his character, conduct, and achievements fare well in comparison with a standard of (moral) excellence. According to how one fares against the standard the result in estimation could range from the highest esteem to disesteem. However, as Darwall points out, not every positive attitude towards another person's character traits qualifies for appraisal respect; for Darwall, drawing on Kant, appraisal respect involves a "*categorical* attitude, one which is unconditional on the fact that the traits in question happen to serve some particular purpose or interest *of mine*" (Darwall 2004, p. 44). For example, my attitude towards a colleague may be positive or negative; whatever it is, that attitude should be in reference to a standard, e.g., merit, work ethic, productivity, how well s/he works with others, etc., which does not vary according to my particular situation, purposes or goals (e.g., competing for a promotion). As Stephen Hudson notes, "[a] person must have reasons for respecting *x* (in the evaluative sense), and these reasons will be what the person takes to be facts about *x* in virtue of which *x* merits the person's respect" (Hudson 1980, p. 72).

On the other hand, recognition respect involves the acknowledgment of a shared fact or a feature of human beings which places restrictions on how to treat another person irrespectively of any variance in character traits, merits or accomplishments: human dignity. Rather oversimplifying, human dignity essentially refers to human beings having an inherent worth by virtue of being human. It does not depend on fulfilling any criteria other than being human. In Kant's classic formulation, dignity is "an unconditioned, incomparable worth", that is, an inner worth which "constitutes the condition under which alone something can be an end-in-itself" (Kant 2002, pp. 53–54). The grounds of human dig-

---

[3] In the discussion which follows, I draw from Darwall 1977 and 2004 (stating Darwall's new position). For a complete account, see Darwall 2006.

nity vary in different conceptions; nevertheless, all agree that dignity is neither earned nor alienated. One may fail to properly acknowledge it either in others or in oneself (e.g., treating others or one's own self as means and not as an end-in-itself), but it is never lost.

Whereas one cannot demand appraisal respect, one can demand recognition respect; and whereas one's esteem for an individual may vary from person to person with no need for uniformity, recognizing human dignity places uniform restrictions on action across individuals. To put it simply, it is not morally permissible for any person to act without due acknowledgment of, or without giving appropriate weight to, that fact or feature of human beings. Since for Darwall the object of recognition respect is dignity or authority, recognition respect concerns how our relations to a bearer of that feature, that is, dignity or authority, are to be governed by it. Darwall's second-person standpoint thus stresses that to respect dignity in another person is something different from respecting human dignity in general.

According to Darwall, the dignity of a person is the authority to make claims and demands which limit the actions of another person. This means that dignity provides reasons for that (second) person to comply with the claims or demands of another person (e.g., not to engage in behavior that violates her/his dignity); in turn, these reasons for acting hold that (second) person accountable when s/he fails to appropriately take them into consideration, for whatever reason (e.g., maximizing social utility). Being accountable for one's failure to view dignity as a reason for acting should not be taken to mean that one is coerced to respect others, e.g. by being shamed or threatened. It means that a person considers, weighs, and prioritizes the reasons available for action and eventually acts freely on account of those reasons. Darwall thus notes that "[w]hen we hold someone responsible as a person, we also accord him membership in the moral community and thereby acknowledge his authority to make moral demands as a free and rational agent himself" (Darwall 2004, p. 49).

Such an idea finds resonance with what Joel Feinberg maintains in relation to the idea of "respect for persons". In his own words, to respect a person, "or to think of him as possessed of human dignity, simply is to think of him as a potential maker of claims". Human dignity, for Feinberg, "may simply be the recognizable capacity to assert claims" (Feinberg 1970, p. 252). Feinberg's idea seems congenial to the view expressed by John Rawls, who believes that to hold oneself entitled to make claims (on the design of social institutions), that is to count "moral personality itself as a source of claims is an aspect of freedom". For Rawls, "[p]eople are self-originating sources of claims in the sense that their claims carry weight on their own without being derived from prior duties or obligations owed to society or to other persons, or, finally, as derived from, or assigned to, their particular social role" (Rawls 1980, pp. 543–544). This means for Rawls that a person has the moral power to form, to revise, and rationally to pursue a conception of the good without the need to justify her/his claims; that moral power is not bound to any antecedent principles external to their point of view (Rawls 1980, pp. 543, 548). Respect for persons, then, is to think of others as equal, free, rational members of the moral community with no other justification than that they are self-originating sources of valid claims.

In *A Theory of Justice* (1971), John Rawls conducted a well-known criticism of utilitarianism, i.e. that it does not take the distinction between persons seriously (Rawls 1999, p. 24): to the utilitarian, individuals matter only as vessels of pleasure or satisfaction which is the only thing of value; as long as total pleasure or satisfaction is maximized, it does not matter if someone is left worse off (Hart 1979, pp. 829–831). Bernard Williams brought to the surface a further problem involved in subscribing to utilitarian approaches: that to demand of anyone to adopt the perspective of social utility is

> to alienate him in a real sense from his actions and the source of his action in his own convictions. It is to make him into a channel between the input of everyone's projects, including his own, and an output of optimific decision; but this is to neglect the extent to which his actions and his decisions have to be seen as the actions and decisions which flow from the projects and attitudes with which he is most closely identified. It is thus, in the most literal sense, an attack on his integrity. (Smart and Williams 1973, pp. 116–117)

The idea of a violation of one's individual identity (an idea which the abovementioned scholars take to be consequent upon the adhesion to a utilitarian view of morals) also has serious implications at the level of human inter-subjective relationships. As Geoffrey Scarre, for instance, notes, when human dignity is violated, "[o]ur revulsion springs from a deeper level", not in that violating dignity may potentially make society less secure or less happy, but in that the person who does not recognize the claims of others to respect them as persons "falls well short of the human ideal". So for Scarre, in short, "[t]he question for the utilitarian is how, if at all, he can accommodate this ideal" (Scarre 1992, p. 29). In reality, the question that the utilitarian is called upon to answer is two-pronged: not only that s/he can accommodate the idea of inviolability of human dignity, but that inviolability is valuable for its own sake. In what follows, I examine whether or not John Stuart Mill's utilitarian theory has the resources to respond to this challenge.

2

The phrase "respect for persons" does not occur in John Stuart Mill's corpus. In the 19th century, to be a "respecter of persons" meant that one allowed oneself to be prejudiced, partial or biased according to status, privilege or gifts. The phrase was found in translations of, and commentaries on, Paul's *Epistle to the Romans* (II.11) as well as the *Acts of the Apostles* (X.34) (see, e.g., Haldane 1842: III.316–317; Livermore 1853, p. 158n) – that is, God is no respecter of persons. Of course, the idea had taken root in legal rhetoric as well – that is, the law is no respecter of persons (see, e.g. Brougham 1828, p. 46).

Acknowledging the influence of both traditions, Mill invoked this maxim in *Subjection of Women* to argue for impartiality between the sexes (*Subjection*, CW: XXI.261). According to Mill, the "*a priori* presumption is in favour of freedom and impartiality". For Mill, positive reasons – the general good, expediency, justice – had been used to restrain individual liberty and justify unequal treatment between individuals. The prevalent justification for restraints on liberty and unequal treatment did not rest on argument but on "a mass of feeling" (*Subjection*, CW:XXI.261). In *On Liberty*, Mill had already taken up the herculean task of reducing the positive reasons for restraints and partiality to their proper bounds.[4] In this section, I outline Mill's familiar theory; in the subsequent section, I briefly discuss the implications of that theory for social relationships, especially those of gender, class and race. It is important to note at the outset that Mill's argument was not abstract; he aimed to challenge and, ultimately, reshape "commonplace" morality.[5] Regretfully, I can only provide a sketch of Mill's distinct arguments here – one that oversimplifies Mill's complex views on these issues.[6]

According to Mill, since people live together in a society, it is imperative to define appropriate limits on how one treats others, a treatment which "consists … in not injuring the interests of one another; or rather certain interests, which, either by express legal provision or by tacit understanding, ought to be considered as rights" (*On Liberty*, CW:XVIII.276). The principle was simple:

---

[4] Interestingly, Mill's contemporaries had missed the link between *On Liberty* and *Subjection* (see Nicholson 1998).

[5] For Mill's "Socratic" concern with reshaping "Commonplace", see Demetriou and Loizides 2013 and Loizides 2013: chs. 4 and 6.

[6] For more details on Mill's feminist thesis, see, e.g., Burgess-Jackson 1995; cf. Moller Okin 1979: ch. 9; for Mill on individuality and the marketplace, see Milgate and Stinson 2009: ch. 12; for Mill on race and the American civil war, see Varouxakis 1998 and 2013.

> the only purpose for which power can be rightfully exercised over any member of a civilized community, against his will, is to prevent harm to others. His own good, either physical or moral, is not a sufficient warrant. He cannot rightfully be compelled to do or forbear because it will be better for him to do so, because it will make him happier, because, in the opinions of others, to do so would be wise, or even right.

Unless there is a claim of self-protection from society against the individual, individuals have absolute independence in conduct which concerns only themselves: "[o]ver himself, over his own body and mind, the individual is sovereign" (*On Liberty*, CW:XVIII.223–224).

A person, Mill argued, exercises her/his full faculties, especially those "which are the distinctive endowment of a human being", i.e., the faculties of "perception, judgment, discriminative feeling, mental activity, and even moral preference" only in making a choice (*On Liberty*, CW:XVIII.262). Without the protection of diversity in modes of life, individuals "neither obtain their fair share of happiness, nor grow up to the mental, moral and aesthetic stature of which their nature is capable" (*On Liberty*, CW:XVIII.270). To set, revise and pursue one's own projects (i.e., self-regarding interests), a person should be given free scope to engage in different experiments in living. "To give any fair play to the nature of each", Mill noted, "it is essential that different persons should be allowed to lead different lives". A person, according to Mill, is not accountable for her/his actions to others in so far as these actions concern her/his own interests. But the rights and interests of others limit self-development, when the development of one individual takes place at the expense of the development of others (*On Liberty*, CW:XVIII.261, 266).

A "just regard for the good of all" (Diary, 9 Apr. 1854, CW:XXVII.667) entails allowing for as many "independent centres of improvement as there are individuals" – a circle around each individual "within which the individuality of that person ought to reign uncontrolled either by any other individual or by the public collectively" (*Principles of Political Economy* (1848), CW:III.938). Mill added that "when there is more life in the units there is more in the mass which is composed of them" (*On Liberty*, CW:XVIII.272, 266). Here, Mill was building on the groundwork of *A System of Logic* (1843, CW:VIII.879): "[t]he laws of the phenomena of society are, and can be, nothing but the laws of the actions and passions of human beings united together in the social state." Social well-being consists in the aggregate of individual well-beings, since "[h]uman beings in society have no properties but those which are derived from, and may be resolved into, the laws of the nature of individual man". Trying to explain the related section of *Utilitarianism* in a letter, Mill noted: "since A's happiness is a good, B's a good, C's a good, &c., the sum of all these goods must be a good" (letter to H. Jones, 13

Jun. 1868, CW:XVI.1414; *Utilitarianism*, CW:X.234). Thirty years earlier, Mill had told Thomas Carlyle:

> Though I hold the good of the species (or rather of its several units) to be the *ultimate* end, [...] I believe with the fullest Belief that this end can in no other way be forwarded but by the means you speak of, namely by each taking for his exclusive aim the development of what is best in *himself*. (Letter to T. Carlyle, 12 Jan. 1834, CW:XII.207–208)

As we saw, a person has free scope to use her/his experience to find a meaningful mode of life. According to Mill, "it is the privilege and proper condition of a human being, arrived at the maturity of his faculties, to use and interpret experience in his own way" (*On Liberty*, CW:XVIII.262). It being a privilege, individuals are not bound by duty to others; that is, others lack a claim against anyone's choice in pursuing a particular mode of life. But this is not *carte blanche* to act against social interests. When one's chosen means of development encroach on another's capability for self-development, the first loses her/his "asylum ... for individuality of character" (*Principles*, CW:II.209) and the second gains a claim against her/him: when individuals lose their "asylum", that is, when they lose the right to claim immunity, others are no longer in a position of disability. By endangering vital social interests, individuals bring themselves under the power of society, that is, they bring themselves into a position where they lack the capacity to claim "immunity from [...] suffering" from the actions of others (*On Liberty*, CW:XVIII.293).

3

Section 2 argued that for Mill diversity and individuality ought to be protected by society, as they are essential components of a person's well-being, i.e., they are vital interests. For this, society needs to accord to concomitant liberties the status of legal and moral rights. The appropriate region of human liberty is threefold: (a) of thought, feeling and expression; (b) of tastes and pursuits; (c) of association. Barring the instances of mental incapacity, youth, force or deception, Mill argued, individuals are free from "impediment from our fellow-creatures, so long as what we do does not harm them, even though they should think our conduct foolish, perverse, or wrong". For Mill, a society is free when these liberties are respected absolutely (*On Liberty*, CW:XVIII.225–226). So, what are the implications of Mill's argument concerning the immunity of individuality from interference for particular social relationships, i.e. those of gender, class, and race?

In *Subjection*, Mill argued that the *a priori* presumption is in favor of freedom and equality – those who push for limits to freedom and equality have the burden of proof. A principle of perfect equality, Mill noted, admits "no power or privilege on the one side, nor disability on the other". However, equality between men and women is far from perfect: the "old" principles of privilege and exclusion needed to be replaced both by justice and an enlarged view of the general good. The source of this inequality was the law of the strongest – a principle wrong in itself – (*Subjection*, CW:XXI.261): the authority of man over woman "arose simply from the fact that from the very earliest twilight of human society, every woman (owing to the value attached to her by men, combined with her inferiority in muscular strength) was found in a state of bondage to some man". Society came to convert this physical fact into a legal right: the masters bound "themselves to one another for common protection, guaranteed by their collective strength the private possessions of each" – women were part of those possessions, just as slaves were (*Subjection*, CW:XXI.264). But such institutions "can have no place in any society [...] founded on justice, or on fellowship between human creatures" (*Principles*, CW:II.233). History, Mill noted, "gives a cruel experience of human nature, in shewing how exactly the regard due to the life, possessions, and entire earthly happiness of any class of persons, was measured by what they had the power of enforcing" (*Subjection*, CW:XXI.265). Women were entirely without any such power; not only was the state of total disability on the part of women considered natural; it was also considered consensual – a host of social beliefs, institutions and customs were at work to make women "willing slaves".[7] In 1869, Mill was building on the momentum created by his contributions in favor of the abolition of slavery in America. All that Mill had to do was to show that women's disability was a species of the genus "human beings held in bondage" – the "civilized world" had already made its mind up on the inherent injustice of the latter.

For Mill, women's disability was one which laws and institutions assigned at birth, "and ordain[ed] that they shall never in all their lives be allowed to compete for certain things" (*Subjection*, CW:XXI.274). As mentioned, Mill thought that placing barriers on how persons use "their faculties for their own benefit and for that of others" was both unjust and socially inexpedient (*Subjection*, CW:XXI.294). According to Mill, "[t]he joint influence of Roman civilization and of Christianity [...] declared the claims of the human being, as such, to be paramount to those of sex, class, or social position" (*Subjection*, CW:XXI.261).

---

[7] For the relation between Mill's *Subjection* and his ethology, the science of character formation, see Ball 2000.

However, the recognition of equal moral worth was not extended to all members of the community. Limiting the options of women to specific occupations and roles is, for Mill, "a flagrant social injustice" (*Principles*, CW:III.765). At the same time, women's lack of self-dependence went against "the fruit of a thousand years of experience": that "things in which the individual is the person directly interested, never go right but as they are left to his own discretion, and that any regulation of them by authority, except to protect the rights of others, is sure to be mischievous". Mill reiterated the idea that "freedom of individual choice is now known to be the only thing which procures the adoption of the best processes, and throws each operation into the hands of those who are best qualified for it" (*Subjection*, CW:XXI.273).

The same idea regarding the primacy of liberty persisted in Mill's view as regards the relations between the rich and poor: the "old" theory of dependence on superiors was to be replaced by the "modern" idea of "self-dependence". The "old" theory views the rich as parents to the poor – guiding, restraining, and providing food, clothes, housing, and amusement to the poor in return for labor and attachment. However, not only is dependence unjustified under the rule of law – one who possesses or earns an independent livelihood, Mill noted, requires no "other protection than that which the law could and ought to give"; also, being in a position of liability to some powerful individual, "instead of being as formerly the sole condition of safety, is now, speaking generally, the only situation which exposes to grievous wrong". Mill was clear: "[a]ll privileged and powerful classes, as such, have used their power in the interest of their own selfishness, and have indulged their self-importance in despising, and not in lovingly caring for, those who were, in their estimation, degraded, by being under the necessity of working for their benefit" (*Principles*, CW: III.760 – 761).

The aim in an advanced state of society is to enable human beings "to work with or for one another in relations not involving dependence" (*Principles*, CW: III.768). Since social happiness, Mill repeated, "must exist by means of the justice and self-government, the *dikaiosynê* and *sôphrosynê*, of the individual citizens", reason and virtue must become common properties to all members of community. For Mill, the cardinal virtue of *sôphrosunê*, i.e., self-government, referred to the ability of individuals to use their reason to set their own direction (*On Liberty*, CW:XVIII.263, 265 – 266, 271 – 272. See further Loizides 2013: ch. 8). Hence, in the current state of advancement of modern nations, Mill argued, the laboring classes, and the poor more generally, must "come out of leading-strings". Whatever advice or encouragement is directed to them must be "accepted by them with their eyes open". Treating the poor as equals calls for allowing them to judge for themselves the direction they should go. The increasing unwillingness of the poor to be led and governed by the mere authority and prestige of superiors, Mill noted, ought not to be confused with their ability to acknowledge epistemic authority (*Principles*, CW:III.763–765). Essentially, Mill stressed the point that the poor have a claim to receiving, weighing and acting on reasons rather than being made dependent on the will of others. To allow for a regard for justice or fairness, in the relations between rich and poor, means that both take on responsibilities towards the other (*Principles*, CW:III.767), acknowledging their respective claims; only then can they secure social well-being.

Mill's rhetoric as regards race equality was markedly different than the question of gender and class equality: as long as a person is recognized as a human being, Mill argued, that person is "entitled to human rights" ("The Contest in America" (1862), CW:XXI.138). In the case of gender and class equality, the law was severely lacking, as it fostered dependence of some on (the will of) others, rather than self-dependence (or independence), thus undermining a person's ability to pursue her/his happiness. Mill thus focused on convincing the powerful to forego their privileges sanctioned by law, and, at the same time, on inspiring action by the disadvantaged to demand change both in the legal system and social mores. His argumentation was doubly limited: considerations of social expediency were mainly directed at the privileged and considerations of justice at the excluded (letter to A. Bain, 14 Jul. 1869, CW:XVII.1623. See further McCabe 2014). But this did not hold in the case of slavery. Already by 1807, the Slave Trade Act had been passed and enforced throughout the British Empire. The "civilized world has in general made up its mind on" treating human beings as property (*Principles*, CW:II.233): the cause of justice called for the abolition of slavery. In 1850, Mill expressed his surprise that there were some who wanted to undo "the best and greatest achievement yet performed by mankind": rescuing human life "from the iniquitous dominion of the law of might" ("The Negro Question" (1850), CW:XXI.88, 87). In 1862, he had an answer to why the younger generations underestimated the importance of this "summing-up and concentration" of all social evils: being received opinion for more than a generation, it had lost its vitality (alluding here to *On Liberty*) and thus its hold over their feelings. Still, for Mill, the "universal [rights] of humanity" as well as "the general law of right" prohibited the exercise of "permanent dominion over any human beings as subjects, or on any other footing than that of equal citizenship" ("The Slave Power" (1862), CW:XXI.158; letter to W.M. Dickson, 1 Sep. 1865, CW:XVI.1100).

Treating slaves as human beings, Mill admitted, would lead slave-owners to ruin ("Contest in America", CW:XXI.134). But their liability to ruin did not count as grievance enough to prevent slave emancipation (though it merited some form of compensation): "those who rebel for the power of oppressing others", Mill argued, do not "exercise as sacred a right as those who do the same thing to resist oppression practised upon themselves" ("Contest in America", CW:XXI.137). No person, Mill proclaimed, is born servant to another ("Negro Question", CW: XXI.92). Even if one grants that the differences between individuals are due to an original difference of nature – which Mill denied – the 'morality of the question' is not affected:

> were the whites born ever so superior in intelligence to the blacks, and competent by nature to instruct and advise them, it would not be the less monstrous to assert that they had therefore a right either to subdue them by force, or circumvent them by superior skill, to throw upon them the toils and hardships of life, reserving for themselves, under the misapplied name of work, its agreeable excitements ("Negro Question", CW:XXI.93).

However, those who have "no moral repugnance to the thought of human beings born to the penal servitude for life", Mill argued twelve years later, were partly responsible for the inconsistency of the moral attitude of the English public opinion as regards the American civil war ("Contest in America", CW:XXI.128– 129; "Slave Power", CW:XXI.157–158). But, for Mill, there should not be any scruple: slave owners are "in rebellion not for simple slavery, they are in rebellion for the right of burning human creatures alive"; for that, they are "enemies of mankind" ("Contest in America", CW:XXI.136–137).

4

Sections 2 and 3 attempted to show that Mill did believe that individuality ought to be inviolable. The second prong of the question to the utilitarian was that whether or not that inviolability is valuable in itself; the sketch of Mill's responses to two contemporary debates suggested not; only against slavery was he adamant that it was a matter of human rights. Still, in *On Liberty*, Mill stated:

> It is proper to state that I forego any advantage which could be derived to my argument from the idea of abstract right, as a thing independent of utility. I regard utility as the ultimate appeal on all ethical questions: but it must be utility in the largest sense, grounded on the permanent interests of man as a progressive being (*On Liberty*, CW:XVIII.224).

If, for Mill, utility was the ultimate appeal, how could justice trump questions of social expediency? Mill admitted that references to "universal" or "human" rights, and the "general law of right" provided a *rhetorical* advantage in arguments on the proper grounds of social interference; so, how could he claim that the inviolability of individuality was not merely skin deep?

Mill's "ultimate appeal" drew from his theory of an "Art of Life", the *philosophia prima* which consists in the first principles of conduct. According to Mill, the Art of Life is divided into three domains: morality (the right), prudence (the expedient) and aesthetics (the beautiful, noble). All three domains fall under the Principle of Utility (general expediency). The Art of Life thus deals with questions which concern the final and intermediate ends of conduct, how acts (and their ends) can be grouped according to some common attribute (including how they are divided according to other common attributes) and how they relate within a hierarchy, both at the level of each domain separately and at that of the Principle of Utility (*Logic*, CW:VIII.949–951. See further Loizides 2013: ch. 7). Mill argued that "there are different orders of expediency; all expediencies are not exactly on the same level". More importantly, he argued that considerations of justice are a branch of expediency of the highest level (Speech on "Admission of Women to Franchise", 20 May 1867, CW:XXVIII.152). The reference to expediency did not mean that Mill had failed to award a special place to justice.

According to Mill, "the right to life, to reputation, to the free disposal of one's person and faculties, to exemption from bodily harm or indignity, and to any external thing of which one is the legal owner", among others, are rights *in rem* ("Austin on Jurisprudence" (1863), CW:XXI.196). These rights are held against all persons, who have the obligation to refrain for acting in ways which infringe upon these rights. So, for Mill, whether or not an individual is fit to "exist as one of the fellowship of human beings" is decided by that individual's ability to fulfill the obligations of justice: avoiding acts of wrongful aggression, abstaining from wrongful exercise of power over some other individual, and refraining from wrongfully withholding from others something which is their due. In all these cases, individuals harm others, either by causing direct suffering, or by depriving some good (including social goods) which others had reasonable ground for counting upon (*Utilitarianism*, CW:X.256). All these cases, however, are violations of "duties of perfect obligation": not only has a wrong been done but also there is some assignable person who did it: "[j]ustice implies something which it is not only right to do, and wrong not to do, but which some individual person can claim from us as his moral right" (*Utilitarianism*, CW:X.247; see also Hart 1982).

Rights, Mill argued, create valid claims on society for protection (*Utilitarianism*, CW:X.250). But there's the rub. This is no ordinary claim; it is the foundation of security, the "most indispensable of all necessaries" and the "most vital of all interests":

> Our notion [...] of the claim we have on our fellow-creatures to join in making safe for us the very groundwork of our existence, gathers feelings round it so much more intense than

those concerned in any of the more common cases of utility, that the difference in degree [...] becomes a real difference in kind. (*Utilitarianism*, CW:X.251)

"The claim", Mill went on, "assumes that character of absoluteness, that apparent infinity, and incommensurability with all other considerations" (*Utilitarianism*, CW:X.251). For Mill, justice refers to moral rules which concern the "essentials of human well-being more nearly, and are therefore of more absolute obligation, than any other rules for the guidance of life". This absolute originates in the feelings of self-protection and sympathy which extend self-protection to families, groups and societies. The sense of justice becomes moral, Mill noted, through a concern with the claims of others; the need to retaliate either for revenge or self-protection itself was amoral – it could become either moral or immoral according to the harm produced to the interests of others (*Utilitarianism*, CW:X.255; *On Liberty*, CW:XVIII.276), i.e. general expediency.

Originating in the very nature of human beings, justice comes to be "guarded by a sentiment not only different in degree, but also in kind; distinguished from the milder feeling which attaches to the mere idea of promoting human pleasure or convenience, at once by the more definite nature of its commands, and by the sterner character of its sanctions" (*Utilitarianism*, CW:X.259). In the choice between justice and the idea of promoting pleasure or convenience, "all or almost all who have experience of both give a decided preference, irrespective of any feeling of moral obligation to prefer it", to the first. Mill's associationist psychology allowed for justice to be

> placed so far above [the promotion of "human pleasure or convenience"] that they prefer it, even though knowing it to be attended with a greater amount of discontent, and would not resign it for any quantity of the other pleasure which their nature is capable of, we are justified in ascribing to the preferred enjoyment a superiority in quality, so far outweighing quantity as to render it, in comparison, of small account. (*Utilitarianism*, CW:X.212)

In *Logic*, Mill argued that kinds are divided by "an unfathomable chasm" that cannot be bridged (CW:VII.65–69, 73–75, 123; VIII.787–788). In this way, the life of an innocent person can never be sacrificed for entertainment – no gain in social utility can justify such a sacrifice (see Riley 2010a, 2010b). Mill argued that individuals know the difference between kinds of sensations just by "observation and experiment upon the kind itself" (*Logic*, CW:VIII.719, 659; see Riley 2014). Not only did Mill apply the test of experience to questions of personal pursuits – attachments are a direct outcome of individuals having numerous experiences – but also to considerations of justice. Having both the experience of being *wronged* and being *inconvenienced*, all individuals are competent alike (i.e., drawing on their sensations, emotions, thoughts and volitions) in acknowledging the higher value of vital interests; consequently, they award them the status of legal and moral rights which society ought to protect, leaving the regulation of other, minor inconveniences to the individuals themselves (*Utilitarianism*, CW:X.211; *Logic*, CW:VII.123; *Examination of Sir William Hamilton's Philosophy* (1865), CW:IX.430 ff.). Hence, Mill's view of justice as involving a distinction in kind rather one of degree renders his references to "human rights" substantial, not merely rhetorical. Most importantly, as we shall see presently, the preference for the life of justice is grounded in a sense of dignity.

5

Sections 2, 3, and 4 argued that Mill had the resources to respond to the two-prong challenge of what recognition al respect entails. Further, Scarre suggested that a person who does not recognize the claims of others to respect them as persons falls short of the human ideal. Fulfilling or falling short of an ideal of doing or being is a form of appraisal respect; Mill's reference to a sense of dignity had much to do with defining such an ideal.

For Mill, the morality of an action and the moral estimation of the agent that performed it are not the same thing. A person's conduct in a given situation, Mill argued, can be appraised according to the feelings it stimulates. These feelings can be of three sorts: moral, aesthetic and sympathetic – individuals estimate particular actions and agents in different ways, since "the moral view of actions and characters", albeit unquestionably having priority, is not the only one "by which our sentiments towards the human being may be, ought to be, and without entirely crushing our own nature cannot but be, materially influenced". Moral approbation "addresses itself to our reason and conscience", aesthetic approbation to our imagination, and, lastly, sympathy, to our human fellow-feeling. As Mill noted: "[a]ccording to the first, we approve or disapprove; according to the second, we admire or despise; according to the third, we love, pity, or dislike. The morality of an action depends on its foreseeable consequences; its beauty, and its loveableness, or the reverse, depend on the qualities which it is evidence of" ("Bentham", CW:X.112).

Reason can grasp arguments on how to live virtuously, according to Mill; however, reason alone cannot create the desire for such a life – unless one already desires such a life, having experienced it, s/he cannot be made to feel how that life would be experienced. As Mill put it: "[i]t is impossible, by any arguments, to prove that a life of obedience to duty is preferable, so far as respects the agent himself, to a life of circumspect and cautious selfishness" ("Plato's Gorgias" (1834), CW:XI.97, 149). In *Autobiography*, Mill recorded that even though he was convinced of the truth of his teachers' belief that the social feelings which aimed at the good of others "were the greatest and surest sources of happiness", by the end of 1820s, he came to realize that "to know that a feeling would make me happy if I had it, did not give me the feeling" (*Autobiography*, CW:I.139, 143).

Mill admitted that a person is "capable of pursuing spiritual perfection as an end; of desiring, for its own sake, the conformity of his own character to his standard of excellence, without hope of good or fear of evil from other source than his own inward consciousness". Mill was referring to the feeling of approbation or disapprobation towards ourselves; but respect and admiration, approval and disapproval, Mill argued, can also be directed to "our fellow-creatures" (*Utilitarianism*, CW:X.220n, 220–221; "Bentham", CW:X.95–96). Mill thus did not seem to believe that people are influenced by a mode of action simply by approving it, unless they already desire the ends such an action advances. For people to be influenced to act similarly, when they are not already inclined to do so, actions have to be admirable and loveable, to work on their imagination and excite care for the well-being of others – not to work on their rational faculties alone. Irrespective of what original circumstances influenced the formation of their character, individuals ought to strive by education and training to direct their conduct toward virtuous pursuits; according to Mill, it is "paralysing to our desire of excellence" as well as humiliating to our sense of dignity to feel unable to do so (*Logic*, CW:VIII.838, 841; *Utilitarianism*, CW:X.212).

Both society and education, Mill argued, are necessary for the improvement of mankind: "the duty of man is to co-operate with the beneficent powers", germs of which can be found in human nature, "by perpetually striving to amend the course of nature – and bringing that part of it over which we can exercise control, more nearly into conformity with a high standard of justice and goodness" ("Nature" (1874), CW:X.402). Both self- and other-regarding virtues can be cultivated so that they become consistently present in human conduct. When such virtues are cultivated "the most elevated sentiments of which humanity is capable become a second nature, stronger than the first, and not so much subduing the original nature as merging it into itself" ("Nature", CW: X.393–396). Self-culture or self-education consist thus in half of morality ("Bentham" (1838), CW:X.98). In *Utilitarianism*, Mill famously argued "no intelligent human being would consent to be a fool, no instructed person would be an ignoramus, no person of feeling and conscience would be selfish and base, even though they should be persuaded that the fool, the dunce, or the rascal is better satisfied with his lot than they are with theirs". No one would "really wish to sink into what he feels to be a lower grade of existence". The higher kinds of life are associated with a sense of dignity, "which all human beings possess in one form or other" (*Utilitarianism*, CW:X.211–212, 231).

A person's own desire to shape her/his character in some way is an important circumstance that can influence the process of character formation; as Mill put it, "[w]e are exactly as capable of making our own character, *if we will*, as others are of making it for us". By working on some of the means of character formation, individuals can do much to modify their "future habits or capabilities of willing" (*Logic*, CW:VIII.840; *Autobiography*, CW:I.177). Individuals wish to change their character when their sense of dignity is prompted by their experience of the lower kind of life to which their habits were leading them or once they have experienced a strong feeling of admiration, e.g. witnessing the virtuous exertions of some other individual. Unless individuals wish to alter their character, they do not feel the desperation that they cannot – they have already lost their capacity to experience the higher kinds of life (*Logic*, CW:VIII.840–841). Hence Mill claimed that:

> There is besides, a natural affinity between goodness and the cultivation of the Beautiful. When it is real cultivation, and not a mere unguided instinct. He who has learnt what beauty is, if he be of a virtuous character, will desire to realize it in his own life – will keep before himself a type of perfect beauty in human character, to light his attempts at self-culture. ("Inaugural Address Delivered to the University of St. Andrews" (1867), CW:XXI.255)

A proper education takes individuals beyond considerations of expediency: life should be viewed as any work "which is done as if the workman loved it, and tried to make it as good as possible, though something less good would have answered the purpose for which it was ostensibly made" ("Inaugural Address", CW:XXI.256). Mill considered the development of personal worth to which such a comprehensive education leads as a reward in itself:

> there is one reward which will not fail you, and which may be called disinterested, because it is not a consequence, but is inherent in the very fact of deserving it, the deeper and more varied interest you will feel in life, which will give it tenfold its value, a value which will last to the end. ("Inaugural Address", CW:XXI.257)

The gains of self-development in terms of respect for ourselves and for others as persons was thus "obvious without being specified" ("Theism" (1874), CW:X.489. See Ryan 1970, pp. 250–255).

6

"[R]espect for persons is mandatory, not optional", Leslie Green notes, "and though its requirements and expression are shaped by culture and history, it is not dependent for its ultimate binding force on such contingencies and not on any contingency like consent or agreement" (Green 2010, p. 216). I have shown that Mill's utilitarian theory has the resources to incorporate the idea of the respect for persons. I also suggested that the question the utilitarian is called upon to answer is two-pronged: not only that s/he can accommodate the ideal of inviolability of human dignity; but that inviolability is valuable for its own sake. On one hand, for Mill the individual is sovereign in all that concerns one's self; simply, one has immunity in the self-regarding sphere. When an individual has immunity, that individual is not in a position of disability with reference to some other person. As Mill put it, "[o]ver himself, over his own body and mind, the individual is sovereign". To be sovereign means to be in a position to claim control over how one's self, body and mind function; in turn, this creates the duty to others to refrain from actions which undermine the person's "asylum of individuality". Not only is giving full scope to individuality to assert itself in the private sphere (or in the market place) socially expedient, Mill argued, but protecting individuality eliminates a long-standing practice wrong in itself: the law of whoever is stronger. On the other hand, as far as the second part of the question is concerned (whether or not invoking expediency undermines the inviolability of dignity), for Mill questions of justice were inherently weightier than questions of simple expediency: individuality should never be violated. The difference between justice and expediency is one of kind, not of degree. As such, no matter what gain in the latter, justice always prevails – and this was grounded, as we saw, "on the permanent interests of man as a progressive being". Finally, coming full circle, I tried to show that for Mill "[a]mong the works of man, which human life is rightly employed in perfecting and beautifying, the first in importance surely is man himself" (*On Liberty*, CW: XVIII.263). Once an individual leads a life of justice, s/he will refrain from anything that fails to respect valid claims of others – her/his sense of dignity will not allow that person "to sink into what he feels to be a lower grade of existence", that is, one which falls "well short of the human ideal".

Bibliography

Ball, T. (2000): "The Formation of Character: Mill's 'Ethology' Reconsidered", *Polity* 33 (1), pp. 25–48.
[Brougham, H.] (1828): *Present State of the Law*, 2nd ed, London: Henry Colburn.
Burgess-Jackson, K. (1995): "John Stuart Mill, Radical Feminist", *Social Theory and Practice* 21 (3), pp. 369–396.
Darwall, S.L. (1977): "Two Kinds of Respect", *Ethics* 88 (1), pp. 36–49.
Darwall, S.L. (2004): "Respect and the Second-Person Standpoint", *Proceedings and Addresses of the American Philosophical Association* 78 (2), pp. 43–59.
Darwall, S.L. (2006): *The Second-Person Standpoint: Morality, Respect, and Accountability*, Cambridge, MA: Harvard University Press.
Demetriou, K.N. and Loizides, A. (2013): "Introduction". In K.N. Demetriou and A. Loizides: *John Stuart Mill: A British Socrates*, Basingstoke: Palgrave Macmillan: pp. 1–16.
Feinberg, J. (1970): "The Nature and Value of Rights", *Journal of Value Inquiry* 4, pp. 243–257.
Green, L. (2010): "Two Worries about Respect for Persons", *Ethics* 120 (2), pp. 212–231.
Haldane R. (1842): *Exposition of the Epistle to the Romans*, new ed., 3 vols., Edinburgh: William Whyte.
Hart, H.L.A. (1979): "Between Utility and Rights", *Columbia Law Review* 79 (5), pp. 828–846.
Hart, H.L.A. (1982): "Natural Rights: Bentham and John Stuart Mill". In H.L.A. Hart: *Essays on Bentham: Studies in Jurisprudence and Political Theory*, Oxford: Oxford University Press, pp. 79–104.
Hudson, S.D. (1980): "The Nature of Respect", *Social Theory and Practice* 6 (1), pp. 69–90.
Kant, I. (2002): *Groundwork for the Metaphysics of Morals*, ed. and trans. by A.W. Wood, New Haven/London: Yale University Press.
Livermore, A. (1853): *The Acts of the Apostles with Commentary*, London: Sampson Low.
Loizides, A. (2013): *John Stuart Mill's Platonic Heritage: Happiness through Character*, Lanham, MD: Lexington Books.
McCabe, H. (2014): "John Stuart Mill's Philosophy of Persuasion", *Informal Logic* 34 (1), pp. 38–61.
Milgate, M and Stimson S.C. (2009): *After Adam Smith; A Century of Transformation in Politics and Political Economy*, Princeton: Princeton University Press.
Mill, J.S. (1963–1991): *Collected Works of John Stuart Mill*, 33 vols., ed. by J.M. Robson, Toronto: Toronto University Press.
Moller Okin, S. (1979): *Women in Western Political Thought*, Princeton: Princeton University Press.
Nicholson, P. (1998): "The Reception and Early Reputation of Mill's Political Thought". In J.M. Skorupski (Ed.): *The Cambridge Companion to Mill*, Cambridge: Cambridge University Press, pp. 464–496.
Rawls, J. (1980): "Kantian Constructivism in Moral Theory", *The Journal of Philosophy* 77 (9), pp. 515–572.
Rawls, J. (1999): *A Theory of Justice*, rev. ed., Cambridge, MA: Belknap Press.
Riley, J. (2010a): "Justice as Higher Pleasure". In G. Varouxakis and P. Kelly (Eds.): *John Stuart Mill: Thought and Influence – The Saint of Rationalism*, London/New York: Routledge, pp. 119–145.

Riley, J. (2010b): "Mill's Extraordinary Utilitarian Moral Theory", *Politics, Philosophy & Economics* 9, pp. 67–116.
Riley, J. (2014): "Different Kinds of Pleasure". In A. Loizides: *Mill's A System of Logic: Critical Appraisals*, London/New York: Routledge, pp. 170–191.
Robson, J.M. (1968): *The Improvement of Mankind*, London: Routledge and Kegan Paul.
Rosen, F. (2013): *Mill*, Oxford: Oxford University Press.
Ryan, A. (1970): *The Philosophy of John Stuart Mill*, London: Macmillan.
Scarre, G. (1992): "Utilitarianism and Self-Respect", *Utilitas* 4 (1), pp. 27–42.
Smart, J.C. and Williams B. (1973): *Utilitarianism: For and Against*, Cambridge: Cambridge University Press.
Varouxakis, G. (1998): "John Stuart Mill on Race", *Utilitas* 10 (1), pp. 17–32.
Varouxakis, G. (2013): "'Negrophilist' Crusader: John Stuart Mill on the American Civil War and Reconstruction", *History of European Ideas* 39 (5), pp. 729–754.

Manuel Knoll
The Cardinal Role of Respect and Self-Respect for Rawls's and Walzer's Theories of Justice[1]

Abstract: The cardinal role that notions of respect and self-respect play in Rawls's *A Theory of Justice* has already been abundantly examined in the literature. On the other hand, however, it has hardly been noticed that these notions are also central to Michael Walzer's *Spheres of Justice*. Respect and self-respect are not only central topics of his chapter "Recognition", but constitute a central aim of a "complex egalitarian society" and of Walzer's theory of justice. This paper substantiates this thesis and elucidates Walzer's criticism of Rawls according to which" we need to distinguish between "self-respect" and "self-esteem".

1 Introduction

The cardinal role that notions of respect and self-respect play in Rawls's *A Theory of Justice* has already been abundantly examined in the literature (Bernick 1978, Eyal 2005, Keat and Miller 1974, Nielsen 1979, Shue 1975, Zaino 1998; recently in the context of Rawls's argument for stability Zink 2011). On the other hand, it has hardly been noticed that these notions are also central for Michael Walzer's *Spheres of Justice*.[2] While Walzer clearly distinguishes between "self-respect" and "self-esteem", Rawls uses the two terms as synonyms (Walzer 1983, p. 274; Rawls 1971, p. 440, § 67). Rawls's failure to distinguish between these two notions has frequently been criticized and discussed.[3]

---

[1] For helpful comments on this paper I thank Tuğba Sevinç Yücel. For some improvements in style I am grateful to Barry Stocker.
[2] The volume *Pluralism, Justice, and Equality*, edited by David Miller and Michael Walzer, deals with recognition and respect only on the sidelines (Miller and Walzer 1995). The articles in the volumes *Reading Walzer* and *Freiheit, soziale Güter und Gerechtigkeit* do not examine these notions at all (Benbaji and Sussmann 2014, Nusser 2012). A cooperative commentary edited on *Spheres of Justice* contains one article on recognition (Knoll and Spieker 2014). However, the author does not argue for a central role for recognition and respect in Walzer's theory of justice (Schütz 2014). The same is true for Russell Keat's and Arto Laitinen's articles (Keat 1997, Laitinen 2014).
[3] Walzer 1983, pp. 274, 277, 335 (fn. 42); Darwall 1977; for more literature on this criticism and discussion see Zaino 1998, p. 738, n. 5. In a footnote to *Spheres of Justice*, Michael Walzer refers

It is evident that notions of respect and self respect play a cardinal role in John Rawls's *A Theory of Justice*. For him, "self-respect (or self-esteem)" is, as he repeatedly states, "perhaps the most important primary good" (Rawls 1971, pp. 440, 544; § 67, § 82). Rawls claims that the fact that his conception of justice as fairness "gives more support to self-esteem than other principles is a strong reason" that it would be adopted in the "original position" and chosen over competing conceptions (Rawls 1971, p. 440, § 67; cf. pp. 178–79, § 29).[4] Similarly, in *Political Liberalism* Rawls talks about "the fundamental importance of self-respect" and asserts "that self-respect is most effectively encouraged and supported by the two principles of justice" (Rawls 2005, p. 318, VIII, § 6). Rawls's conception of self-respect and its role in his theory of justice as fairness seem to undergo no significant modifications or developments after *A Theory of Justice*. However, Rawls's statements on self-respect and in particular the "bases of self-respect" and their status as primary goods in *A Theory of Justice* and *Political Liberalism* are sometimes unclear and confusing.

After a short and partly critical second section on Rawls's understanding of respect and self-respect, this essay substantiates the thesis that notions of respect and self-respect play a cardinal role in Walzer's *Spheres of Justice*. Self-respect and self-esteem are not only central topics in his chapter "Recognition", but constitute a central aim of his whole theory of justice. Section three provides a very short introduction to Walzer's theory of distributive justice and to his chapter "Recognition". The fourth section examines his concepts of public honor and individual desert and shows that, in this context, Walzer advances a strong argument against Rawls's theory of justice. Section five substantiates the thesis that self-respect and self-esteem constitute a central aim of a "complex egalitarian society" and of Walzer's theory of justice.

2 John Rawls on Self-Respect

John Rawls not only claims that his conception of justice as fairness gives more support to self-respect than others, but argues that every conception of justice "should publicly express men's respect for one another" (Rawls 1971, p. 179,

---

to David Sachs's distinction between "self-respect" and "self-esteem" (Sachs 1981) and comments: "David Sachs is one of the few contemporary philosophers who has written about this distinction" (Walzer 1983, p. 334, n. 38).

4 In *A Theory of Justice*, Rawls understands the "original position" mainly as a favorable interpretation of an "initial choice situation" for principles of justice (Rawls 1971, pp. 11–19, 118–192; § 3, § 4, §§ 20–30).

§ 29). Respect leads to self-respect and *vice versa*. Self-respect is "reciprocally self-supporting". This means that "those who respect themselves are more likely to respect each other and conversely" (Rawls 1971, p. 179, § 29). For Rawls, "self-respect (or self-esteem)" is opposed to "self-contempt" and has two crucial aspects that are related to each other (Rawls 1971, p. 179, § 29). He defines these aspects in § 67 of *A Theory of Justice*. First, self-respect

> includes a person's sense of his own value, his secure conviction that his conception of the good, his plan of life, is worth carrying out. And second, self-respect implies a confidence in one's ability, so far as it is within one's power, to fulfill one's intentions (Rawls 1971, p. 440, § 67).

These two aspects describe the desirable mental state of a person who has self-respect. A person's sense of her own value cannot be achieved by an isolated individual because it essentially depends on an intersubjective or social dimension. For Rawls, "our self-respect normally depends upon the respect of others. Unless we feel that our endeavors are honored by them, it is difficult if not impossible for us to maintain the conviction that our ends are worth advancing" (Rawls 1971, p. 178, § 29). Self-respect depends on "finding our person and deeds appreciated and confirmed by others" (Rawls 1971, p. 440, § 67).

For Rawls, a person's sense of her own value is not primarily linked to her job, income or wealth, but to her conception of the good or her plan of life. According to his theory, human beings are equal as moral persons. Moral persons are defined by both their capabilities of having a sense of justice and of having a "conception of their good (as expressed by a rational plan of life)" (Rawls 1971, pp. 19, 505; § 4, § 77).[5] In the modern world, individuals "have different plans of life" and "there exists a diversity of philosophical and religious belief" (Rawls 1971, p. 127, § 22). According to Rawls's "thin theory" of the good, "a person's good is determined by what is for him the most rational plan of life given reasonable favorable circumstances" (Rawls 1971, pp. 395–396, § 60). If a person's rational plan of life is recognized or approved by the other members of society, the person develops the conviction that her plan is worth carrying out and, as a consequence, develops a sense of her own value.[6]

---

5 Cf. Rawls 2005, pp. 310–324, VIII, §§ 5–6. For Rawls, "the capacity for moral personality is a sufficient condition for being entitled to equal justice" (Rawls 1971, p. 505, § 77).
6 Rawls declares about the opposite scenario, in which a person's rational plan of life is not socially recognized or approved: "When we feel that our plans are of little value, we cannot pursue them with pleasure or take delight in their execution" (Rawls 1971, p. 440, § 67).

The social recognition or approval of the different plans of life in a just society is in particular expressed by Rawls's first principle of justice that calls for "an equal right to the most extensive total system of equal basic liberties" (Rawls 1971, p. 302; § 46). The first principle, which includes the equal liberty of conscience and the right to vote and to be eligible for public office, ensures equal citizenship and thus a similar and secure status for all members of society. On this basis, "a variety of communities and associations" or "free communities of interest" can be established that allow all citizens to carry out their plans of life (Rawls 1971, pp. 441, 544; § 67, § 82). In a just society, the equal distribution of the fundamental rights and liberties guaranteed by the first principle constitutes the basis for self-respect (Rawls 1971, p. 544, § 82).

Rawls emphasizes that among his two principles it is in particular the equal liberty principle that is supposed to promote and sustain self-respect: "The basis for self-esteem in a just society is not then one's income share but the publicly affirmed distribution of fundamental rights and liberties" (Rawls 1971, p. 544; § 82; cf. Rawls 2005, p. 318, VIII, § 6). Rawls's argument from self-respect is not only an important argument for his conception of justice as fairness in general, but in particular for the priority of liberty among the two principles (Rawls 1971, pp. 541–548, 544–546, § 82; cf. Shue 1975, Taylor 2003). Critics have rightly objected that individual self-respect depends to a considerable amount also on one's income share and that the importance Rawls gives to self-respect among the primary goods calls for less socioeconomic inequality than Rawls's difference principle allows (Barry 1973, p. 32[7]; Eyal 2005; Keat and Miller 1974; Miler 1978, p. 18; Nielsen 1979; Zaino 1998). In modern work and market societies, the social status and self-respect of a person depends to a high degree on her job and on being able to buy a certain set of commodities.[8]

---

[7] Barry criticizes Rawls: "That equality of self-respect may be as much or more hindered by inequalities of wealth or power themselves apparently does not occur to him" (Barry 1973, p. 32). This criticism is exaggerated because Rawls clearly states about his idea that the "precedence of liberty entails equality in the social bases of self-respect": "Now it is quite possible that this idea cannot be carried through completely. To some extend men's sense of their own worth may hinge upon their institutional position and their income share" (Rawls 1971, p. 546, § 82; cf. p. 534, § 80; cf. Zaino 1998).

[8] Cf. Walzer's analysis of sociologist Lee Rainwater's studies on the "social meaning of income", according to which in industrial societies money buys membership (Walzer 1983, pp. 105–106). Walzer also quotes another sociologist and refers to the difference between the society of feudal Europe and modern bourgeois society: "Status, Frank Parfin argues, is a function of place, profession, and office, not of particular recognitions of particular achievements. The abolition of titles is not the abolition of classes. Conceptions of honor are more controversial than they

According to the second aspect, "self-respect implies a confidence in one's ability, so far as it is within one's power, to fulfill one's intentions". This second aspect is related to the first one in terms of being its prerequisite. A person must have the confidence that she has the ability to fulfill her particular plan of life in order to follow it through and to have "the will to strive for" it. If we are "plagued by failure and self-doubt" we cannot "continue in our endeavors" (Rawls 1971, p. 440, § 67).

Both aspects of self-respect, and in particular the first, are associated with what Rawls calls the "Aristotelian Principle". This principle "is a principle of motivation" and "runs as follows: other things equal, human beings enjoy the exercise of their realized capacities (their innate or trained abilities), and this enjoyment increases the more the capacity is realized, or the greater its complexity" (Rawls 1971, pp. 426–427, § 65). Rawls illustrates this principle referring to people who are able to play both checkers and chess. As chess is a more ingenious and complicated game than checkers, it leads to more enjoyment. Therefore, such kinds of people are more motivated to play the former than the latter (Rawls 1971, p. 426–427, § 65). Analogously, people enjoy their plans of life much more if these plans succeed as a

> call upon their natural capacities in an interesting fashion. When activities fail to satisfy the Aristotelian Principle, they are likely to seem dull and flat, and to give us no feeling of competence or a sense that they are worth doing. A person tends to be more confident of his value when his abilities are both fully realized and organized in ways of suitable complexity and refinement (Rawls 1971, p. 440, § 67).

The more a person's plan of life allows her to develop and exercise her capacities and abilities and the more this plan of life is recognized or approved by the other members of society, the more she will be able to develop a sense of her own value or self-respect.

Rawls discusses the objection that the high demands of the Aristotelian Principle make it difficult for less gifted individuals to gain recognition for their personal life plans from others. However, he counters this objection by claiming that it "normally suffices that for each person there is some association (one or more) to which he belongs and within which the activities that are rational for him are publicly affirmed by others. In this way we acquire a sense that what we do in everyday life is worthwhile" (Rawls 1971, p. 441, § 67). Rawls does not give concrete examples of the kind of associations and communities

---

were under the old regime, but distributions are still patterned, now dominated by occupation rather than blood or rank" (Walzer 1983, p. 256).

he has in mind. In all likelihood he thinks of a variety of clubs, societies, unions, corporations and such like. Being a member of such kinds of associations also has a beneficial effect on self-respect: Associative "ties strengthen the second aspect of self-esteem, since they tend to reduce the likelihood of failure and provide support against the sense of self-doubt when mishaps occur" (Rawls 1971, p. 441, § 67).

As a Kantian, Rawls not only talks about "principles of justice for institutions", but also about "principles of natural duty and obligations that apply to individuals" (Rawls 1971, p. 333, chap. VI). His theory claims that in an "original position of equality", free and rational persons would also choose principles of natural duty. One important natural duty is the "duty of mutual respect": "This is the duty to show a person the respect which is due to him as a moral being" (Rawls 1971, p. 337, § 51). As already mentioned, moral beings are defined as persons with a sense of justice and with a conception of their good. In correspondence to the two aspects of moral personality, mutual respect is shown "in our willingness to see the situation of others from their point of view, from the perspective of their conception of their good; and in our being prepared to give reasons for our actions whenever the interests of others are materially affected" (Rawls 1971, p. 337, § 51).[9] Rawls convincingly claims that everyone benefits "from living in a society where the duty of mutual respect is honored" and that such a duty supports everyone's sense of her own value and thus self-respect.

This short clarification and critique of Rawls's view of respect and self-respect allows for a final criticism of his central term "bases of self-respect". Rawls introduces this term together with his "general conception of justice", from which he derives his two principles of justice. This "general conception" reads: "All social values – liberty and opportunity, income and wealth, and the bases of self-respect – are to be distributed equally unless an unequal distribution of any, or all, of these values is to everyone's advantage" (Rawls 1971, p. 62, § 11; cf. p. 303, § 46). In this important section of Rawls's book the term "bases of self-respect" remains opaque. After introducing his "general conception", Rawls tells his readers that "liberty and opportunity, income and wealth"

---

[9] Rawls further explains his statement: "When called for, reasons are to be addressed to those concerned; they are to be offered in good faith, in the belief that they are sound reasons as defined by a mutually acceptable conception of justice which takes the good of everyone into account. Thus to respect another as a moral person is to try to understand his aims and interests from his standpoint and to present him with considerations that enable him to accept the constraints on his conduct" (Rawls 1971, pp. 337–338, § 51). In this context, in a footnote that says "On the notion of respect" Rawls refers to Bernard Williams 1962, pp. 118–119.

are "primary goods, that is, things that every rational man is presumed to want" and that these primary goods are distributed by "the basic structure of society"[10] (Rawls 1971, p. 62, § 11). At this point, he mentions for the first time that also self-respect is an important primary good. However, he does not only stay silent about what exactly the social bases of this primary good are, but also does not indicate whether these bases should also be considered as a primary good.[11] On the one hand, these bases are listed among the primary goods that are to be distributed equally;[12] on the other, he only mentions self-respect and not its bases in his enumeration of the chief primary goods on this page.

Only much later in the book, when Rawls introduces the grounds for the priority of the equal liberty principle, he makes clear what he means with his term "bases of self respect". He mentions that "the precedence of liberty entails equality in the social bases of self-respect" and – as already mentioned – states: "The basis for self-esteem in a just society is not then one's income share but the publicly affirmed distribution of fundamental rights and liberties" (Rawls 1971, pp. 546, 544; § 82). Therefore, the social bases of self-respect are primarily identical with the rights and liberties secured by the first principle of justice. This late clarification demonstrates that Rawls was not careful when he phrased his "general conception of justice" because his enumeration of those social values that "are to be distributed equally" lists "liberty and opportunity, income and wealth,

---

[10] The basic structure of the society is composed out of its most important institutions: "By major institutions I understand the political constitution and the principal economic and social arrangements. Thus the legal protection of freedom of thought and liberty of conscience, competitive markets, private property in the means of production, and the monogamous family [...]. Taken together as one scheme, the major institutions define men's rights and duties and influence their life-prospects, what they can expect to be and how well they can hope to do" (Rawls 1971, p. 7, § 2).

[11] Nir Eyal claims that Rawls mentions only five social primary goods including the social bases of self-respect (Eyal 2005, p. 195). However, in the context of his "general conception of justice" Rawls designates only self-respect as a primary good. Eyal seems to be unaware of this problem regarding the difference between self-respect and its social bases.

[12] It seems that Nir Eyal, who has been mention in the preceding footnote, is also not aware of Rawls's "general conception of justice" because he asserts that Rawls nowhere states how the bases of self-respect should be distributed (the first reference to self-respect in the context of the "general conception" has been overlooked in creating the index of *A Theory of Justice*). Eyal claims in his paper that the distributive principle of the social bases of self-respect is Rawls's "covert" principle of justice and undertakes to reconstruct it. The result of this reconstruction is that "justice mandates that each social basis for self-respect be equalized" (Eyal 2005, p. 195–196). However, already in his "general conception of justice" Rawls's states clearly that the bases of self-respect should be "distributed equally unless an unequal distribution of any, or all, of these values is to everyone's advantage" (Rawls 1971, p. 62, § 11; cf. p. 546, § 82).

and the bases of self-respect" (M.K.'s italics). The word "*and*" before "the bases of self-respect" suggests or implies that these bases are something different from all of the afore-mentioned primary goods, which is not the case. Liberty is a primary good that is also the main social basis for self-respect. Therefore, both self-respect and its bases are primary goods. In *Political Liberalism*, Rawls pronounces that also "fair equality of opportunity" counts as a social basis for self-respect (Rawls 2005, p. 203, V, § 7; for several other bases see Eyal 2005, pp. 196, 212). In *Political Liberalism*, Rawls also states clearly that the social bases of self-respect count as one out of five primary goods. However, confusingly enough, now he doesn't list self-respect anymore as a primary good (Rawls 2005, pp. 308–309, 319, VIII, § 4, § 6). In *Justice as Fairness. A Restatement*, Rawls declares "that it is not self-respect as an attitude toward oneself but the social bases of self-respect that count as a primary good" (Rawls 2001, p. 60).[13]

3 Walzer's Theory of Distributive Justice and his Chapter on Recognition

In the preface of the German edition of *Spheres of Justice*, Michael Walzer points out what he holds to be the main difference between his and Rawls's theory of justice. According to Rawls, his two principles of justice are sufficient to regulate the distribution of all desirable social goods, like liberty, opportunity, income and offices. Against this claim, Walzer argues that the broad range of different social goods – membership, welfare, security, free time, education, recognition, political power, etc. – cannot be reduced to "a short list of basic goods", and neither are two principles of justice sufficient to regulate the just distribution of all these social goods (Walzer 1983, p. 5; Walzer 1992, p. 12). Rather, Walzer calls for a diverse set of rules, standards and principles for the distribution of all different social goods. While "from Plato onward" the majority of philosophers who have written about justice assume that "there is one, and only one, distributive system", Walzer argues for a pluralist approach that encompasses a variety of distributions and distributive principles. He claims "that the principles of justice are themselves pluralist in form; that different social goods ought to be distributed for different reasons, in accordance with different procedures, by different agents" (Walzer 1983, pp. 5–6). For him, there is only one universal procedural

---

[13] In the corresponding footnote he states: "*Theory* is ambiguous on this point. It fails to distinguish between self-respect as an attitude, the preserving of which is a fundamental interest, and the social bases that help to support that attitude" (Rawls 2001, p. 60).

rule: each social good should be distributed according to the criteria valid for its own sphere (Walzer 1992, p. 12). Walzer's main suggestion for the multiplicity of social goods and the complexity of distributive systems is his idea of "complex equality". This remarkable idea reconciles the common egalitarian demand for social equality with the recognition of a large number of social inequalities. According to Walzer's republican theory of distributive justice, a just distribution of all social goods leads to a "complex egalitarian society" in which every citizen is equally free from domination and tyranny (Walzer 1983, p. 17; cf. Knoll 2014).

According to Walzer's relativist approach, social goods tend to have different meanings in different societies. The claim of his interpretative method is that the proper distributive criteria of social goods are intrinsic to each particular social good. It is the meaning of each social good that determines the criterion of its just distribution.[14] Walzer argues, for example, that the appropriate understanding of the meaning of medical care and welfare reveals to us that these goods should not be sold but allocated according to need (Walzer 1983, pp. 64–90). The consequence of Walzer's claim that the meaning of each social good determines its criterion of just distribution is that each social good and its distinct meaning constitutes – as he puts it metaphorically – a separate and relatively autonomous sphere of justice: "When meanings are distinct, distributions must be autonomous. Every social good or set of goods constitutes, as it were, a distributive sphere within which only certain criteria and arrangements are appropriate" (Walzer 1983, p. 10). In the case of medical care and welfare in general, these constitute a sphere in which the proper criterion for a just distribution is need. Office, on the other hand, constitutes a sphere in which the suitable criterion is qualification (Walzer 1983, pp. 135–139, 143–147). If all social goods are distributed autonomously and according to their meanings, a "complex egalitarian society" has been reached.

In *Spheres of Justice*, Walzer examines questions of self-esteem and self-respect mainly in the chapter "Recognition". Walzer is aware that the modern philosophy of recognition goes back to Hegel who he quotes twice: "they recognize themselves as mutually recognizing each other" (Walzer 1983, pp. 259, 278). For Hegel, self-consciousness and personal identity depend on recognition by others, which is usually the result of some kind of struggle. In line with this, Walzer calls his first subchapter, in which he approaches his topic from a historical perspective, "The Struggle for Recognition".[15] Like Hegel in the famous chapter on

---

[14] For the difficulties of Walzer's claim that the meaning of each social good determines its criterion of just distribution see Miller 1995, pp. 5–10.
[15] Likewise, the title of Axel Honneth's Habilitationsschrift, which also draws on Hegel's early Jena writings, is *Kampf um Anerkennung* (Honneth 1992).

master and servant, Walzer is interested in the changes that go along with the progress from hierarchical society of feudal Europe to modern bourgeois society. In the former society, social ranks and hereditary titles go along with a certain degree of honor: "Titles are instant recognitions" (Walzer 1983, p. 250). In the latter societies, titles based on blood lose their central importance. The hierarchy of titles among men is substituted by the single title "Master" or "Mister":

> In a society of misters, careers are open to talents, recognitions to whoever can win them. To paraphrase Hobbes, the equality of titles breeds an equality of hope and then a general competition. The struggle for honor that raged among aristocrats [...] is now entered by everyman. It is not, however, aristocratic honor that everyman is after. As the struggle is broadened, so the social good at issue is infinitely diversified, and its name is multiplied. *Honor, respect, esteem, praise, prestige, status, reputation, dignity, rank, regard, admiration, worth, distinction, deference, homage, appreciation, glory, fame, celebrity* [...] (Walzer 1983, p. 252).

In modern bourgeois society, people have no fixed places and ranks, and there exists a plurality of methods by which a variety of forms of recognition can be gained from others. People usually are preoccupied with their own claims to recognition and thus are reluctant to recognize others. However, Walzer is right in observing that people also have the need to give recognition: "we need heroes, men and women whom we can admire without negotiation and without constraint" (Walzer 1983, p. 254). Nevertheless, as recognition is a scarce good and as everyone can compete to obtain it, in modern society life becomes – as probably Hobbes noticed for the first time – a race for better places and more recognition. For Walzer, this is an ambivalent development: "A society of misters is a world of hope, effort, and endless anxiety" (Walzer 1983, p. 254). Recognition is a social good that is mostly distributed unequally. People have different skills and talents and will thus obtain different degrees of recognition. Modern bourgeois society does not promise "equality of outcomes" but "equality of opportunity" (Walzer 1983, p. 256).

Walzer is aware that modern societies do not make good on this promise. He criticizes the social reality that there are still classes and that social status does not depend mainly on individual qualities and "particular achievements", but on the achievement of professional status or an "office"[16]. Walzer condemns

---

16 Walzer defines *office* "as any position in which the political community as a whole takes an interest, choosing the person who holds it or regulating the procedures by which he is chosen" (Walzer 1983, p. 129). According to this definition, most jobs in the modern world have turned into offices because "the state controls licensing procedures and participates in the enforcement

that "office holders command respect in the same way that they command high salaries, without having to prove their worth to their fellow workers or to their clients" (Walzer 1983, p. 256). As he shows in the chapter "Office", the distribution of this social good is so important because "so much else is distributed along with office (or some offices): honor and status, power and prerogative, wealth and comfort" (Walzer 1983, p. 155). As a consequence, in modern societies the struggle for recognition becomes a struggle for office or for jobs and income (Walzer 1983, p. 256).

Walzer speculates on a better alternative to the existing social situation, in which recognition is closely tied to professional status or to holding an office. If these ties were cut, the result could be what he calls "the free appraisal of each person by each other person" (Walzer 1983, p. 257). In such a social arrangement, particular performances and achievements would lead to particular recognitions. For example, respect would not be tied to mere office holding, but to "helpfulness in office" (Walzer 1983, p. 257). The highest honor would only come "to office holders who perform well" (Walzer 1983, p. 272). However, Walzer admits that we don't exactly know how "such world would look like" (Walzer 1983, p. 257).

4 Walzer on Public Honor and Individual Desert. A Strong Argument against Rawls's Theory of Justice

In the subchapter "The Struggle for Recognition", Walzer refers primarily to "individual distributions" of respect, honor, and esteem. However, he is aware that there are also "a variety of collective distributions: rewards, prices, medals, citations, wreaths of laurel" (Walzer 1983, p. 259). Public honor is the reward for outstanding performances, accomplishments or works attributed to an individual or a group of individuals. One of Walzer's main examples for the distribution of public honor is the Nobel Prize in literature. According to his theory, every social good should be distributed in regard to its meaning. Public honor constitutes a separate sphere in which the appropriate criterion for distributions is individual desert: "The crucial standard for public honor is desert" (Walzer 1983, p. 259). Analogously, "punishment, the most important example of public dishonor",

---

of standards for professional practice. Indeed, any employment for which academic certification is required is a kind of office" (Walzer 1983, pp. 130–131).

should be allotted to those individuals who deserve it (Walzer 1983, p. 268). Walzer understands desert not as a subjective or relative criterion but as an "objective measure": "Hence it is distributed by juries, whose members deliver not an opinion but a verdict – a "true speech" about the qualities of the recipients. And on juries thought is not free; it is bound by evidence and rules" (Walzer 1983, p. 259, cf. 268).

Desert is one of three criteria that Walzer distinguishes in his first and pivotal chapter "Complex Equality".[17] An important characteristic of desert is that it "seems to require an especially close connection between particular goods and particular persons" (Walzer 1983, p. 24). In his chapter "Office", in which he distinguishes between qualification and desert, Walzer outlines his concept of desert:

> *Desert* implies a very strict sort of entitlement, such that the title precedes and determines the selection, while *qualification* is a much looser idea. A prize, for example, can be deserved because it already belongs to the person who has given the best performance; it remains only to identify that person. Price committees are like juries in that they look backward and aim at an objective decision. An office, by contrast, cannot be deserved because it belongs to the people who are served by it, and they or their agents are free (within limits I will specify later) to make any choice they please (Walzer 1983, p. 136; Walzer's italics).

If an author has written a novel that is generally agreed to be the best novel of this year, he is entitled to or deserves the Nobel Prize in literature for this year (Walzer 1983, p. 137).

In the literature, it has not always been noticed that Walzer's subchapter "Public Honor and Individual Desert" contains a strong argument against a core element and central moral intuition of Rawls's theory of justice. For Rawls, the "inequalities of birth and natural endowment are undeserved": "No one deserves his greater natural capacity nor merits a more favorable starting place in society" (Rawls 1971, p. 100, 102, cf. 103–104; § 17). Rawls introduces his principle of fair opportunity that provides as much compensation as possible for talented individuals born into less favorable social positions as a consequence of this moral judgment. He also introduces his difference principle as a consequence of this moral intuition (Rawls 1971, pp. 73–75, 100–108; § 12,

---

[17] Like "free exchange" and "need", "desert" is a criterion that meets Walzer's "open-ended distributive principle. *No social good x should be distributed to men and women who possess some other good y merely because they possess y and without regard to the meaning of x*" (Walzer 1983, pp. 20–21).

§ 17).¹⁸ The difference principle should be understood as the principle of the welfare state because its social application requires the redistribution of social income towards the less favored members of society (cf. Knoll 2013). For Rawls, the less favored members of society are also defined by having less capabilities and talents and thus less resources to generate a high income (Rawls 1999, p. 83). However, such an "outcome of the natural lottery" is "arbitrary from a moral perspective" (Rawls 1971, p. 74, § 12). Therefore, it gives rise to "claims of redress" (Rawls 1971, p. 101, § 17). The undeserved bad luck of the less fortunate in the distribution of natural talents has to be compensated: "Those who have been favored by nature, whoever they are, may gain from their good fortune only on terms that improve the situation of those who have lost out" (Rawls 1971, p. 101, § 17). Rawls justifies this with his claim that the favored individuals do not deserve their superior endowments and talents.

Against this claim, Walzer argues that public honor "cannot exist as a good unless there are deserving men and women" (Walzer 1983, p. 261).¹⁹ In his critique of Rawls, Walzer partly follows Nozick's criticism (Nozick 1974, pp. 213–216, 228). Walzer attacks Rawls:

> Advocates of equality have often felt compelled to deny the reality of desert. The people we call deserving, they argue, are simply lucky. [...]. How are we to conceive of these men and women once we have come to view their capacities and achievements as accidental accessories, like hats and coats they just happen to be wearing? How, indeed, are they to conceive of themselves? The reflective forms of recognition, self-esteem and self-respect, our most important possessions [...] must seem meaningless to individuals all of whose qualities are nothing but the luck of the draw (Walzer 1983, pp. 260–261).

Rawls abstracts persons from their individual qualities and capabilities. Against this abstraction, Walzer argues firstly that it does not leave "us with *persons* at all" (Walzer 1983, p. 261; Walzer's italics). Secondly, he claims that we cannot be proud of our achievements if the qualities that led to them are not an integral part of our personality. If we don't deserve any recognition for who we are and for our achievements, and if we cannot be proud of ourselves, we cannot develop self-esteem and self-respect. The fact that Walzer calls self-esteem and self-re-

---

18 The final statement of the difference principle in *A Theory of Justice* reads: "Social and economic inequalities are to be arranged so that they are [...] (a) to the greatest benefit of the least advantaged, consistent with the just savings principle" (Rawls 1971, p. 302, § 46).

19 Walzer advocates the questionable thesis that the "recognition of deserving men and women, and of all deserving men and women, is possible only in a democracy" (Walzer 1983, p. 267). The validity of this thesis cannot be discussed in this paper.

spect "our most important possessions" demonstrates how important these notions are for him and his theory of justice.

5 The Importance of Self-Respect for Walzer's Theory of Justice

As already mentioned, Walzer criticizes Rawls for not distinguishing between self-esteem and self-respect. For his own distinction between these two concepts, Walzer is indebted to David Sachs's article "How to Distinguish Self-Respect from Self-Esteem" (Sachs 1981). If the jury for the Nobel Prize in literature pronounces its verdict about the best novel of the year, it expresses its esteem for the work and the author. The author internalizes this judgment and develops as its reflective-form "self-esteem", which the Oxford English Dictionary defines as "a favorable appreciation or opinion of oneself". Like esteem, self-esteem "is a relational concept": "men and women value themselves – just as they are valued – in comparison with others" (Walzer 1983, p. 274). Of course, usually there is no official jury that judges our value, and therefore we have to make our own judgments about ourselves:

> In order to enjoy self-esteem, we probably have to convince ourselves (even if this means deceiving ourselves) that we deserve it, and we can't do that without a little help from our friends. But we are judges in our own case; we pack the jury as best we can, and we fake the verdict whenever we can. About this sort of thing, no one feels guilty; such trails are all-too-human (Walzer 1983, p. 278).

Even if we successfully convince ourselves of our own value, self-esteem depends to a large degree on the opinion of others. It also depends on social value judgments that are connected to different kinds of jobs and salaries. Therefore, like in the hierarchical society of feudal Europe, in the modern bourgeois society there exists no equality of esteem and self-esteem (cf. Walzer 1983, pp. 255–256, 279).

In line with the Oxford English Dictionary, Walzer defines "self-respect" as "a proper regard for the dignity of one's person or one's position" (Walzer 1983, p. 274). A person regards the dignity of her position – e.g. as a teacher or a doctor – and thus herself, if she measures up to the professional code or the general norm that is valid for this position in her society: "What is at stake is the dignity of the position and the integrity of the person who holds it. He ought not lower himself for some personal advantage; he ought not sell himself short; he ought not to endure such-and-such an affront" (Walzer 1983, pp. 274–275). Contrary to self-esteem, self-respect is not a relational concept or the outcome of a competitive practice. It is enough that I know the norm and measure myself against it. Whether I succeed in measuring up to the norm or not is independent from others succeeding or failing to do so. Self-respect is "a normative concept, dependent upon our moral understanding of persons and positions" (Walzer 1983, p. 274).

While the valid norms and standards for the diverse professional positions and social ranks differ, in democracies general and equal norms also exist for the proper regard of all persons as citizens. In order to achieve self-respect as citizens, persons have to be publicly recognized as such by the political community. The community has to show equal respect to its members by giving them "the same legal and political rights", like equal voting rights (Walzer 1983, p. 277). As a result of the equal respect among members of the political community, persons can have proper regard for their dignity as citizens. Self-respect in "any substantive sense" is "a function of membership" (Walzer 1983, p. 278; cf. Walzer's chapter "Membership", 1983, pp. 31–63). Self-respect also presupposes that persons are considered to be owners of their qualities and their character and thus responsible for their actions (Walzer 1983, p. 279).

Self-respect requires "some substantial connection" to the groups one belongs to as a member, like one's professional group, one's political community, or a political movement:

> That's why expulsion from the movement or exile from the community can be so serious a punishment. It attacks both the external and the reflective forms of honor. Prolonged unemployment and poverty are similarly threatening: they represent a kind of economic exile, a punishment that we are loathe to say that anyone deserves. The welfare state is an effort to avoid this punishment, to gather in the economic exiles, to guarantee effective membership. But even when it does this in the best possible way, meeting needs without degrading persons, it doesn't guarantee self-respect; it only helps to make it possible. This is, perhaps, the deepest purpose of distributive justice. When all social goods, from membership to political power, are distributed for the right reasons, then the conditions for self-respect will have been established as best as they can be. But there will still be men and women who suffer from a lack of self-respect (Walzer 1983, p. 278).

In *Spheres of Justice*, Walzer conceives of a just society as a democratic welfare state. In the book, he argues for "an expanded American welfare state", in which each citizen receives welfare benefits "according to his socially recognized needs" (Walzer 1983, pp. 90–91). The quote above demonstrates that a democratic welfare state is in particular necessary in order to allow citizens to develop self-respect. To enable self-respect is, for Walzer, "perhaps, the deepest purpose of distributive justice". In a "complex egalitarian society", in which all social goods are distributed according to their social meanings, "the conditions for self-respect will have been established as best as they can be". The "experience of complex equality will breed, though it can never guarantee, self-respect" (Walzer 1983, p. 280). These important statements elucidate that the notions of respect and self-respect play a central role in Walzer's *Spheres of Justice*.

That the development of citizen's self-respect is a fundamental aim of Walzer's theory of justice is also demonstrated by the fact that he comes back to this topic in the concluding paragraph of his book. In the passage, Walzer states that the unequal distribution of goods in a "complex egalitarian society" is "no affront to our dignity, no denial of our moral or political capacity" (Walzer 1983, p. 321). As citizens have the possibility to succeed and experience recognition in many different spheres, failings in some spheres do not constitute an affront to their dignity. The "deep strengths of complex equality" are, as Walzer declares in the concluding sentence of his work, "mutual respect and a shared self-respect", which together are "the source of its possible endurance" (Walzer 1983, p. 321).

6 Conclusion

This essay has demonstrated that notions of respect and self-respect play a central role in Rawls's and Walzer's theories of justice. As these two theories are amongst the most important works in contemporary political theory and philosophy, the paper has also shown that respect and self-respect are amongst the most important topics in this field. Rawls's and Walzer's theories of justice are the result of different approaches to political philosophy. While Rawls speculates on the ideal of a well-ordered society, Walzer interprets the world we live in and the moral norms it contains. In their approaches to respect and self-respect, both mainly focus on the equal respect that is due to citizens of a democracy. However, also in this context, Walzer rightfully criticizes Rawls for not distinguishing between self-esteem and self-respect (Walzer 1983, pp. 272, 277, 335, fn. 42). As a consequence of this flaw, Rawls's theory does not catch sight of the many different forms of recognition distributed in modern societies and its corresponding effects on the self or on individual persons. This blind spot might also be the result of Rawls's focus on the basic structure of society as the only agent distributing social goods.

Although both political philosophers argue for a welfare state, only Walzer succeeds in showing that such a social arrangement is essential for safeguarding self-respect.[20] A main reason for this is that Rawls assigns an exaggerated role to classical rights and liberties for promoting and sustaining self-respect and underestimates the role that jobs or income play for achieving this goal. Finally, as Walzer's criticism of Rawls's concept of persons implies, this concept is hardly compatible with the role that Rawls ascribes to self-respect and self-esteem in his theory of justice.

Bibliography

Barry, B. (1973): *The Liberal Theory of Justice: A Critical Examination of the Principal Doctrines in "A Theory of Justice" by John Rawls*, Oxford: Clarendon.
Benbaji, Y. and Sussmann, N. (Eds.) (2014): *Reading Walzer*, London-New York: Routledge.
Bernick, M. (1978): "A Note on Promoting Self-Esteem", *Political Theory* 6 (1), pp. 108–118.
Darwall, S.L. (1977): "Two Kinds of Respect", *Ethics* 88 (1), pp. 36–49.
Eyal, N. (2005): "'Perhaps the most important primary good': Self-respect and Rawls's principles of justice", *Politics, Philosophy & Economics* 4 (2), pp. 195–219.
Honneth, A. (1992): *Kampf um Anerkennung: Zur moralischen Grammatik sozialer Konflikte*, Frankfurt a.M.: Suhrkamp.
Keat, R. (1997): "Colonisation by the Market: Walzer on Recognition", *Journal of Political Philosophy*, 5 (1), pp. 93–107 (reprinted in: R. Keat: *Cultural Goods and the Limits of the Market*, London: Palgrave 2000, pp. 70–85).
Keat, R. and Miller, D. (1974): "Understanding Justice", *Political Theory* 2 (1), pp. 3–31.
Knoll, M. (2013): "An interpretation of Rawls's difference principle as the principle of the welfare state", *Sofia Philosophical Review* 2, Vol. VII, pp. 5–33.
Knoll, M. (2014): "Das Verhältnis von Freiheit, Gleichheit und Herrschaft in Michael Walzers Theorie der Verteilungsgerechtigkeit. Eine republikanische Interpretation von *komplexer Gleichheit*". In M. Knoll and M. Spieker (Eds.): *Sphären der Gerechtigkeit. Ein kooperativer Kommentar*, with a preface by M. Walzer, Stuttgart: Steiner, pp. 51–72.
Knoll, M. and Spieker, M. (Eds.) 2014: *Sphären der Gerechtigkeit. Ein kooperativer Kommentar*, with a preface by M. Walzer, Stuttgart: Steiner.
Laitinen, A. (2014): "Michael Walzer on Recognition as a Dominant Good". In H. Ikäheimo, P. Niemi, P. Lyyra and J. Saarinen (Eds.): *Sisäisyys ja suunnistautuminen: juhlakirja Jussi Kotkavirralle*, Jyväskla: SoPhi, pp. 586–621.

---

[20] Cf. Knoll 2013. In *Justice as Fairness. A Restatement*, Rawls emphasizes "the distinction between a property-owning democracy, which realizes all the main political values expressed by the two principles of justice, and a capitalist welfare state, which does not. We think of such a democracy as an alternative to capitalism" (Rawls 2001, p. 135–136). He also states that this "distinction is not sufficiently noted in *Theory*" (Rawls 2001, p. 135). This article has mainly focused on Rawls's account of self-respect in *A Theory of Justice*. It does not discuss whether some of the above mentioned criticisms of this account could be mitigated by including Rawls's last revisions of his theory.

Miller, D. (1978): "Democracy and Social Justice", *British Journal of Political Science* 8 (1), pp. 1–19.
Miller, D. (1995): "Introduction". In D. Miller and M. Walzer (Eds.): *Pluralism, Justice and Equality*, Oxford: Oxford University Press, pp. 1–16.
Miller, D. and Walzer, M. (Eds.) (1995): *Pluralism, Justice and Equality*, Oxford: Oxford University Press.
Nielsen, K. (1979): "Radical Egalitarian Justice: Justice as Equality", *Social Theory and Practice* 5 (2), pp. 209–226.
Nozick, R. (1974): *Anarchy, State, and Utopia*, New York/Oxford: Basic Books/Basil Blackwell.
Nusser, K.-H. (Ed.) (2012): *Freiheit, soziale Güter und Gerechtigkeit. Michael Walzers Staats- und Gesellschaftsverständnis* (Staatsverständnisse, 45), Baden: Nomos VerlagBaden.
Rawls, J. (1971): *A Theory of Justice*, Cambridge, MA: The Belknap Press of Harvard University Press.
Rawls, J. (1999): *A Theory of Justice*, revised edition, Cambridge: Belknap Press of Harvard University Press.
Rawls, J. (2001): *Justice as Fairness. A Restatement*, ed. by E. Kelly, Cambridge, MA/London: Belknap Press of Harvard University Press.
Rawls, J. (2005): *Political Liberalism. Expanded Edition*, New York: Columbia University Press (first edition 1993).
Sachs, D. (1981): "How to distinguish Self-Respect from Self-Esteem", *Philosophy and Public Affairs* 10 (4), pp. 346–360.
Schütz, M. (2014): "Anerkennung". In M. Knoll and M. Spieker (Eds.): *Sphären der Gerechtigkeit. Ein kooperativer Kommentar*, with a preface by M. Walzer, Stuttgart: Steiner, pp. 209–224.
Shue, H. (1975): "Liberty and Self-Respect", *Ethics* 85 (3), pp. 195–203.
Taylor, R.S. (2003): "Rawls's Defense of the Priority of Liberty: A Kantian Reconstruction", *Philosophy & Public Affairs* 31 (3), pp. 246–271.
Walzer, M. (1983): *Spheres of Justice. A Defense of Pluralism and Equality*, New York: Basic Books.
Walzer, M. (1992): *Sphären der Gerechtigkeit. Ein Plädoyer für Pluralität und Gleichheit*, Frankfurt a.M./New York: Campus.
Williams, B. (1962): "The Idea of Equality". In P. Laslett and W.G. Runciman (Eds.): *Philosophy, Politics, and Society*, Second Series, Oxford: Blackwell, pp. 110–131.
Zaino, J.S. (1998): "Self-Respect and Rawlsian Justice", *The Journal of Politics* 60 (3), pp. 737–753.
Zink, J.R. (2011): "*Reconsidering the Role of Self-Respect in Rawls's 'A Theory of Justice'*", *The Journal of Politics* 73 (2), pp. 331–344.

List of Contributors

Christine Bratu is Assistant Professor at the Chair of Practical Philosophy and Political Theory at the Department of Philosophy of Munich University. She wrote her dissertation on questions of political authority and legitimacy, focusing on the ongoing debate between political liberalism and perfectionism. Her other areas of expertise include constitutivist arguments in ethics, the value of personal relationships, Kant's practical philosophy and feminist philosophy. She is the author of *Die Grenzen staatlicher Legitimität. Zum Verhältnis von Liberalismus und Perfektionismus* (Mentis, 2014), and numerous articles in international journals.

Giovanni Giorgini is Professor of Political Philosophy at the University of Bologna and Life Member of Clare Hall College, Cambridge. Giorgini is a member of the scientific board of *Il Pensiero Politico* and a member of the board of directors of *Filosofia Politica* and *Etica & Politica*. He is the author of *La città e il tiranno* (Giuffrè, 1993), *Liberalismi eretici* (Edizioni Goliardiche Trieste, 1999), *I doni di Pandora* (Bonomo, 2002) as well as of a translation and commentary of Plato's *Politicus* (Rizzoli, 2005), numerous essays, translations and entries in encyclopedias.

Marie Göbel is a research assistant and PhD-candidate in the research project "Human Dignity as the Foundation of Human Rights?" at the Ethics Institute of Utrecht University. Her main areas of expertise include Kant's practical philosophy, theories of human rights and human dignity, and the relationship between morality and politics / law. Other publications include: "Die Notwendigkeit der Menschenwürde" [The "Necessity" of Human Dignity], together with Marcus Düwell, forthcoming 2017.

Elena Irrera is Lecturer in Ancient Philosophy and Research Fellow in Political Philosophy at the University of Bologna. She has been research unit director in Bologna for the FIRB project "Feeding Respect. Food Policies and Minority Instances in Multicultural Societies", in partnership with the Universities of Pavia and Milan (March 2012–March 2015). She is the author of *Il bello come causalità metafisica in Aristotele* (Mimesis, 2011), *Sulla bellezza della vita buona: fini e criteri dell'agire umano in Aristotele* (Carabba, 2012) and several essays in international journals.

Manuel Knoll is Professor of Philosophy at Istanbul Şehir University, Instructor (Lehrbeauftragter) in Political Theory at the Munich School for Political Science, Member of the Instituto "Lucio Anneo Séneca" of Universidad Carlos III de Madrid, and Co-Publisher of *Widerspruch. Münchner Zeitschrift für Philosophie*. He has lectured and published widely on topics pertaining to ancient, modern and contemporary political philosophy and ethics, in particular ancient and contemporary theories of justice, Plato, Aristotle, Machiavelli, Nietzsche, Rawls and Walzer, social philosophy and critical theory.

Arto Laitinen is Professor of Social Philosophy at the University of Tampere. His main area of research is the philosophy of recognition. His interests include philosophical anthropology, theories of practical reason, value, normativity and solidarity. He is the author of *Solidarity: Theory and Practice* (Lanham 2014), co-edited with A.B. Pessi. He has also published numerous articles in international journals and companions, among them *MacIntyre and Taylor: Traditions, Rationality, and the Modern Predicament* (Routledge Companion of Hermeneutics).

Antis Loizides teaches Political Theory and History of Political Thought at the University of Cyprus. His main areas of expertise include the philosophy of John Stuart Mill and James Mill. He is the author of several books, among them *John Stuart Mill's Platonic Heritage: Happiness Through Character* (Lexington Books, 2013) and *A British Socrates*, co-edited with K.N. Demetriou (Palgrave Macmillan, 2013). He is also the author of numerous essays in international journals.

Christopher J. Rowe is Emeritus Professor of Greek at Durham University. He was appointed OBE in the 2009 Queen's Birthday Honours List for services to scholarship. His publishing activity has included co-editing, with Malcolm Schofield, *The Cambridge History of Greek and Roman Political Thought* (2000); writing monographs, first, with Terry Penner, on Plato's *Lysis* (on friendship: CUP 2005), then on Plato more generally (*Plato and the Art of Philosophical Writing*, CUP 2007); and translating Aristotle's *Nicomachean Ethics* (with Sarah Broadie: OUP 2002) and Plato's *Republic* (Penguin 2012).

Simon Weber teaches Ancient and Political Philosophy as Wissenschaftlicher Mitarbeiter at the University of Bonn. He has been Guest Lecturer at the Universities of Lodz and Luzern. His main area of interest is Plato's and Aristotle's ethical and political thought. He is the author of *Herrschaft und Recht bei Aristoteles* (De Gruyter, 2015). He has also written several essays and articles on issues of Ancient Philosophy in journals and edited volumes.

Index

Accountability/accountable   5, 8, 18, 27, 120, 128, 175, 190, 193
Aidôs (shame, self-respect)   9, 41, 44f., 48, 52-55, 57–59,63,67
Aischynê (shame)   45
Amour de soi (positive self-love)   28–30
Amour propre (negative self-love)   30
Anagnôrisis (recognition)   26
Aretê (virtue)   27, 48, 50, 56–57
Aristotle   3f., 10, 19, 25–27, 35, 41, 43, 45–47, 49–51, 53, 61, 69, 83, 85–103
– *Metaphysics*   87, 96–97
– *Nicomachean Ethics*   75, 117
– *Poetics*   26
– *Politics*   10, 43, 46, 53, 83, 86, 89–102
– *Rhetoric*   26
Atimia (institutionalized lack of honor)   9, 41, 45, 59–62
Autonomy   85, 164
Axia (value, worth, dignity)   50, 90

Cairns, D.L.   44, 53, 61
Carter, I.   1
Cicero   69, 109
– *De Finibus*   69
– *De Officiis*   45
Community   2, 11, 19, 36, 52f., 59–61, 69, 92f., 100, 120, 144f., 155, 184, 190f., 193, 196, 216, 221
– Moral ~   144f., 190f.
– Political ~   11, 120, 216, 221
Conflict   1, 11, 28, 46, 48f., 86, 109, 111, 115–117, 119f., 123f., 126
Consciousness/conscience/*Bewußtsein*   25, 33f., 68, 126, 136, 172, 178, 201f., 210, 213, 215
Cooperation   93, 98, 115, 124
Cranor, C.   4

Darwall, S.   2, 4–8, 83–85, 118, 120, 124f., 131, 140, 142, 189f., 207
Dignity   1, 3, 12f., 32–33, 36, 43, 47–50, 52, 86, 120, 125, 131f., 140–147, 149, 151f., 164–166, 176, 187–191, 201–204, 216, 220–222
Dikê/dikaiosynê (right/justice)   56
Dikê/dikaiosynê (right/justice)   48f., 51
Distributive justice   15, 127, 208, 215, 221
Drive   12, 93, 159–161, 178
– Sensual ~   161
– *Triebfeder* (Kant)   12, 33, 159
Duty   6, 32f., 43, 84, 102, 131, 133, 136, 138f., 141–147, 153, 157, 160–162, 165, 194, 201f., 204, 212
– In conformity with ~ (see *Pflicht*)   160–162
– Natural ~   212

End
– ~ in itself   31, 152, 164, 189
Epistemic authority   8, 124, 197
Equality
– ~ before the law (*Isonomia*)   154
– ~ in virtue   27
– Moral ~   3, 42
– ~ of entitlements   8
– ~ of treatment   28, 41
Esteem (*Schätzung*)   2f., 7, 10f., 13, 15, 17, 29, 33, 50, 85, 109f., 115, 118, 171f., 179, 189f., 207–210, 212, 215, 217, 219–223
– Self-~   15, 207–210, 212f., 215, 219–223
Esteem (*Schätzung*)   216
Eudaimonia (happiness; well-being)   88, 96f., 99f., 103
Eugeneia (nobility of birth)   46

Fairness   2, 18, 49, 197, 208
– Justice as -   18, 208, 210, 214, 223
Family   9, 13, 18, 29, 35, 43, 47, 69, 75, 77–79, 82, 98f., 171f., 172, 180–184, 213
Fear   26, 44, 46, 67, 109, 115, 125, 127f., 202
Freedom   1, 12f., 20, 28, 30f., 33–35, 43, 50, 97, 152, 154f., 171–176, 179–181, 183, 190, 192, 195f., 213

Galeotti, A.E. 1f., 18
Glory 45, 52, 115f., 119, 122f., 216
Good and evil 111, 114

Hegel, G.W.F. 4, 13, 19f., 28, 34f., 171–181, 183f., 215
– *Phenomenology of Spirit* 172f.
– *Philosophy of Right* 13, 171–173, 177
Hill, T.E. Jr. 2f., 131, 160
Hobbes, T.
– *De Cive* 110f., 120, 122
– *Leviathan* 11, 110–112, 120, 123
– The Elements of Law. Natural and Politic 11, 110, 112, 116, 120, 125, 127
Hobbes, T. 4, 11, 19, 28, 109–128, 216
Homer 9, 19f., 41, 44, 55, 62
– *Iliad* 44
– *Odyssey* 20
Honneth, A. 1, 13, 35f., 171f., 179–182, 215
Honor 7, 9–11, 15, 17, 41, 45, 47, 50, 52, 54, 57, 59–62, 85, 109f., 115f., 119f., 144, 208, 210, 216f., 219, 221
Humiliation 33, 78, 134
Hybris (insolence, arrogance) 26, 44, 50, 56f., 61f.

Impartiality 88, 192
Imperative 126, 160, 162, 192
– Categorical ~ 31f., 141, 156–158, 160–162, 164–166
– Hypothetical ~ 126, 160
Individuality 13, 35, 178, 184, 187f., 192–194, 198, 204
Isêgoria (equal right of speech) 51
Isonomia (equality of treatment before the law) 41, 47, 51

Kant, I. 3f., 10–12, 19f., 24f., 31–34, 42, 83f., 86f., 102, 131–147, 149–166, 176, 189
– *Critique of Practical Reason* 32f., 132
– *Critique of Pure Reason* 24f.
– *Groundwork of the Metaphysics of Morals* 132
– *Metaphysics of Morals* 31f., 132, 163

Law 1, 3, 7, 11–13, 19, 32f., 41, 45f., 49–51, 53f., 59–63, 81, 91, 97f., 114, 127, 133, 135–138, 150–154, 157, 160f., 164, 181, 192, 195–198, 204
– Moral ~ 3, 12f., 32f., 86, 102f., 133, 135f., 146, 150, 159–162
– ~ of nature 123, 126–129
– Philosophy of ~ 1
– Practical ~ 33
Liberty 31, 123–124, 127, 171f., 180, 187f., 192, 194, 196, 210, 212–214, 223
– Absolute ~ 127
– Equal basic ~ 210
– Natural ~ 124
– Negative ~ 171f., 180
– Restraints on ~ 192
Liberty

Merit 30, 43, 49, 84f., 132, 189, 197, 218
Mill, J.S. 13f., 187–189, 191–204
– *On Liberty* 14, 187f., 192–194, 196–198, 200, 204
– *Principles of Political Economy* 14, 188, 193
– *Subjection of Women* 14, 187, 192
– *Utilitarianism* 14, 187, 193, 199–202

Obligation 12, 32, 44, 84, 86, 88, 90, 101–103, 133, 146, 153, 156, 158–160, 162–165, 199f., 212
– (Categorical) moral ~ 12, 86, 88, 90, 101–103, 153, 156, 158–160, 162–165, 200
– Level of ~ 162f.
– ~ to respect 84, 88, 90, 159f., 163–165
Obligation 163
Observantia (respect, conformity) 12, 131f., 139, 146
Oikeiôsis/oikeion/oikeiôtikos (appropriation, affinity and/or self-realization) 10, 42, 67, 68–70, 72, 73, 75, 76, 77, 79, 80, 81
Oligôria (lack of respect) 26

Parrhêsia (freedom of speech) 51, 62
Pathological feelings 137–139
Personhood 13, 171–173, 177–184
Pflicht (in Kant)
– *aus Pflicht* („from duty") 160

– *pflichtgemäß* („in conformity with duty") 160
Pflicht (in Kant) 160
Plato 3 f., 9 f., 21, 23, 43–45, 48, 53 f., 67, 69 f., 72 f., 77–82, 87, 92, 201, 214
– *Charmides* 72
– *Gorgias* 201
– *Lysis* 67, 70 f., 72–74, 76–80
– *Protagoras* 48, 70, 73
– *Republic* 43, 70, 88
– *Sophist* 72
– *Symposium* 67
– *Theaetetus* 21 f., 70, 73, 80
Polis 49, 60, 93 f., 100
Pride 1, 57, 75, 122–123
Private property 171, 173, 179 f., 183, 213

Rational 3, 12, 27, 31, 33, 69, 79–81, 85, 96, 101, 112 f., 115, 121 f., 124–126, 133 f., 137, 146, 159, 161, 163, 175, 190 f., 202, 211–213
– ~ being 12, 32 f., 68, 85, 89, 94–97, 101, 133, 149 f., 152, 155, 159–161, 175
– ~ faculty 27
– ~ plan of life 209
– Practical rationality 34, 95, 102
Rational 112
Rawls, J. 2, 4, 8, 14 f., 18, 36, 121, 142, 172 f., 189–191, 207–214, 217–220, 222 f.
– *A Theory of Justice* 14, 121, 191, 208, 213, 217, 219 f., 223
– *A Theory of Justice* 8, 207–209
– *Political Liberalism* 208, 214
Rawls, J. 15
Raz, J. 1, 6, 182
Reciprocity 3, 84, 127, 154
Recognition 1–3, 7 f., 10–15, 17–28, 30–36, 41, 43, 46, 50, 61, 70, 83–85, 90, 109 f., 113, 120–122, 124–126, 128, 131, 140, 143, 153, 155, 161, 171 f., 175–177, 182–184, 196, 201, 207, 210 f., 214–217, 219, 222
Regard 5, 9, 11, 14, 17, 32, 36, 69, 83, 90, 92, 94, 98, 103, 110, 116, 126 f., 133–134, 149, 151, 153 f., 156, 158–161, 163, 165 f., 175 f., 182, 187, 193, 195, 197 f., 216–218, 220 f.
Respect 1, 3–9, 11–14, 17, 26, 28, 31–33, 35, 42–44, 46–49, 52, 54–59, 61, 63, 67, 69, 77, 81, 83, 85 f., 88 f., 101–103, 110, 113, 115, 117–121, 124 f., 127, 131–134, 139, 142–147, 151, 158–166, 171–176, 178–183, 187–191, 201–203, 207–215, 216–217, 219–223
– Appraisal ~ 7, 10, 14, 84 f., 90, 101, 118, 188–190, 201
– ~ as honor 8, 10, 41, 110
– ~ as obstacle 125
– Equal ~ 1–3, 5, 7 f., 11, 13, 15, 18, 27, 31, 36, 42, 61, 109 f., 115, 124–127, 221 f.
– Evaluative ~ 7, 118, 189
– ~ for persons 1–6, 8, 10–15, 31 f., 35, 41, 83–91, 101–103, 109 f., 120, 149 f., 152, 158 f., 162, 164, 184, 187–190, 192, 204
– ~ for the law 32, 33, 138, 150
– Reciprocal/mutual ~ 28, 212, 222
– Recognition ~ 7 f., 10, 14, 83–85, 90 f., 103, 188–190
– reverential r. 2, 18, 28, 33, 119, 133
– Self-~ 3, 8 f., 11 f., 14 f., 28, 33, 35, 41, 109 f., 121–123, 131, 143, 179, 187 f., 207–215, 219–223
Respecter 4–8, 192
Respicere/re-spicere 5 f.
Reverentia 12, 131–133, 139, 146
Rights
– Equal ~ 181
– Human ~ 3, 12, 149, 157, 163, 166, 197 f., 201
Rousseau, J.J. 28–31

Security 29, 109, 145, 199, 214
Self 3, 8 f., 11–15, 19, 23–28, 30 f., 33–35, 41, 48, 53, 61, 68, 71, 80, 82, 92, 102, 112, 117, 121, 135 f., 142, 158, 161, 171–184, 187 f., 190, 193 f., 196 f., 200, 202–204, 208, 210 f., 219 f.
– Other ~ 27, 35
– ~-restraint 44, 49, 56
– Selfhood 13, 171
Sittlichkeit (ethical life) 13, 172 f.

Slavery 46, 48, 49, 86, 89, 91, 97, 102, 175, 181, 195, 197f.
Solon 9, 41, 44, 48–54, 57
Stability 207
State 11, 13, 25, 28f., 31, 35, 51, 55, 59, 61, 95, 115, 128, 131f., 134, 136–138, 141, 143, 153–155, 171f., 174, 176, 180–182, 184, 189, 193, 195f., 198, 209, 216, 219, 221–223
– Civil ~ 11, 28, 31, 113f., 120, 128
– ~ of nature 11, 28f., 109–111, 113–117, 119–121, 123f., 126, 128, 156, 164, 176f., 181
(Subjective) Inclination 29, 31, 33, 56, 116, 119, 127, 128, 129, 134, 135, 136, 137, 143, 161, 173

Technê (craft) 48
Trust 8, 17, 29, 56f., 115–118, 121f.

Walzer, M. 1, 4, 14f., 36, 207f., 210, 214–222
– *Spheres of Justice* 14, 207f., 214f., 221, 222
Weakness of the will 138
Willensbestimmung (determination of the will) 160, 167
Willkür (arbitrary choice) 84

Xenophon 61, 92

www.ingramcontent.com/pod-product-compliance
Lightning Source LLC
Chambersburg PA
CBHW021807230426
43669CB00008B/657